OFFICIAL CHESS HANDBOOK

OFFICIAL

CHESS HANDBOOK

By KENNETH HARKNESS

Author of *The Official Blue Book and Encyclopedia of Chess*
and *Invitation to Bridge*. Co-author of *An Invitation to
Chess*. Formerly Managing Editor of *Chess Review*. Formerly
Business Manager and Rating Statistician of the United
States Chess Federation

Approved by

THE UNITED STATES CHESS FEDERATION

DAVID McKAY COMPANY, INC.

New York

OFFICIAL CHESS HANDBOOK

Third Printing, January 1973

Library of Congress Catalog Card Number: 66-13085

MANUFACTURED IN THE UNITED STATES OF AMERICA

VAN REES PRESS • NEW YORK

Preface

Important changes have been made in the laws of chess during the past decade. The *Fédération Internationale des Échecs* (World Chess Federation) has adopted new laws, revised old laws, issued interpretations amounting to amendments of other laws. There have been so many of these changes that it has been difficult for tournament players and directors to keep track of what was happening. For the first time in a single volume, all the new and amended laws, together with official interpretations of old laws, are included in this successor to *The Official Blue Book and Encyclopedia of Chess,* published in 1956.

Of necessity, some of the material in the *Blue Book* is repeated in the present volume, but many alterations have been made to bring the material up to date, and some sections have been completely rewritten. The chapter on rating systems now includes a complete description of the system currently used by the United States Chess Federation (USCF).

In the chapter on the conduct of chess tournaments I have made some revisions in the Harkness pairing system for Swiss events now employed by most chess organizations in the United States. The final chapter of this new book contains a complete record of competitions for world and national titles from the year each title originated to the present day.

KENNETH HARKNESS

Boca Raton, Florida
1967

Acknowledgments

For much of the information needed to bring the Laws of Chess up to date I am greatly indebted to Mr. Folke Rogard, President of the *Fédération Internationale des Échecs,* who furnished me with the minutes of the FIDE Chess Congresses and the interpretations of the FIDE Committee on Laws.

I am also indebted to Lt. Col. E. B. Edmondson, Executive Director of the U.S. Chess Federation, who read the manuscript of this book and made some valuable recommendations which were incorporated into the finished work.

Mr. Fred Cramer, former President of the USCF, rendered great assistance in the preparation of the chapter on rating systems, especially the section devoted to the Elo-USCF System.

The section on "Chess Ratings in the USSR" is based on a translation by Jack Soudakoff of an article in *Shakhmati v USSR* for May 1946.

I acknowledge with gratitude the valuable research work performed by Eliot Hearst in the history of the Swiss System, the rules of Kriegspiel and a few other types of unorthodox chess. Eliot also made excellent suggestions concerning methods of pairing players in Swiss tournaments.

The splendid photographs in chapter one were produced by Lloyd Wegner of New York.

And a vote of thanks to Joe Reinhardt, my latest successor as Business Manager of the USCF, who found time to answer my letters and provide information on various subjects.

Contents

OFFICIAL CHESS HANDBOOK

CHAPTER I

The Laws of Chess Explained

The earliest printed rules of modern chess appear in a rare book by the Spaniard Lucena. The book is believed to have been published in 1497, just a few years after the moves of the Queen and Bishop were changed and the game began to be played in approximately the same way as it is played today.

Lucena's rules are rather sketchy, but he describes the difference between the old and new styles of chess, gives the moves of the chessmen, some definitions, and advice. One of his "rules" states:

If you play at night, place your candle on your left-hand side, if by day, place your opponent facing the light. It will be the worse for your opponent if you play him when he has just eaten and drunk freely. During a game drink water, not wine. Play for a small stake, so that the thought of it may not trouble you.

The trick of placing your opponent with the light in his eyes was apparently an old Spanish custom, for it is repeated in the code of laws included in the volume by Ruy Lopez published in 1561.

Chess literature of the sixteenth and seventeenth centuries records the rules followed by players in various countries. In those days, there was considerable difference of opinion on the subjects of castling, pawn promotion, stalemate, the *en passant* pawn capture, etc. Some of these differences were still being debated in the nineteenth century.

In the eighteenth and nineteenth centuries, codes were adopted by chess clubs and eventually by national chess associations, but there was no general agreement on the rules of the game. The first international tournament, London, 1851, was played "in accordance with the rules of the chief European Chess Clubs." (*The Chess Tournament*, by Howard Staunton, London, 1852.) In the first national tournament held in this country, New York, 1857, play was governed by the code of chess rules published in Staunton's *Chess Player's Hand-*

3

book (London, 1847). In 1860, a revised code published by Staunton
in his *Chess Praxis* was adopted by the organizers of many tournaments and became generally recognized as the rules of the game for
English and American players.

Although basic chess laws had become fairly well standardized
by the middle of the nineteenth century, the rules governing competitive play were in a state of confusion. In the book of the Fifth
American Chess Congress (New York, 1880), the chess code committee refers to its "delicate and difficult task of dissecting the mass
of disordered and conflicting codes of chess laws at present in operation." This committee prepared a revised code which was adopted
by the Congress, but the code was copied largely from Staunton. It
lasted until 1897, when New York's Manhattan Chess Club obtained
the American rights to laws which had been officially adopted by
the leading chess associations and clubs of Great Britain, and published these laws as "The American Chess Code."

In the meantime, other countries had their own rules and regulations. The organizers of international tournaments had to announce
which code would be followed. There was an obvious need for a
supreme authority to control international competitive play and to
formulate a code of laws which would be recognized throughout
the world.

At Paris in 1924, on the occasion of the first Chess Olympiad,
fifteen of the national associations represented at this event agreed
to become affiliates of an international chess organization. Later in
the same year, the *Fédération Internationale des Echecs* (International Chess Federation) was inaugurated, with headquarters at
The Hague. Dr. A. Rueb of the Netherlands became the first president of the FIDE, and it is largely due to his efforts that it was established and eventually obtained worldwide recognition. (In 1953, more
than fifty national chess organizations were affiliated with the
FIDE.)

At Venice, in 1929, the first international chess code was adopted
by the Council of the FIDE. The code was written in French, the
official language of the FIDE, and the affiliated national associations
(or Units, as they are called) were requested to have the code translated into their languages in order to secure universal adoption. The
British Chess Federation translated the laws into English, and this
version was approved and adopted by the National Chess Federa-

tion of the United States, the American Unit of the FIDE. (In 1939, the National and American Chess Federations consolidated to become the United States Chess Federation, and since that time the USCF has been the American Unit of the FIDE.)

For twenty-three years, the 1929 FIDE Laws of Chess governed play in practically all tournaments and matches. National and local chess associations had their own supplementary regulations and interpretations of the code, but the FIDE laws were accepted throughout the world, by chess organizations and chessplayers alike, as the basic rules of the game.

But laws are made by man, and man is fallible. There were several ambiguities in the 1929 code. As time went on, it became increasingly apparent that the laws would have to be changed. Under the direction of Mr. Folke Rogard, of Stockholm, who became the new president of the FIDE when it was reorganized after World War II, a completely revised code of laws was prepared. This new code was adopted by the General Assembly of the FIDE at its twenty-third Congress in Stockholm, 1952. However, one of the new laws met with violent opposition, and the 1952 code was amended the following year at the twenty-fourth Congress in Switzerland. Later, experience indicated the need for new regulations governing the recording of moves in tournaments and matches, and for new rules covering the procedure of claiming a draw and agreeing to a draw. New laws and amendments of existing laws were adopted by the Congresses of 1956, 1962, 1963, 1964, and 1965.

The international code is divided into two parts. This chapter contains part one, on the fundamental rules of the game—how it must be played, and how games are won and drawn. Section No. 3 of Article 12 on the "draw by repetition" has been amended, but this is the only change that has been made in part one of the laws. All the other alterations are in the regulations for tournaments and matches in part two.

Throughout the first and second chapters, the laws are printed in *italics*. Our comments and explanations appear in roman type.

THE LAWS OF CHESS
Article 1

INTRODUCTION. The game of chess is played between two op-
ponents by moving men on a square board called a "chessboard."

Sounds simple enough. The "men" you push around the chessboard
are described later.

Article 2

THE CHESSBOARD AND ITS ARRANGEMENT

1. The chessboard is composed of 64 equal squares alternately
light (the "white" squares) and dark (the "black" squares).

The squares may be any combination of two colors, such as white
and green, yellow and black, buff and brown, maple and walnut;
but, whatever the two colors may be, the squares with a light shade
of color are called "white" squares, and the squares with a dark
shade of color are called "black" squares.

2. The chessboard is placed between the players in such a way
that the corner square to the right of each player is white.

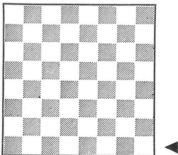

The Chessboard

Before putting the chessmen on the board, check to see that the
board is placed right—with a white square at the right-hand corner
nearest to you. (See pointer above.)

3. The eight rows of squares running from the edge of the chess-board nearest one of the players to that nearest the other player are called "files."

4. The eight rows of squares running from one edge of the chess-board to the other at right angles to the files are called "ranks."

5. The straight rows of squares of one color, touching corner to corner, are called "diagonals."

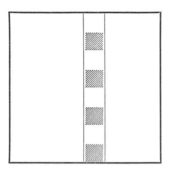

This is one of the 8 rows of squares called *files*. They run "up and down" the board between the two players.

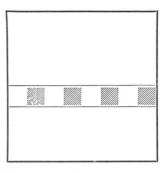

This is one of the 8 rows of squares called *ranks*. They run "sideways" across the board, at right angles to the files.

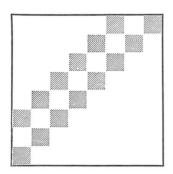

This diagram shows two of the 13 black diagonals and one of the 13 white diagonals.

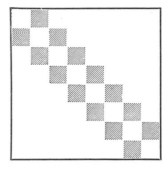

The diagonals run in two directions, crossing at right angles. Note the long white diagonal from upper left to lower right.

Article 3

THE CHESSMEN AND THEIR ARRANGEMENT. At the beginning of the game, one player commands 16 light-colored men (the "white" men), the other 16 dark-colored men (the "black" men). These men are as follows:

One white King	*with the usual symbol in print of*	♔
One white Queen	" " " " " " "	♕
Two white Rooks	" " " " " " "	♖
Two white Bishops	" " " " " " "	♗
Two white Knights	" " " " " " "	♘
Eight white Pawns	" " " " " " "	♙
One black King	" " " " " " "	♚
One black Queen	" " " " " " "	♛
Two black Rooks	" " " " " " "	♜
Two black Bishops	" " " " " " "	♝
Two black Knights	" " " " " " "	♞
Eight black Pawns	" " " " " " "	♟

The initial position of the men on the chessboard is as follows:

In chess diagrams the men are indicated by symbols. The photo on the next page illustrates actual chessmen in the same position as the above diagram.

The chessmen in the above picture are placed on the board in the starting position. The "white" men are in the foreground, the "black" men in the rear.

From left to right on the first rank (at bottom of picture) are placed a white Rook, Knight, Bishop, Queen, King, Bishop, Knight, and Rook. These men are usually called "pieces" to distinguish them from the Pawns. In front of the eight white pieces stand the eight white Pawns.

In the rear, the eight black pieces are placed in the same order as the white pieces. The black Pawns stand in front of the black pieces.

Note that each Queen "goes on its own color"—the white Queen on a white square, the black Queen on a black square.

Chessmen may be any combination of two colors, but the light-colored men are called "white" men and the dark-colored "black" men.

Article 4

CONDUCT OF THE GAME

1. The two players must alternate in making one move at a time. The player with the white men commences the game.

2. A player is said to "have the move" when it is his turn to play.

This article is self-explanatory, but readers who are accustomed to the old rules should note the change in terminology. In these new laws, the terms "player" and "opponent" have no unusual significance.

In our comments on the laws, the terms "White" and "Black" (capitalized) are used when referring to the players with the white and black men, respectively.

Article 5

GENERAL DEFINITION OF THE MOVE

1. With the exception of castling (Article 6), a move is the transfer of a man from one square to another square which is either vacant or occupied by an enemy man.

2. No man, except the Rook when castling, and the Knight (Article 6), may cross a square occupied by another man.

3. A man played to a square occupied by an enemy man captures, in the same move, this enemy man, which must be removed immediately from the chessboard by the player making the capture. See Article 6 for capturing "en passant."

To beginners: These rules are difficult to understand before you learn how the chessmen move. They will be clarified later.

To tournament players: Under section 3 above, it makes no difference which man you touch first—the enemy man you are capturing, or your own man that is doing the capturing. As we shall see later, however, the man you touched first would be the deciding factor if you made an illegal capture.

The Rook moves in any one of these four directions.

Article 6

MOVES OF THE INDIVIDUAL MEN

THE ROOK

The Rook moves to any square (except as limited by Article 5, No. 2) on the file or rank on which it stands.

The picture above illustrates the directions in which a Rook moves on the chessboard. It may move up or down the file it stands on; or it may move left or right on the rank it stands on.

The distance the Rook may travel is limited by the condition stated in Article 5, No. 2. This is illustrated in the picture on the next page. Here the Rook may move one, two, or three squares to the left; or it may move one or two squares to the right, but it is not allowed to jump over the white King and go to the square beyond. With certain exceptions which do not apply to the ordinary movement of the Rook, "no man ... may cross a square occupied by another man."

The Rook may move to any one of the ten vacant squares indicated by circles, or it may move to the square occupied by the black Bishop and capture this enemy man.

Instead of moving to the left or right, the Rook in the pictured position may move one or two squares down the file; or it may move one, two, three, or four squares up the file, the fourth square being occupied by a black Bishop. Although the Rook is not permitted to jump over the Bishop, it may capture this enemy man. The method of capturing, as defined in Article 5, No. 3, is illustrated below and in the examples on the next page.

After Capturing

This diagram shows the position after the Rook in the picture above has captured the Bishop. The Rook is on the square where the Bishop stood, and the captured piece is off the board.

Before Capturing

This black Rook may capture the white Pawn on the rank or the white Knight on the file.

After Capturing

The Rook has captured the white Knight by moving to the square the Knight occupied.

Before Capturing

The Bishop and Pawn are on the same rank as the Rook, so either may be captured.

After Capturing

The Rook has moved two squares to the left on the rank and has captured the Pawn.

Before Capturing

The white Rook can move in only one direction—up the file. The other white men prevent the Rook from moving sideways or down the file.

After Capturing

The white Rook moved two squares up the file and captured the black Rook. The captured man was immediately removed from the board.

The Bishop moves in any one of these four directions.

THE BISHOP

The Bishop moves to any square (except as limited by Article 5, No. 2) on the diagonals on which it stands.

The picture above illustrates the directions in which a Bishop moves on the chessboard. It may move up or down either of the two diagonals on which it stands.

When a game starts, each player has two Bishops, one on a white square and the other on black. The "white-square" Bishop moves only on white squares, the "black-square" Bishop on black squares. Its diagonal movement prevents a Bishop from moving to a square of the opposite color.

The distance the Bishop may travel in a diagonal direction is limited by an obstructing man in the same way as a Rook's movement is restricted. The Bishop is not permitted to cross a square occupied by another man, white or black.

This Bishop may move to any one of nine vacant squares or it may
capture the black Knight.

An example of the Bishop's move is shown in the position pictured
on this page. This Bishop may move one, two, or three squares
up the diagonal to the right, but only one square down the diagonal
to the left. In the latter direction the Bishop is obstructed by the
white Pawn.

On the other diagonal, the Bishop may move one, two, or three
squares down to the right; or it may move one, two, or three squares
up to the left. The third square up to the left is occupied by a black
Knight. The Bishop is not allowed to jump over the Knight but it
may capture this enemy man. To make the capture, the Bishop is
placed on the square occupied by the Knight, and the Knight is removed from the board.

Note that chess captures are optional. If he wishes, a player may
take an enemy man, but he is not compelled to do so. There is one
exception to this rule: a capture must be made by a player who has
no other legal move.

Examples of Captures by the Bishop

Before Capturing

The Bishop may capture the black Knight or the black Rook.

After Capturing

The Bishop has captured the black Rook which is now off the board.

Before Capturing

The Bishop may capture the Rook, Knight, or Pawn. The Rook is on one diagonal, the Pawn and Knight on the other diagonal on which the Bishop stands.

After Capturing

The Bishop has captured the black Pawn. Note that this Bishop travels on black squares. Its diagonal movement keeps a Bishop on squares of the same color.

The Queen moves in any one of these eight directions.

THE QUEEN

The Queen moves to any square (except as limited by Article 5, No. 2) on the file, rank, or diagonals on which it stands.

' The directions in which a Queen moves on the chessboard, as illustrated above, are those of a Rook and Bishop combined. Like a Rook, the Queen may move up or down the file, or to the left or right on the rank. Or, like a Bishop, the Queen may move up or down either of the two diagonals.

The limitation of Article 5, No. 2, also applies to the Queen. This piece is not permitted to cross a square occupied by another man, white or black.

An example of the Queen's move is shown in the position pictured on the next page. Here the white Queen may move to any one of 22 vacant squares on the file, rank, and diagonals on which this Queen stands. Or it may move to the square occupied by the black Queen, or to the square occupied by the black Pawn. If it moves to either of these squares, the enemy man is captured and removed from the board.

The white Queen may move to any of the vacant squares indicated, or it may capture the black Queen or Pawn.

There are only two restrictions on the movement of this white Queen in any of the eight directions the piece may travel. To the right on the rank, it is not allowed to cross the square occupied by

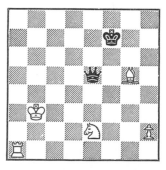

This white Queen may move up the file and capture the Bishop; or it may move down the diagonal and capture the Rook.

This black Queen may capture any one of the four white men on the rank, file, and diagonals on which the Queen stands.

the white Pawn. Up the diagonal to the left, it is not permitted to cross the square occupied by the black Queen.

Examples of Captures by the Queen

Before Capturing

The black Queen may capture the Bishop on the file or the Knight on the diagonal.

After Capturing

The Queen has moved down the file, like a Rook, and has captured the Bishop.

Before Capturing

This Queen, hemmed in by its own men, cannot go along the rank or up the file.

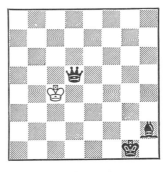

After Capturing

Being able to move in only one direction, the Queen has captured the white Bishop.

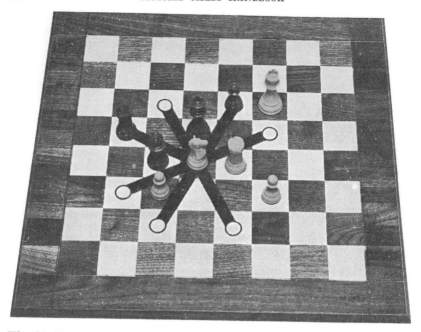

The Knight may leap over and capture Rook or Pawn, or land on
any of the five vacant squares indicated.

white or black men and land on a square within its range on the
next rank or file.

The Knight may leap over the
white Pawn and capture the
Bishop; or it may leap over the
black Rook and capture the
white Rook.

The Knight may jump over the
white King and capture the
black Rook; or it may jump
over the black Pawn and capture the Bishop.

Examples of Captures by the Knight

Before Capturing

The Knight may leap over the Pawns and capture the Rook or Queen.

After Capturing

The Knight has moved to the square that was occupied by the Queen.

Before Capturing

The Knight may jump over white or black men and capture Rook or Bishop.

After Capturing

The Knight has jumped over the black King and captured the Rook.

Each player moves his Pawns forward. When first moved, any Pawn
may be advanced one or two vacant squares.

THE PAWN

The Pawn moves forward only.

*a) Except when capturing, it advances from its original square
one or two vacant squares along the file on which it is placed, and
on subsequent moves only one vacant square along the file. When
capturing, it advances to either square, contiguous to its own, on
the diagonal.*

When a Pawn moves or captures it must advance toward the
opponent's side of the board—directly forward on the file if it moves
without capturing, diagonally forward if it captures.

As illustrated in the picture above, a Pawn may advance either
one or two vacant squares on its first move. This option holds good
throughout the entire game. Provided a Pawn has not moved from
its original square (on the player's second rank), it may go forward
either one or two vacant squares.

After a Pawn has moved one or two squares from its original position, it may advance on the file only one vacant square on each subsequent move.

Each player has moved a Pawn. The white Pawn advanced two squares, the black Pawn one square. Hereafter each of these moved Pawns may advance only one square per move.

Each player has moved a Pawn two squares. Now they block each other and cannot move. To advance on the file, the square in front of a Pawn must be vacant.

The white Pawn cannot move, for it is blocked by the black King. The black Pawn may advance one or two squares, for this Pawn has not moved from its original square.

It is White's turn to play. If he wishes to move his advanced Pawn, he may push it forward one square on the file, or he may capture the black Pawn (see next page).

Note that a Pawn, on its first move or on any subsequent move, is not allowed to advance on the file if the square immediately in front of the Pawn is occupied. Even if the square is occupied by an enemy man, the Pawn is blocked.

It is White's turn to play. He cannot take the black Pawn, but he may capture the Rook or the Knight.

Before Capturing

This black Pawn may advance one square on the file (down the page) or it may capture either the Bishop or Knight.

After Capturing

The black Pawn has captured the white Knight. The Knight is off the board and the Pawn has taken its place.

A Pawn is blocked by an enemy man because the Pawn does not capture in the direction it moves to a vacant square. In this respect, the Pawn differs from all the other types of chessmen. As illustrated on the previous page, the Pawn captures on either of the two squares *diagonally* in front of the Pawn.

The "En Passant" Capture

Occasionally, a Pawn is able to capture an enemy Pawn in an unusual way, defined in the laws as follows:

b) *A Pawn attacking a square crossed by an enemy Pawn, which has been advanced two squares in one move from its original square, may capture this enemy Pawn, as if the latter had been advanced only one square. This capture may only be made on the move immediately following such advance and is called taking "en passant."*

This sounds rather complicated; but the following illustrations and captions demonstrate the simplicity of this type of capture. In these pictures it is the black Pawn that makes the "en passant" capture. Note that Black's Pawn is on his fifth rank (which is White's fourth rank). Black would not be allowed to make this type of capture if his Pawn were on any other rank.

1 Black's Pawn is on his fifth rank. White's Pawn has not moved from its original square. The two Pawns are on adjacent files. It is White's turn to play. See next page.

2 White's Pawn has advanced two squares in one move, thereby passing through the square on which the black Pawn could have captured it. Now it is Black's turn to play.

3 Black has taken the white Pawn "en passant." The black Pawn has moved to the square the white Pawn *passed through,* capturing as though White had advanced his Pawn only one square. Black was not forced to capture, but any other reply would have forfeited the right to capture that Pawn "en passant."

Pawn Promotion

c) Any Pawn reaching the last rank must be exchanged imme-diately, as part of the same move, for a Queen, Rook, Bishop, or Knight of the same color, at the choice of the player and without reference to the other men still remaining on the chessboard. This

Before Promotion	After Promotion

It is White's move. His Pawn is on the seventh rank. He advances the Pawn to the last square on the file.

As part of the same move, White substitutes a Queen for the Pawn. Black is checkmated (see page 44).

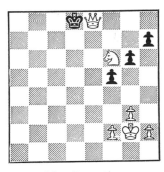

Before Promotion	After Promotion

It is White's move. His Pawn on the seventh rank is blocked by the black King.

White's Pawn reached the last rank by capturing the Rook. The Pawn is promoted to a Queen.

*exchange of a Pawn is called "promotion" and the action of the
promoted man is immediate.*

As illustrated in the examples on these pages, a Pawn can reach
the last rank by advancing from the player's seventh rank to the last
square on the file, or by capturing an enemy man on the last rank.

As a rule, a promoted Pawn is exchanged for a Queen, so that
Pawn promotion is usually called "queening a Pawn." However, a
player may exchange for a Rook, Bishop, or Knight. This is called
"under-promotion."

Before Promotion

It is Black's move. He can
advance his Pawn on the
seventh rank and exchange it
for a Queen, Rook, Bishop, or
Knight. See diagram at right.

After Promotion

Black has advanced his Pawn
to the last square on the file
and exchanged it for a Knight
which checks the King and
attacks the Queen.

Note that a Pawn, on reaching the eighth rank, *must* be promoted;
it cannot remain a Pawn.

Back in the eighteenth century, some codes of chess laws stated
that a promoted Pawn could only take the place of a captured piece.
The latest edition of any book in English containing this rule is
believed to have been published about 100 years ago. Nevertheless,
there are thousands of players in this country who seem to think that
the rule is still in effect. Chess organizations and clubs are constantly
being asked this question: "Can a player have two Queens on the
board at the same time?" The answer is yes. In fact, he can have
more than two Queens. And he can have three or more Rooks,
Knights, or Bishops. Pawn promotion has nothing to do with the
pieces on the board or the pieces that have been captured.

The white King may move to any one of seven adjacent squares but not to the square attacked by the Pawn.

THE KING

Except when castling, the King moves to any adjacent square that is not attacked by an enemy man.

The paragraph of the laws on castling will be explained later. Meantime, the position pictured above illustrates the ordinary move of the King. Here the white King may move to any one of seven adjacent squares but is not permitted to advance one square on the file because this adjacent square is attacked by the black Pawn. If it were Black's move in this position, the black King could move to any one of the eight squares adjacent to this King, for none of these squares is attacked.

The object of the game is to "checkmate" the enemy King. The King is checkmated when it can be captured and there is no way of preventing the capture. Consequently, a player is not allowed to expose his King to attack. The law prevents a King from committing suicide.

The white King is not allowed to advance one square on the file. This adjacent square is "attacked" by the pinned Knight.

It is White's move. The King must move to the left. The two squares in front of the white King are "attacked" by the black King.

A King must never be moved to a square that is under attack by an enemy man. Ordinarily, this means that the King must not go on a square to which an enemy man may move and capture. However, the diagram above, at the left, illustrates a type of position in which a square is "attacked" within the meaning of the law but not in the usual sense. Thus, the black Knight in the diagram is "pinned" by the white Rook. As we shall see later, it would be illegal for this Knight to move and thereby expose the black King to attack by the Rook. Nevertheless, the white King must not advance one square on the file, for this square is "attacked" by the Knight within the meaning of the law. The Knight *could* move to this square if it were not pinned, and that constitutes an "attack" on the King.

The other diagram illustrates the fact that a King must not move to a square adjacent to the enemy King.

Captures by the King

As shown in the next examples, the King may capture an enemy man on a square adjacent to the King, provided the square is not attacked by another enemy man. In other words, the King may capture an unguarded man, but not a guarded man. In the position of the right-hand diagram, the "guard" is pinned and cannot move.

Despite this, the King is not permitted to capture the black Pawn. The square the Pawn stands on is attacked, within the meaning of the law.

The white King may capture the Pawn but not the Knight. The Pawn guards the Knight. To capture, the King moves to the square occupied by the Pawn, and the Pawn is removed from the board.

The white King may capture the Rook, but not the Pawn. The pinned Bishop cannot move but it "attacks" the square the Pawn stands on, so the Pawn is "guarded" and immune from capture.

The Castling Move

The paragraph of the laws describing the King's castling move reads as follows:

Castling is a move of the King and either Rook, counting as a single move (of the King), executed as follows: The King is transferred from its original square to either of the nearest squares of the same color in the same rank; then that Rook toward which the King has been moved is transferred over the King to the square which the King has just crossed. Castling is permanently impossible if the King or castling Rook has previously moved. Castling is momentarily prevented: a) if the King's original square, or the square which the King must cross, or that which it will occupy, is attacked by an enemy man; b) if there are any men between the King and the Rook toward which the King must move.

Castling on the King's Side

1. The King moves two squares toward the King-Rook.

2. The King-Rook goes to the square the King crossed.

Pictured above are the two steps of castling on the King's side of the board (the four files to the right of the player with the white men). White moves his King two squares toward the King-Rook (at the player's right), then transfers this Rook to the square the King just crossed. The two steps count as one move.

Black castles on the King's side in the same way. However, from the viewpoint of this player, the King's side of the board, and the King-Rook, are at his left.

Castling on the Queen's Side

1. The King moves two squares toward the Queen-Rook.

2. The Queen-Rook goes to the square the King crossed.

Pictured above are the two steps of castling on the Queen's side of the board (the four files to the left of the player with the white men). White moves his King two squares toward the Queen-Rook (at the player's left), then transfers this Rook to the square the King just crossed. The two steps count as one move.

Black castles on the Queen's side in the same way. However, from the viewpoint of this player, the Queen's side of the board, and the Queen-Rook, are at his right.

Castling is an illegal move (of the King) if executed by a player who has forfeited the right to castle. Thus, a player is not permitted to castle:

(a) With either Rook if he previously moved his King from its original square. His previous move of the King entirely forfeited the right to castle.

(b) With a Rook he previously moved from its original square. The previous move of the Rook forfeited the right to castle with that Rook.

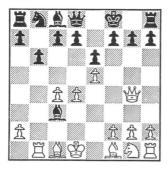

Both players have moved their Kings. Therefore, they have lost entirely the right to castle throughout the game.

White has moved his Queen-Rook, losing the right to castle with that Rook. But White may castle on the King-side.

The diagrams on the next page show positions in which a player has not forfeited the right to castle but is not allowed to castle under the existing conditions. The fact that a player is prevented from castling under these conditions has no effect on his right to castle in the future.

As illustrated in these diagrams, castling is an illegal move (of the King):

(a) If a player's King is in check (attacked by an enemy man). He must parry the check, but not by castling. If he parries by moving his King, he forfeits the right to castle later (see above). If he does not move his King, he retains the right to castle later with an unmoved Rook.

(b) If the King crosses a square that is attacked by an enemy man.

(c) If the King moves to a square that is attacked by an enemy man.

(d) If there are any men between the King and the Rook toward which the King moves.

There is no rule against castling with a Rook that is attacked by an enemy man.

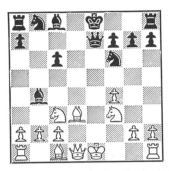

White's King is in check. It would be illegal to get out of check by castling. White must interpose or move his King. If the latter, he forfeits the right to castle later.

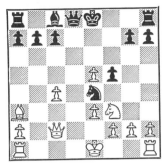

White may castle K-side but not Q-side. Black's Queen attacks the square the King would cross. If Black's move, castling is illegal. White's Bishop prevents castling.

White is not allowed to castle. Black's bishop attacks the square the King would occupy. Note that Black has castled on the K-side.

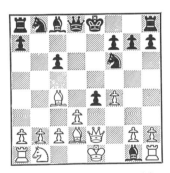

White cannot castle on either side. The squares between the King and the castling Rook must be vacant. If Black's move, he may castle K-side.

Comments for Tournament Players

When castling, the King must be moved first, then the Rook. This is clearly stated in Article 6 and confirmed in Article 7, c. According to the Laws, a player is castling illegally and should be forced to move his Rook if he castles by moving the Rook first. This interpretation was proposed at the 1952 FIDE Congress, but a majority of the delegates at the 1953 Congress held that such an interpretation is undesirable and too harsh.

Article 7

COMPLETION OF MOVE

A move is completed:

a) in the transfer of a man to a vacant square, when the player's hand has released the man;

b) in a capture, when the captured man has been removed from the chessboard and the player, having placed on its new square his own man, has released the latter from his hand;

c) in castling, when the player's hand has released the Rook on the square crossed by the King; when the player has released the King from his hand, the move is not yet completed, but the player no longer has the right to make any other move than castling;

d) in the promotion of a Pawn, when the Pawn has been removed from the chessboard and the player's hand has released the new man after placing it on the promotion square; if the player has released from his hand the Pawn that has reached the promotion square, the move is not yet completed, but the player no longer has the right to play the Pawn to another square.

Comments for Noncompetitive Players

The rules of Article 7 are extremely important to tournament contestants, for winning or losing a game may hinge on whether or not a player has completed his move. In serious play, a contestant is never allowed to "take a move back." Once completed, the move stands.

Even when chess is played for fun, taking moves back is a bad habit as well as being illegal. It can also produce nervous disorders in your opponent. He may have laid a nice trap which you fell into because you did not see as far ahead as he did. He is not going to like it if you take your move back after he reveals what he had in mind. You will keep more friends, and play better chess, if you stand by your blunders.

If you really want to know how to play chess legally, read the rules on completion of the move carefully, and the comments for tournament players on the following pages.

Comments for Tournament Players

In the supplementary rules for chess competitions, Article 14, No. 4, it is stated that "upon the execution of the prescribed number of moves, the last move is not considered as being completed until after the player has stopped his clock." Comments on this important section of the laws will be found on page 57.

The laws avoid all reference to the touchy subject of what to do about players who move a piece to one square, then change their minds and move it to another square, hanging on to the piece until they finally decide what to do with it.

For better or worse, the ambiguity of the 1929 code has been removed. It is now legal for a player to shift a man around the board before alighting somewhere. There is no law that states what a player should or should not do between the time he grabs hold of a man and the time he lets it go.

This does not mean, however, that reprehensible conduct on the part of players is now legalized. Some players are extremely annoyed when their opponents move in a vacillating manner. Therefore, a Director may impose penalties under Article 18.

To avoid disputes, and to protect himself from the possibility of being penalized, a player should develop the habit of moving each man directly and unhesitatingly to the square to be occupied. A good practice is to write down a move before making it.

Almost all the old codes contained laws or admonitions on this subject. One of the simplest dates back to 1497 when Lucena declared: "If the player touches a square with the piece, he must move to that square." Some players would like to revive this rule—but it would be unfair and unenforceable. For instance, almost every strong player slides his Queen, Rooks, and Bishops along the board, and would break the rule automatically. Who would like to be the Director who tells Reshevsky he has to move his Bishop back from KN5 to Q2 because it touched Q2 first? To move legally under such a rule, a player would have to pick up each man in a dainty, ladylike fashion and place it on the square it was to occupy. It just wouldn't work.

For twenty-three years, the 1929 FIDE code had a milder rule stating that a man must be moved directly toward the square to be occupied, but this rule was hardly ever enforced. How is "directly" to be interpreted? Is a momentary hesitation to be penalized, or is the Director supposed to hold a stop watch in his hand and time the hesitation? If a rule has been on the books for twenty-three years and has seldom been enforced, there must be something wrong with it. If it cannot be put into effect, it is better to repeal it—and that is what the FIDE has done.

Article 7, c: See comments on castling, page 37. If a player is permitted to reverse the order of castling, we will have to assume that the move is completed when he releases the King. However, it does not follow that a player can be forced to castle when he moves his Rook to KB1 or Q1, as the case may be. That would be absurd. But if a player moves his Rook and then touches his King, it is obvious that he intended to castle and must do so.

For correct castling the rule is clear. When the King is moved two squares toward the castling Rook and the player's hand releases the King, he must castle; the move is completed when the castling Rook is released. Of course, if a player moves his King two squares toward a Rook with which he cannot castle, it is just an illegal move of the King. Finally, if a player moves his King two squares and, without releasing it, moves it back one square and then lets go, he has just moved his King under Article 7, a. It would be up to the Director to decide if the player annoyed his opponent by such maneuvers, and whether or not he should be penalized.

Article 7, d: Players who get into time-trouble should note that the promotion move is not completed until the hand is released from the new man on the promotion square. The last part of the rule covers the situation in which a player has the option of advancing a Pawn to the last square on the file or capturing on the eighth rank. The fact that the move is not completed does not permit the player to change his mind after he has advanced or captured, and his hand has released the Pawn. However, under Article 8, he would be forced to capture if he touched the enemy man before touching his Pawn.

Article 8
THE TOUCHED MAN

Provided that he first warns his opponent, the player having the move may adjust one or more men on their squares.

Except for the above case, if the player having the move touches one or more men, he must make his move by moving or capturing the first man touched which can be moved or captured.

No penalty is entailed if the opponent does not claim a violation of this rule before himself touching a man, or if none of the moves indicated above can be made legally.

A tournament player says "adjusting" or "J'adoube" (the international expression) to warn his opponent that he is touching a man or men for the purpose of adjustment. Note that the player having the move may adjust his opponent's men as well as his own. Nothing is said about the player who does not have the move, but this player should keep his hands off the men on the board.

If a player wishes to adjust men when his opponent is not present, the FIDE has ruled that he may do so provided he first informs the Director of his intention. It follows from this ruling that it is unethical to take advantage of an opponent's absence by touching a man and then not moving or capturing it. A player may not break the touch-move rule when his opponent is absent, even though the opponent is now permitted to overlook such a violation if he is present.

The second paragraph of Article 8 simplifies the provisions of the 1929 code. If a player touches a man that can be moved he must move it, or if he touches an opponent's man that can be captured he must capture it. If he touches more than one man, he must move (or capture) the first man he touched that can be moved (or captured).

The third paragraph indicates that the rule requiring a player to move (or capture) a touched man can be enforced only if a violation is immediately claimed by the opponent. A legal move or capture infringing the touch-move rule stands as played if the opponent makes no protest before touching a man.

It is now up to each contestant to make sure that his opponent obeys the touch-move rule. Unless a claim is made at the proper time, it is not the responsibility of the Director to see that the rule is observed. If he wishes to do so, a player may condone a breach of the touch-move rule by his opponent.

Although these laws have been in effect since 1952, there is still some confusion in the minds of tournament players as to the meaning of the third paragraph of Article 8. There is a prevalent notion that this paragraph now makes it legal to take a move back in a tournament game. It should be noted, therefore, that Article 8 refers only to the touch-move rule of chess and has nothing to do with taking moves back. The latter subject is covered in Article 7.

If a player completes a legal move, and his opponent makes no claim that the touch-move rule was violated, the rules of Article 8 do not apply. The completed move stands. If the player takes his move back and substitutes another, he is breaking the rules of Article 7. The opponent cannot condone such an offense, nor does the absence of a claim legalize it.

Article 9

ILLEGAL POSITIONS

1. If, during a game, it is found that an illegal move was made, the position shall be reinstated to what it was before the illegal move was made. The game shall then continue by applying the rules of Article 8 to the move replacing the illegal move. If the position cannot be reinstated, the game shall be annulled and a new game played.

All five sections of Article 9 were incorporated into the laws in 1953, replacing the rules governing illegal positions adopted in 1952. In the earlier and now extinct version of the first section, an illegal move would not be corrected if either player made another move! There were violent objections to this rule on the obvious grounds that it would encourage and reward cheating. It is surprising that the rule was ever proposed, and still more surprising that it was adopted by the FIDE Congress in 1952.

As the law now reads, an illegal move must be corrected, provided the illegality is found and verified *before the game ends*. A finished game is not affected by the law; if illegal moves were made, they stand as played.

The procedure is outlined clearly in section No. 1. The illegal move and all moves thereafter are canceled, the position reinstated to what it was before the illegal move was made, and the game continued. The player who made the illegal move must substitute a legal move, and the rules of Article 8 apply to this move.

The clarification of the first move in the continuation of such a game is welcomed. In the past, there have been many arguments as to whether or not the player who made the illegal move must move the man he touched, etc. There can be no doubt on this point in the future. The player who made the illegal move is in the situation of the player who has touched one or more men, as described in Article 8.

2. If, during a game, one or more men have been accidentally displaced and incorrectly replaced, the position shall be reinstated to what it was before the displacement took place and the game shall be continued. If the position cannot be reinstated the game shall be annulled and a new game played.

In this situation no illegal move is involved but the procedure is the same as that outlined in Section No. 1. Although not specifically stated, it must be assumed that Article 8 applies to the first move in the continuation of the game.

3. If, after an adjournment, the position has been reinstated incorrectly, it shall be re-established to what it was at the adjournment and the game shall be continued.

With the exception of the sealed move, any moves that were played from the incorrect adjourned position would, of course, be canceled. The clocks would be set back to the time recorded when the game was adjourned.

4. If, during a game, it is found that the initial position of the men was incorrect, the game shall be annulled and a new game played.

According to an interpretation made by FIDE, this paragraph can apply in the case of a game which was incorrectly started with the players' colors reversed.

5. If, during a game, it is found that the board has been wrongly placed, the position reached shall be transferred to a board correctly placed and the game shall be continued.

This paragraph contradicts section 4 above. If the board has been wrongly placed, then the initial position of the men was incorrect. At the next FIDE Congress, the USCF intends to propose that section 5 be canceled.

It will be noted that the provisions of all these rules apply "during a game." If a game is finished, any irregularities are not corrected. However, in the case of adjudicated games, the FIDE has ruled that a game is not finished until the adjudicator has given his decision.

The white King is mated and Black wins the game.

Article 10
CHECK

   1. The King is in check when the square on which it stands is attacked by an enemy man; the latter is then said to give check to the King.

   2. Check must be parried by the move immediately following. If check cannot be parried, it is said to be "mate." (See Article 11, No. 1.)

   3. A man intercepting a check to the King of its own color can itself give check to the enemy King.

Article 11
WON GAME

   1. The game is won by the player who has mated the enemy King. (See Article 10, No. 2.)

   2. The game is won by the player whose opponent resigns the game.

In the example pictured, the white King is checkmated ("mated"). The King is in check, the square on which it stands being attacked by the black Queen. The King cannot move out of check and the black Queen cannot be captured, for it is guarded by a Rook. The check cannot be parried, so the King is mated and Black wins the game.

As stated in Article 10, No. 2, when a player's King is in check (attacked by an enemy man), the check must be "parried" by the move immediately following. If the check cannot be parried, the King is mated.

The important point here is that a player whose King is in check must immediately make a move which gets his King out of check, if such a move is available to him. Any other move would be illegal.

The diagrams below and on the next page show examples of parrying a check. In each position, the black King is in check. Therefore Black must make a move which gets his King out of check.

As shown in the four examples, a check may be parried by:

(a) moving the King to a square that is not attacked by an enemy man; or

(b) capturing the man that is giving the check; or

(c) interposing a man between the King and the enemy man that is giving check.

Black's King is checked by the Rook. Black must parry the check, is not allowed to move his Pawn. He can get out of check by moving the King to a square that is not under attack by an enemy man.

Black's King is checked by the Knight and the check must be parried. Black has the option of moving his King to an unattacked square or capturing the Knight with his Bishop.

The last method can never be used when the checking piece is a Knight, for a Knight may cross a square occupied by another man. The Laws do not require a player to announce check. However, it is customary to say "check!" when making a move which attacks the opponent's King.

Black's King is checked by the Bishop. Black may move his King to an unattacked square, or capture the Bishop with his Knight, or interpose his Bishop between his King and the white Bishop.

Black's King is checked by the Rook. If Black parries the check by interposing his Bishop, placing it between the King and Rook, the white King will then be checked by the black Bishop.

Section 3 of Article 10 is illustrated in the right-hand diagram above. If the black Bishop is interposed to parry the check by the

It is White's move. It would be illegal to move Bishop or Knight and expose the King to check. Both of these white men are pinned. White must move his King.

White's move. His King must not move to a white square, for this exposes the King to check by the black Bishop, even though the Bishop is pinned and has no legal moves.

white Rook, this Bishop will itself give check to the white King, despite the fact that the Bishop will be pinned and unable to move.

It is illegal for a player to expose his King to check in any manner whatsoever. As we have seen before, the King must not move to (or capture on) a square that is attacked by an enemy man. It would be just as illegal to move a pinned man and thereby expose the King to check. Thus, in the diagram at the lower left, White's Bishop and Knight are both pinned. To move either of these pieces in this position would expose the King to check, which is illegal.

Comment for Tournament Players

As stated in the Supplementary Rules for Competitions (Article 17), a game is also won by a player whose opponent (1) does not complete the prescribed number of moves in the time specified; (2) arrives at the chessboard more than one hour late; (3) seals a move the real significance of which it is impossible to establish; (4) refuses to comply with the laws of chess.

Article 12

DRAWN GAME

The game is drawn:

1. When the King of the player who has the move is not in check, but such player cannot make any legal move. The King is then said to be "stalemated."

2. By agreement between the two players. (See Article 17a.)

3. Upon demand by one of the players when the same position appears three times, provided that the same player has the move after each of the three appearances of the same position on the chessboard. The position is considered the same if men of the same kind and color occupy the same squares, and the possible moves of all the men are unchanged. The right to claim the draw belongs exclusively to the player who—

(a) is in a position to play a move leading to such repetition provided that he indicates the move and claims the draw before making the move;

(b) must reply to a move which has produced the repeated position, provided that he claims the draw before executing his move.

If a player's claim of a draw proves to be incorrect (Article 17a), and the game continues, then the player who has indicated a move according to clause (a) above is obliged to execute this move on the chessboard.

If a player makes a move without having claimed a draw in the manner prescribed in clauses (a) and (b) above, he loses the right to claim a draw; this right is restored to him, however, if the same position appears again, the same player having the move, and the possible moves of all men being unchanged.

(Note: For the sake of clarity we have reworded section 3 above so that it combines the original Article 12, No. 3, and the several interpretations of this section by the FIDE Committee on Laws.)

4. When a player having the move demonstrates that at least fifty moves have been made by each side without the capture of any man, or the movement of any Pawns.

This number of fifty moves may be increased for certain specific positions, provided that this increase in number and these positions have been clearly established prior to the commencement of the game.

The draw by stalemate (Article 12, No. 1) is illustrated in the two diagrams below. For the benefit of beginners: A position cannot be a stalemate if the King is in check. It is only when the King of

It is Black's move. His King is not in check and every square adjacent to the King is attacked by White's Queen or Bishop. Black has no legal moves so the position is a draw by stalemate.

It is White's move. His King is not in check and every square adjacent to the King is attacked by Black's Queen or Pawn. The Pawns are blocked. White has no legal moves. A draw by stalemate.

the player on the move is *not* in check, and the player has no legal moves, that stalemate is reached.

A question often asked is: "Am I forced to capture a Pawn "en passant" to get out of stalemate?" The answer is yes. When the "en passant" capture (or any other capture) is a player's only legal move, he must make the capture or resign. This also applies to positions in which a player's King is *in check* and the check can be parried only by a capture ("en passant" or otherwise). In such positions the player whose King is in check must capture or resign.

The draw by agreement (section No. 2) has been the subject of much discussion at the Congresses of the FIDE. This is covered in the next chapter.

The draw by repetition (section No. 3) is clarified by these new regulations. The most recent modification was adopted in 1964 at Tel Aviv, following a suggestion by International Master Joseph Porath. Hitherto, a position was considered as being repeated if men of the same kind and color occupied the same squares, and the same player had the move. It is now added that the possible moves of all the men must also be the same; an earlier right to castle or capture "en passant" must not be lost.

The fifty-move rule (section No. 4) is designed to put a reasonable limit on efforts to win theoretically drawn games, or even games that can be won but require a knowledge of the technique. The last paragraph of this section is intended to take care of possible future developments in chess theory.

Noncompetitive players will not be too concerned about these technicalities. In social games, players seldom agree to a draw until there is no hope of winning. Beginners have been known to keep on playing games in which it would be impossible for either player to mate the other. In case there are any readers who do not know it, checkmate cannot be forced when all the Pawns are off the board unless one player is ahead at least a Rook or two minor pieces (two Bishops, or Bishop and Knight). A King and two Knights cannot checkmate a lone King by force, but the mate is possible against weak defense.

CHAPTER II

The Laws of Chess, Part Two

The World Chess Federation has made significant changes in the laws governing the conduct of tournaments and matches. The Congress of 1956 amended Article 13 and added a new Article 17a. In 1962, a new section was added to 17a, and in 1963 this new section was changed. Still another revision was made in 1964. A section of Article 17 was amended in 1965.

Article 13 on Recording Moves: The amended Article 13 is a big improvement, and the interpretation of this Article by the FIDE Committee on Laws, issued in 1959, is most welcome. The interpretation appears under Article 13 in this chapter.

Article 17a on the Drawn Game: In its original form, as adopted in 1956, the purpose of this new Article was to clarify the procedure of proposing and claiming a draw. The law still contains these clarifications; but in response to continued criticism of short, agreed draws between players in important tournaments (particularly the Soviet players in the Interzonal and World Championship Candidates' Tournaments), the FIDE added clauses to Article 17a in an attempt to develop legislation that would prohibit premature draws and penalize players who engage in unethical practices in this respect.

This matter of agreeing to a draw after making a few moves on the board for the sake of appearances (but fooling nobody) has plagued competitive chess for decades. There is a case on record of a player in one of the early American tournaments who lost his last-round game, then complained to the tournament committee that his opponent had welched on their advance agreement to draw and split the prize. He had the nerve to ask the committee to declare the game a draw and give him half the prize money!

The 1929 code required players to complete thirty moves before they could agree to a draw, but this rule was abandoned in the laws of 1952. The Congress of 1954 rejected a proposal to reinstate the thirty-move rule but stated that it is unethical and unsportsmanlike to agree to a draw before a serious contest has begun. The Congress declared that FIDE Grandmasters and International Masters must be examples to other players, and that the Director of a tournament must discipline any player who repeatedly fails to respect his duty toward the tournament organizers and the chess public. This had no observable effect on tournament players.

The subject was discussed from time to time, and various proposals were made. In 1962, the thirty-move rule was revived and the following section added to Article 17a:

An agreement to a draw may not be made before the thirtieth move unless on account of quite exceptional circumstances the referee of the competition confirms it. Infringement of this regulation entails loss of the game for both players.

This rule was given a trial period of one year to determine its value. It went into effect at the 15th Olympics in Bulgaria, 1962, "with lamentable results" (to quote the *British Chess Magazine*). Many players agreed to draw before the thirtieth move without being penalized; others circumvented the principles of the rule by an agreed repetition of moves.

The 1963 Congress made a second attempt to clamp down on unethical and chickenhearted players. Effective until 1964, section No. 3 of Article 17a was changed to read as follows:

A draw by agreement before the thirtieth move is forbidden. Contravention is to be punished by the loss of the game for both players.

The referee should take care that this regulation is not circumvented. For example, in the case of a draw by repetition of moves, the referee has the right to investigate whether the circumstances are not equivalent to a direct draw by agreement.

This rule was just as ineffective as the first, and was abolished by the Congress of 1964 at Tel Aviv. Grandmaster Isaac Kashdan, delegate of the United States, led the fight for its repeal. The Russians strongly favored the rule, but the majority agreed with Kashdan that the thirty-move rule was too mechanical and deprived players of their right to judge for themselves if and when an agreement to draw was indicated. It was also decided that the rule had not encouraged aggressive play.

2. If, extremely pressed for time, a player is obviously unable to meet the requirements of section No. 1 above, he should nevertheless endeavor to indicate on his score sheet the number of moves made. As soon as his time-trouble is over, he must immediately complete his record of the game by writing down the omitted moves. However, he will not have the right to claim a draw, on the basis of Article 12, No. 3, if the moves in question were not recorded in conformity with the stipulation of section No. 1 above.

The new Article 13 makes it clear that players in time-trouble are permitted to make check marks on their score sheets instead of writing down the moves. They are not even *required* to make check marks, but they must endeavor to do so. Other than losing the right to claim a draw by repetition of moves, a player in serious time-trouble is not penalized if he does not record the moves on his score sheet or even make check marks. However, the FIDE Committee on Laws has issued an important interpretation of Article 13. In 1959, the Committee ruled as follows:

"1. The words 'extremely pressed for time' in Article 13, No. 2, cannot be precisely defined. It is the referee's task to decide (after considering the time on the clock, the number of moves to be made, and the character of the position at the moment) whether these words apply to a player's situation. In this matter, the referee's opinion decides. If the referee thinks the words do not apply, he may require the player to write down the moves, in the manner specified in Article 13, No. 1. If the player refuses to do this, the referee may rule that the player has lost the game by refusing to comply with the Laws of Chess (Article 17, No. 4).

"2. If the referee instructs a player to write down the moves as described above, and the player declares that he cannot fill in the missing moves without consulting his opponent's score sheet, the request for this sheet must be made to the referee, who will estimate if the player's form can be completed before the time control without embarrassing the opponent. The latter cannot refuse his score sheet for two reasons: the form belongs to the organizers of the tournament, and the player who has been instructed to complete his form must do so on his own time.

"3. In all other cases, the score sheets can only be completed after the time control. There are then two possibilities:

(a) One player alone has not completed his score sheet, in which case he will do so on his own playing time.

(b) The two players have not completed their score sheets. In this case, both clocks will be stopped until the two forms are completed, if necessary with the help of a chessboard under the control of the referee who will, beforehand, have noted the final position.

"If, in the case (a), the referee sees that the player's complete score sheet cannot help in reconstituting the game, he will act as in case (b)."

The Tournament Rules Committee of the U. S. Chess Federation has added its interpretation that, if the referee cannot determine how many moves have been made, the game shall proceed from the final position as if the next time control had commenced.

The USCF has also ruled as follows:

"In those USCF tournaments which do not qualify any contestants into a FIDE event, the referee or tournament director should announce in advance whether he will forfeit players for not keeping a game score or whether such players will only lose their right to claim a draw by repetition of moves or a win by time forfeiture."

The recording of games is closely related to the subject of time forfeits. This relationship will be discussed in the comments under Article 17.

Article 14

USE OF THE CHESS CLOCK

1. Each player must make a certain number of moves in a given period of time, these two factors being specified in advance.

2. Control of each player's time is effected by means of a clock equipped with special apparatus for this purpose.

3. At the time determined for the start of the game, the clock of the player who has the white men is set in motion. In the continuation of the game, each of the players, having made his move, stops his own clock and starts his opponent's clock.

4. Upon the execution of the prescribed number of moves, the last move is not considered as being completed until after the player has stopped his clock.

5. Every indication given by a clock or its apparatus (the flag attached to some chess clocks) is considered as conclusive in the absence of evident defects. The player who wishes to claim any such defect is required to do so as soon as he himself has become aware of it.

6. If the game must be interrupted because of some situation for which neither player is responsible, the clocks shall be stopped until the situation has been adjusted. This should be done, for example, in the case of an illegal position to be corrected, in the case of a defective clock to be exchanged, or when the man which a player has announced he wishes to exchange for one of his Pawns that has reached the last rank, is not immediately available.

7. When, in the case of Article 9, Nos. 1 and 2, it is not possible to establish the time used by each player up to the moment of irregularity, each player shall be allotted up to that moment an amount of time proportional to that indicated by the clocks when the irregularity is observed. Example: After Black's 30th move it is found that an irregularity took place at the 20th move. If, for these 30 moves, the clocks indicate 90 minutes for White and 60 minutes for Black, it shall be assumed that the times used by the two players for the first 20 moves were in proportion, thus:

$$\text{White} \qquad \frac{90 \times 20}{30} = 60 \text{ minutes}$$

$$\text{Black} \qquad \frac{60 \times 20}{30} = 40 \text{ minutes}$$

The time limit for each tournament is announced in the program of the contest. For example, the U. S. Chess Federation uses different time limits for the various championships under its jurisdiction. In the U. S. Open, each player must make 50 moves in the first 2½ hours registered on his clock; if games are adjourned, the number of moves is increased by 20 for each additional hour (70 moves in 3½ hours, 90 moves in 4½ hours, etc.). In the U. S. Amateur Championship, the time limit is 50 moves in two hours. In other tournaments, different time limits may be announced.

With regard to Article 14, No. 3, the FIDE has ruled that the clock of the player with the white men must be started at the time specified for the commencement of a game, even though both players may be absent.

The FIDE was asked to rule on a question in connection with

Article 14, No. 4. A player's last move mated his opponent. The player's flag dropped after he released the mating piece but before he punched his clock. Had he "completed" his move, or had he lost the game on time? In reply, the Committee on Laws pointed out that the general laws of part one state that a move is completed when the player's hand has released the man moved (Article 7). This is not overruled by Article 14, No. 4. The purpose of the latter special regulation for competition is to take care of situations when the Director is not present just at the moment when a player has completed his move on the board with his clock still running. In the case in question, the last move was a mating move that finished the game and won for the player who had executed the mate. It was of no importance whether one or the other clock was running after the end of the game. The player who mated his opponent was ruled to have won the game. Under similar circumstances, it follows that a final move (completed under Article 7) that stalemates the opponent draws the game. The same ruling would also apply to a situation in which a player's final move (completed under Article 7) enables him to correctly claim a draw under the provisions of Article 12, No. 3.

Ordinarily, Article 14, No. 4, enables the referee to decide whether a player's last move was made within the time limit, even if the referee was not present. The clock's flag and the score sheets are usually sufficient evidence to make a decision. However, as pointed out above, a player may have completed his last move (under Article 7) with a mating or drawing move, even though his flag dropped after his hand released the man moved. Therefore the Director should be sure to witness the final moves of a player in time-trouble if there is any possibility that the player may be able to mate, stalemate, or claim a draw by repetition of moves.

With regard to section 5, the players are responsible for the operation of their clocks. Each contestant should make sure that his own clock stops and his opponent's starts every time he punches the lever. He should also check to see that the clocks are keeping reasonably accurate time, and that the flag attached to each clock is functioning properly. Any delay in reporting a defect cannot be remedied by an adjustment of time. A player's claim that his own clock should be set back, or his opponent's set ahead, should be disallowed. (In the 1954 USA-USSR match, Reshevsky claimed that a time adjustment should be made because Smyslov's clock had stopped for 35 minutes. His claim was rejected.)

Although it is up to each player to see that his clock is not defective, the Director should halt a game if he sees that a clock is not operating properly. After the clock has been repaired, or a new clock substituted, the game should be continued with the times recorded by the defective clock when the game was interrupted. No adjustment in time should be made. Note, however, that this intervention by the Director applies only to the case of a defective clock. Under no circumstances should the Director (or any other person) call a player's attention to the fact that he has failed to punch his clock.

In section 6 of Article 14 it is stated that "the clocks shall be stopped . . ." Note that the players do not have the right to stop the clocks during the progress of a game; this must be done by the Director. The only time a player may stop both clocks is at adjournment, as provided in Article 15, No. 1.

Article 15

ADJOURNMENT OF THE GAME

1. If a game is not finished upon conclusion of the time prescribed for play, the player having the move shall write his next move in unambiguous notation on his score sheet, place his and his opponent's score sheets in an envelope, seal the envelope, and then stop the clocks. If the player has made the said move on the chessboard, he must seal this same move on his score sheet.

2. Upon the envelope shall be indicated:

(a) the name of the players;

(b) the position immediately before the sealed move;

(c) the time used by each player;

(d) the name of the player who has sealed the move, and the number of that move.

3. Custody of the envelope must be assured.

At the end of a playing session, a signal is given informing contestants that play must cease. The Director and his assistants then go from board to board and check the number of moves that have been made in each unfinished game. At each board where the prescribed number of moves has been completed, the player on the move is given an envelope and instructed to seal his move. Care should be taken to make sure that the move is written correctly. Unabridged notation should be used, for this protects the player from recording an ambiguous move. The carbon copy of a score sheet should not be enclosed in the sealed-move envelope.

In addition to the information listed in Article 15, No. 2, to be written on the outside of the envelope, it is a good idea to write the date and time the game is to be resumed. To make sure that both players have checked the position and agreed on the details written on the outside of the envelope, the Director should ask both players to sign the envelope. The Director then keeps custody of the envelope until the game is resumed.

Article 16

RESUMPTION OF AN ADJOURNED GAME

1. When the game is resumed, the position immediately before the sealed move shall be set up on a chessboard, and the time used by each player at the time of adjournment shall be indicated on the clocks.

2. The envelope shall be opened only when the player having the move (the player who must reply to the sealed move) is present. That player's clock shall be started after the sealed move has been made on the chessboard.

3. If the player having the move is absent, his clock shall be started, but the envelope shall be opened only at the time of his arrival.

4. If the player who has sealed the move is absent, the player having the move is not obliged to reply to the sealed move on the chessboard. He has the right to record his move in reply upon his score sheet, to place the latter in an envelope, to stop his clock, and to start his opponent's clock. The envelope should be placed in security, and opened at the time of his opponent's arrival.

5. If the envelope containing the sealed move at the time of adjournment has disappeared, and it is not possible to re-establish, by agreement of the two players, the position and the times used for the adjourned game, or if, for any other reason, the said position and said times cannot be re-established, the game is annulled, and a new game must be played in place of the adjourned game. If the envelope containing the move recorded in accordance with Section 4 hereof has disappeared, the game must be resumed from the position at the time of adjournment, and with the clock times recorded at the time of adjournment.

6. If, upon resumption of the game, the time used has been incorrectly indicated on either clock, and if such mistake has been established by either player before making his first move, the error must be corrected. If the error is not then established, the game continues without correction.

If players agree on a result before the time specified for resumption, they should notify the Director; otherwise they may become liable to penalty under Article 17, No. 2.

Article 17

LOSS OF THE GAME

A game is lost by a player:

1. Who has not completed the prescribed number of moves in the time specified.

2. Who arrives at the chessboard more than one hour late.

3. Who has sealed a move the real significance of which it is impossible to establish.

4. Who, during the game, refuses to comply with these laws of chess.

If both players arrive at the chessboard more than one hour late, or refuse to comply with these laws of chess, the game shall be declared lost by both players.

Article 17 enumerates the ways in which a game can be lost, apart from resignation or being mated. The commonest way is covered in the first section; a player is forfeited because he fails to complete the prescribed number of moves in the time specified. If both players have kept their score sheets up to date, and agree on the number of moves made, there should be no occasion for dispute. If the score sheets are not completed, the procedure outlined in the FIDE interpretation of Article 13 should be followed to determine the number of moves played and thereby decide whether one of the players has lost on a time forfeit.

As an additional clarification, the USCF has made the following rule for its tournaments:

"Whenever a player claims a win on time he must produce a score which, upon verification by the director or referee, proves that the player's opponent failed to make the required number of moves in the allotted time."

In the absence of an evident defect, the dropping of a clock's flag should be regarded as marking the moment at which the time control period expires. According to the current tournament rules of the U. S. Chess Federation, a claim that a flag has fallen prematurely should be accepted only if there is a clear white space between the minute hand and the left side of the hour marker when the flag drops. If there is no flag on a clock, the time control is deemed to have expired when there is a clear white space between the right side of the hour and the minute hand.

The FIDE was asked if a player could lose a game by overstepping the time limit when the position was such that mate could not be given, no matter how the players continued. The committee ruled that the player who oversteps the time limit loses the game, even if his opponent did not have enough material to win under any conditions. In this connection, it should be realized that a player invariably loses the game if, in making the last of the specified number of moves, his hand does not release the man before his flag drops, i.e., if the move is not completed as defined in Article 7 before the time period ends. This would apply to a move that would have mated or stalemated the opponent if it had been completed in time.

Note also that the announcement of mate or stalemate or perpetual check has no legal standing. Unless the opponent resigns or agrees that the game is drawn, mating moves or moves forcing a draw must be executed on the board. A player about to overstep the time limit cannot avoid losing the game by announcing the moves he intends to make, even if they lead to a mate or a forced draw.

With regard to Article 17, No. 2, and the final subclause stating that a game is lost by players arriving at the chessboard more than one hour late, the FIDE has ruled that these regulations apply to both the commencement of a game and the resumption of play after an adjournment. When the player who sealed the move is absent at the time of resumption, while his opponent presents himself at the chessboard, and the former is still absent after the lapse of one hour, the game is lost for him unless it has been decided previously by one of the following circumstances:

(a) the absent player has won the game because the sealed move is checkmate;

(b) the absent player has drawn the game because the sealed move produces a stalemate; or

(c) the player present at the chessboard has lost the game under Article 17, No. 1, by exceeding his time limit.

This interpretation by the FIDE merely confirms the basic fact that what happens as a result of an action or an omission after the termination of a game is of no importance.

The third section of Article 17 was amended in 1965, the new wording being shown above. Prior to this year, this section read:

Who has sealed an illegal move, or one so inaccurately or vaguely defined as to render impossible the establishment of its true meaning.

According to this old wording, the Director has no discretion in the case of a sealed illegal move; he must declare the game lost if a player makes a mistake and writes down an illegal move, even though his intention may be obvious. Only in the case of an impossible or ambiguous move is the Director supposed to make an effort to establish the real meaning of the move as written.

Some time ago, the FIDE was asked to clarify this section of Article 17, but it refused to do so. It was the Committee's contention that it is the duty of the referee to make the necessary decision in accordance with the circumstances of each particular case. From this we could only conclude that the referee is permitted to disregard the actual wording of Article 17, No. 3, and use his own judgment.

Since it would seem much simpler and better to change the wording of the section, the writer communicated with Mr. Folke Rogard, President of the FIDE, on the subject. He submitted our observations to the Committee on Laws at its session during the week preceding the 1965 Congress at Wiesbaden. The Committee then changed the wording of this section. The new version gives much more scope to the referee's judgment and legalizes the previous interpretation by the FIDE.

In using his judgment, the Director or referee should permit an illegal, ambiguous, or impossible sealed move to be corrected only if the player's true intention is *obvious*. For instance, if a player seals "B-QN5" and this move is impossible, the referee may use his judgment to decide that the player intended to write "B-KN5." Or if a player seals "K-B1" and this is an illegal move, the referee may

decide that the player intended to write "K-N1" providing N1 is
the *only* square to which the King may legally move. However, the
referee should declare a game lost by a player who seals an illegal,
ambiguous, or impossible move if the player's intention is not obvious but calls for interpretation based on the playing skill of the
referee himself. For example, a player in a recent tournament sealed
the ambiguous move "B-Q" without specifying which square on
the Q-file was intended. In the adjourned position, the Bishop could
move to either Q6 or Q8, and both were logical moves. To decide
which square the player intended would call for judgment based
on the playing skill of the referee. As it happeens, the referee permitted the player to specify which square was intended and allowed
the game to continue. This was a mistake. The player should have
been forfeited.

Article 17a

DRAWN GAME

*1. A proposal to draw may be made by a player only at the mo-
ment when he has just made a move. On then proposing a draw he
starts the clock of his opponent. The latter may accept or, either
orally or by making a move, reject the proposal. In the interval,
the player who has made the proposal cannot withdraw it.*

*2. If a player claims a draw under the provisions of Article 12,
No. 3, his clock must continue to run until the director has verified
the legitimacy of the claim.*

*If the claim is found to be correct, the game will be declared
drawn, even if the claimant, in the interval, has overstepped the time
limit.*

*If the claim is found to be incorrect, the game will continue, unless
the claimant has, in the interval, overstepped the time limit, in which
case the game will be declared lost by the claimant.*

The history of this Article was explained in the introduction to
this chapter. Although the thirty-move rule on agreeed draws was
repealed by the Congress of 1964, referees are still expected to impose penalties on players who are guilty of clear violations of the
moral principles of chess. In extreme cases, the penalty may be loss
of the game.

Article 18

CONDUCT OF THE PLAYERS

1. (a) *During play the players are forbidden to make use of notes, manuscripts, or printed matter, or to analyze the game on another chessboard; they are likewise forbidden to receive the advice or opinion of a third party, whether solicited or not.*

(b) *No analysis is permitted in the playing rooms during play or during adjournment.*

(c) *Players are forbidden to distract or annoy their opponents in any manner whatsoever.*

2. Infractions of the rules indicated in Section 1 hereof may incur penalties even to the extent of loss of the game.

To remain above criticism, a player should not take chess books or other chess literature into the playing room, and should avoid discussions about chess games or positions with other players or with onlookers, even though the discussions may have nothing to do with the games in progress. Naturally, a player should not be penalized if advice is forced upon him, but he should silence an adviser as quickly as possible and tell him that contestants are not allowed to receive advice or talk about their games. Persistent kibitzers should be reported to the Director.

Bobby Fischer accused the Russian players at Curaçao, 1962, of audibly discussing his games. As Paul Keres declared, "Fischer's repeated protests to the tournament controllers had the ultimate result that a player could not even exchange a few words with his wife." It may be true that the Soviet players were not talking about Fischer's games, but the contestants in such a tournament should give no cause for suspicion, especially when they speak a language not understood by other contestants.

The analysis of adjourned games outside the playing room, and the employment of seconds to assist in such analysis, are not prohibited under Article 18. These questions are being discussed and solutions being sought by the FIDE, as explained in the introduction to this chapter.

The old laws, prior to 1952, named various practices that were to be considered ethical or otherwise. The current rules stick to the essentials and leave it to the Director and the players to decide what is to be considered good or bad conduct in other respects. It would be difficult to legislate against all the ways a player might think up to annoy his opponent. The Director can decide whether or not a player is being "distracted or annoyed" and if necessary impose a penalty under section 1, c. However, one of the commonest pests is the player who is continually begging for a draw. In response to a suggestion by the USSR Chess Federation, the FIDE Committee on Laws made the following interpretation of Article 18, No. 1, c:

"This clause should be applied in the case of a player who has proposed a draw and repeats his proposal without reasons that are obviously well founded, before his opponent has in his turn made use of the right to propose a draw."

Article 19

TOURNAMENT DIRECTOR OR MATCH REFEREE

To manage the competition, a tournament director or match referee must be designated. His duties are:

(a) *to see that these laws of chess are strictly observed.*

(b) *to supervise the progress of the competition; to establish that the prescribed time limit has not been exceeded by the players; to arrange the order of resumption of play in adjourned games; to supervise the arrangements set forth in Article 15, above all to see that the information on the envelope is correct; to assume custody of the sealed envelopes until such time as adjourned games are resumed; etc....*

(c) *to enforce the decisions he has reached in disputes that have arisen during the course of the competition.*

(d) *to impose penalties on the players for all infractions of these laws of chess.*

Here are a few other jobs the tournament director must handle or supervise:

1. Make sure that every player knows the days and times the rounds and adjourned games will be played. The schedule should be displayed prominently in the tournament room.

2. Post prominently any unusual specifications concerning time limits, pairing systems, tie-breaking, etc.

3. Make up a scoreboard in advance on which the players' names and ratings will be listed and the round-by-round results posted daily.

4. Get the local addresses and phone numbers of all players so that they may be reached when necessary.

5. Check all chess clocks for defects before the tournament starts.

6. Provide each player, before each round, with two score sheets and carbon paper, clipped or stapled together.

7. Set all clocks in the starting position before each round.

8. Make the pairings in each round of a Swiss System tournament.

9. Keep custody of all score sheets and records of the tournament.

There are many other chores which the director may have to supervise or perform in cooperation with the local committee. Cards with the names of the players should be prepared, so that they may be attached to the tables before each round. Ropes should be put up to keep the spectators from breathing down the necks of the contestants. The lighting should be checked. The players should be provided with pencils, ashtrays, drinking water. The chessmen and clocks have to be put in position before each round, stowed away in a safe place at the end of each round.

Article 20

INTERPRETATION OF THE LAWS OF CHESS

In case of doubt as to the application or interpretation of these laws, the FIDE shall examine the evidence submitted, nad render official decision. Decisions published in the "Revue de la FIDE" are binding on all affiliated Federations.

In the United States, disputes as to the intention or interpretation of these laws should be forwarded to the USCF.

SUPPLEMENT No. 1

Chess Notation

FIDE Laws at present recognize only the two most generally known systems of notation: the algebraic system and the descriptive systems. Each affiliated unit is free to employ whichever of these two notations it prefers.

This supplement to the FIDE Laws continues with an explanation of the algebraic and descriptive systems of notation. These systems are fully described in the next chapter.

SUPPLEMENT No. 2

Expressions in General Use

Piece. *A general term comprising all chessmen except the Pawn.* (In the United States, a Queen or Rook is called a "major piece," a Bishop or Knight a "minor piece." The collective term "men" is used to designate both pieces and Pawns.)

To Interpose. *To place a man between one's own King and the piece giving check. A check by a Knight cannot be parried by interposing.*

Pinned Man. *The man interposed to parry a check, whose freedom of movement is thereby destroyed, is said to be pinned.* (This refers to an absolute pin. A man shielding an attack is also said to be pinned if its movement would involve loss of material when the shielded man is captured.)

Discovered Check. *Check by a piece whose action has been unmasked by the moving of another man.*

Double Check. *Check simultaneously obtained by moving a man which itself gives check, and which at the same time uncovers the action of a piece which also gives check.*

Long Castling (Queen-side Castling). *Castling with the Rook at a1 or a8* (the Queen-Rook).

Short Castling (King-side Castling). *Castling with the Rook at h1 or h8* (the King-Rook).

Winning the Exchange. *To exchange a Knight or Bishop for a Rook.*

Losing the Exchange. *To exchange a Rook for a Knight or Bishop.*

I adjust (or "J'adoube"). *Expression used when the player adjusts a man on its square.* (See Article 8.)

SUPPLEMENT No. 3

Postal and Telegraphic Notations

This supplement describes and authorizes the use of Correspondence Notation (International Postal Chess Notation) and Telegraphic Notation (the Uedemann Code). Both of these are fully explained and illustrated in our chapter on Chess Notation.

SUPPLEMENT No. 4

Special Rules for Blind Players

1. A blind player is allowed to use a special chessboard and set of chessmen. Each square of the board shall contain a securing aperture for holding the chessmen placed on that square.

The sighted player shall use the normal chessboard and men. The moves made by the two players shall be transferred from one chessboard to the other in the order that they are made according to the following rules.

2. For the blind player the following exceptional rules shall apply.

(a) The blind player is not considered to have touched a man as specified in Article 8 of the Laws until he has taken the man out of its securing aperture.

(b) A move is carried out only when a chessman is placed in a securing aperture and, in the case of a capture, when the captured chessman is removed from the blind player's board.

3. (a) As soon as a move is made the player shall announce it to his opponent, who must immediately transfer it to his board.

(b) A slip of the tongue in announcing a move does not render the teller liable to any penalty.

(c) When clocks are used the player shall stop his clock and start his opponent's as soon as the announcement is made.

4. A blind competitor may employ a deputy (whose employment shall be subject to the approval of the tournament director) who shall

(a) make on the tournament board any move made on the special board by the blind competitor;

(b) announce any move made on the tournament board by the sighted competitor and verify that it is made also on the special board;

(c) state, when requested, the clock time registered by the clock of either competitor;

(d) record a score of all moves made by both competitors;

(e) start and stop the clocks of both competitors.

CHESS CLOCKS AND TIME LIMITS

Chess clocks are made in various sizes and shapes. They may be electrically or mechanically operated. Most players prefer the mechanical type, for it can be used anywhere, has no wiring to trip over, and stops instantly when the lever is punched. (An electric clock continues in motion for a split-second after it is switched off.) However, the mechanical clock must be adjusted and checked occasionally to make sure that it keeps good time.

The "Pal Benko" mechanical clock, manufactured in the United States, is illustrated above. It consists of two movements and dials mounted side by side in a wooden housing. The winders and time-setters are at the back. When either of the push-buttons on top is pressed down, the clock below the button is stopped and the other clock started. When the two buttons are in the neutral position (halfway down) both clocks are stopped. Each clock is equipped with a revolving "ticker" to show whether it is running or stopped. Each clock is also equipped with a "flag" which indicates the exact moment at which the minute hand is pointing vertically upward. As the end of each hour approaches, the minute hand raises the flag to a horizontal position. Then the flag drops when the hand registers the end of the hour.

Before a game begins, the two clocks are set to register the same time. If the session is to last four hours (two hours for each player), the clocks are set so that each registers 11:59 o'clock. If the session is to last five hours (2½ hours for each player), the clocks are set so that each registers 11:29 o'clock. Each player is allowed one extra minute to compensate for a possible defect of a minor nature in the operation of the clock's flag. Until the game begins, the push-buttons are placed in the neutral position.

At the time scheduled for the start of the game, the player with the black men punches the button over his clock, thereby starting his opponent's clock. Then, when the player with the white men has made his first move, he punches the button on his side, thereby stopping his own clock and starting Black's clock. The same procedure is followed throughout the game. After each move, the player stops his own clock and starts his opponent's clock. Therefore each clock registers the amount of time taken by the player to study and make his moves. An unfinished game is adjourned (or adjudicated, if the rules so provide) when the times registered on the two clocks add up to the period specified for the duration of the session.

Each player must make a certain number of moves in a given period of time. The organization or club conducting the tournament specifies these two factors. A player loses the game on a "time-forfeit" if he fails to make the required number of moves in the allotted time.

The flag of a player's clock indicates the expiration of the time limit. For instance, if a player is requried to make 40 moves in 2 hours, he must have completed 40 moves when his clock registers 2 o'clock and the flag drops.

In international tournaments, the time limit is nearly always 40 moves in 2½ hours for each player. In the United States, important tournaments are conducted under the time limit of 40 moves in 2 hours, or 50 moves in 2½ hours—an average rate of 20 moves per hour for each player. In weekend tournaments and other contests in which two or three rounds are played each day, the duration of each round has to be restricted to about four hours, and each player may be required to make 45 or 50 moves in two hours.

A time limit averaging 25 moves per hour for each player is about the maximum for serious play. It is too fast for master chess, but can be used in non-master tournaments. For special events, such as a one-day tournament, it may be necessary to specify a faster average than 25 moves per hour, but these contests are either intended for amusement or for players below the expert class.

In all matches and tournaments in which chess clocks are used, the *number of moves* to be made by each player in a given time should always be specified. This may seem to be laboring the obvious, but inexperienced organizers of some open tournaments have announced rules requiring each player to make "all the moves" of his game in two hours.

If the number of moves is not specified, a game may degenerate into a contest to decide which player is the better performer at "five-minute" or "blitz" chess. For example, a player in a winning position who has made about 50 moves, and has only a minute or so left on his clock, could be forced to attempt an *unlimited* number of additional moves, and might lose the game by coming in second-best in a race with the clock's flags. When the rules specify the number of moves to be completed, this same player could easily make the last two or three moves in the time remaining on his clock, and the game would then be adjourned (or adjudicated).

When clocks are not available for all the games of a tournament, special regulations should be announced, specifying the procedure to be followed. For example, the following time-limit rules governed play in the U. S. Amateur Championship of 1955:

Games Played With Clocks: In each round, the games of the ten top-ranking players will be played with clocks from the first move to the conclusion of each game. In these games, each player must make 50 moves in the first two hours registered on his clock.

Games Started Without Clocks: After two hours of play in each round, all available clocks will be placed at tables where the players have made less than 25 moves. In these games, each player must complete 50 moves in the first hour registered on his clock.

Games Played Without Clocks: Upon conclusion of the time prescribed for play, as announced by the Director, play must cease in all unfinished games played without clocks. The final position must not be disturbed until it has been adjudicated.

CHAPTER III

Chess Notation

To record the moves of games, various systems of notation have been invented during the long history of chess, but only two are now in general use—the descriptive and the algebraic systems.

In the United States, the descriptive system is used almost exclusively by chessplayers and by the publishers of chess books and periodicals. It bears about the same relationship to algebraic notation as the old-fashioned system of weights and measures bears to the metric system—and there is about the same likelihood of worldwide adoption of the more modern method.

Almost everybody admits the defects of descriptive notation, and recognizes the simplicity and accuracy of the algebraic system; but we have been "describing" chess moves for hundreds of years, and will probably continue to do so in the future. The courageous publisher who puts out an English-language chess book with algebraic notation might just as well print it in Greek or Arabic.

Descriptive notation has a colorful background. The contractions and symbols we use today are the result of a long process of evolution which started about a thousand years ago. The fundamental method of identifying the squares of the board and describing the moves of the chessmen was used in the manuscripts of the tenth century.

In printed books up to the nineteenth century, the moves are described in words, with no abbreviations. The names of the chessmen and squares are spelled out in full. For example, in the first English edition of *Chess Analyzed* (London, 1750), Philidor describes the first three moves of a game as follows:

1

WHITE   The King's Pawn two steps
BLACK   The same

2

W.   The King's Knight at his Bishop's third Square.
B.   The Queen's Pawn one Move.

72

3
W. The King's Bishop at the Queen's Bishop's fourth Square.
B. The King's Bishop's Pawn two Moves.

In the early nineteenth century, chess writers started to abbreviate the descriptions of moves. Thus, "The Queen's Pawn" was written "The Q. Pawn," and "The King's Bishop" as "The K. Bishop." Gradually, the use of initials became more extensive. The names of the chessmen were contracted to "K.P." for King's Pawn, "Q.B." for Queen's Bishop. "K.Kt." for King's Knight, etc. Then the word "square" was dropped, and a great deal of space was saved by arranging the white and black moves in two adjacent columns. Thus, in the third and fourth decades of the nineteenth century, the moves of Philidor's game were written as follows:

WHITE	BLACK
1. K.P. two	1. The same
2. K.Kt. to B. third	2. Q.P. one
3. K.B. to Q.B. fourth	3. K.B.P. two

Around the middle of the last century, chess writers began to describe Pawn moves in the same way as piece moves. Instead of giving the number of squares the Pawn moved forward (Q.P. one, K.B.P. two, etc.) the square to which the Pawn moved was named. It also became customary to use figures instead of words for the numbers of the squares. At this stage in the evolution of descriptive notation, Philidor's moves were written:

WHITE	BLACK
1. P. to K.'s 4th	1. P. to K.'s 4th
2. K.Kt. to B.'s 3rd	2. P. to Q.'s 3rd
3. K.B. to Q.B.'s 4th	3. P. to K.B.'s 4th

The above style was used in most publications for about twenty years. Then books and magazines began to save space by dropping the periods after initials and the duplications of move numbers for White and Black. The notation became more condensed, as shown below:

WHITE	BLACK
1 P to K4	P to K4
2 Kt to KB3	P to Q3
3 B to B4	P to KB4

About the end of the nineteenth century, it became the common practice to use a hyphen or dash to represent the word "to" and an "x" to represent the word "captures." Thus, the moves were written:

WHITE	BLACK
1 P–K4	P–K4
2 Kt–KB3	P–Q3
3 B–B4	P–KB4

This type of notation is still used today. However, the similarity between "Kt" for Knight and "K" for King has caused a great deal of confusion. The vast majority of tournament players now use the symbol "N" for Knight. This takes up less space and is much easier to read and write than "Kt." For example, the move "Kt–KKt5" is now written "N–KN5," which is much simpler and clearer. However, tradition dies hard, and there are still many players and editors who stick to the antiquated and confusing "Kt" for Knight.

It will be realized that modern chess notation is a kind of "shorthand" representing the words which describe the moves. Thus, the moves of Philidor's game, as recorded by condensed notation, would be *spoken* as follows:

WHITE	BLACK
One: Pawn to King four	Pawn to King four
Two: Knight to King-Bishop three	Pawn to Queen three
Three: Bishop to Bishop four	Pawn to King-Bishop four

This brief summary of the history of descriptive chess notation may help the learner to read and write chess moves by this system. The method of naming the squares and other details are explained in this chapter.

HOW SQUARES ARE IDENTIFIED

In the description of a move, the square to which a piece or Pawn moves is identified by giving the name of the file and the number of the rank, counting from the player's side of the board. For example, when we say that White plays "Pawn to King four" we mean that White moves a Pawn to the fourth square on the King's file, counting from White's side of the board. Or, if we say that Black plays "Pawn to Queen four" we mean that Black moves a Pawn to the fourth square on the Queen's file, counting from Black's side of the board.

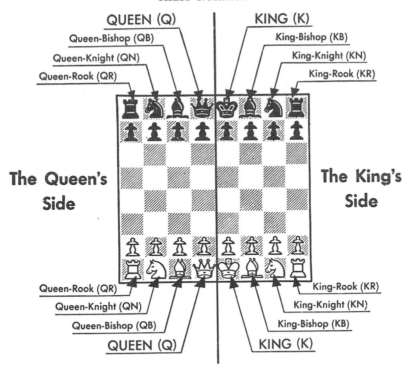

Names of the Files

The files are named after the pieces which occupy these "up and down" rows of squares in the starting position of the game, as illustrated in the diagram. The pieces on the Queen's side of the board are called the *Queen-Rook, Queen-Knight,* and *Queen-Bishop,* to distinguish them from the similar pieces on the King's side of the board—the *King-Rook, King-Knight,* and *King-Bishop.*

The eight files of the board, from left to right in the diagram, are named after the pieces as follows:

Name of File	Notation Symbol
Queen-Rook's file	QR
Queen-Knight's file	QN or QKt
Queen-Bishop's file	QB
Queen's file	Q
King's file	K
King-Bishop's file	KB
King-Knight's file	KN or KKt
King-Rook's file	KR

In descriptive notation, the files are indicated by the initials of their names, as shown above.

How the Ranks Are Numbered

The eight ranks of the board are numbered from 1 to 8. However, when describing a move by White, the count starts from White's side of the board. For a move by Black, the count starts from Black's side.

QUEEN-ROOK'S FILE	QUEEN-KNIGHT'S FILE	QUEEN-BISHOP'S FILE	QUEEN'S FILE	KING'S FILE	KING-BISHOP'S FILE	KING-KNIGHT'S FILE	KING-ROOK'S FILE

The eight files (left to right) are indicated by the initials of their names: QR, QN (or QKt), QB, Q, K, KB, KN (or KKt) and KR.

8	WHITE'S 8TH RANK
7	
6	
5	
4	
3	
2	
1	WHITE'S FIRST RANK

The ranks are numbered from 1 to 8. For a move by White, the count starts from White's side of the board, at the bottom of this diagram.

1	BLACK'S FIRST RANK
2	
3	
4	
5	
6	
7	
8	BLACK'S 8TH RANK

For a move by Black, the ranks are also numbered from 1 to 8, but the count starts from Black's side of the board, at the top of this diagram.

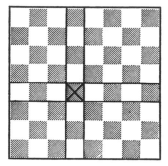

A square is identified by a symbol combining the initials of the file's name and the number of the rank. The marked square is White's Q4 and Black's Q5.

BLACK

			Q8	K8			
			Q7	K7			
			Q6	K6			
			Q5	K5			
			Q4	K4			
			Q3	K3			
			Q2	K2			
			Q1	K1			

WHITE

Notation Symbols for Squares

A square is identified by a symbol combining the initials of the file's name and the number of the rank. Thus, as shown in the diagram above, the squares on the Queen-file are identified by the symbols Q1, Q2, Q3, Q4, Q5, etc. Similarly, the squares on the King-file are indicated by the symbols K1, K2, K3, etc. The number of the rank depends on whether a White or Black move is described. The symbols of the squares, from Black's point of view, may be read by turning the book upside down.

BLACK

QR8	QN8	QB8			KB8	KN8	KR8
QR7	QN7	QB7			KB7	KN7	KR7
QR6	QN6	QB6			KB6	KN6	KR6
QR5	QN5	QB5			KB5	KN5	KR5
QR4	QN4	QB4			KB4	KN4	KR4
QR3	QN3	QB3			KB3	KN3	KR3
QR2	QN2	QB2			KB2	KN2	KR2
QR1	QN1	QB1			KB1	KN1	KR1

WHITE

The above diagram shows the symbols for the squares on the Queen-Rook, Queen-Knight and Queen-Bishop files at the left, for the King-Bishop, King-Knight and King-Rook files at the right. Thus, the squares on the Queen-Rook file, at the extreme left, are identified by the symbols QR1, QR2, QR3, etc., and the squares on the King-Rook file, at the extreme right, are indicated by the symbols KR1, KR2, KR3, etc. In old-fashioned notation, the squares on the Knight files are identified by the symbols QKt1, QKt2, QKt3, etc., for the Queen-Knight file, and by KKt1, KKt2, KKt3, etc., for the King-Knight file.

BLACK

R1 / R8	N1 / N8	B1 / B8			B1 / B8	N1 / N8	R1 / R8
R2 / R7	N2 / N7	B2 / B7			B2 / B7	N2 / N7	R2 / R7
R3 / R6	N3 / N6	B3 / B6			B3 / B6	N3 / N6	R3 / R6
R4 / R5	N4 / N5	B4 / B5			B4 / B5	N4 / N5	R4 / R5
R5 / R4	N5 / N4	B5 / B4			B5 / B4	N5 / N4	R5 / R4
R6 / R3	N6 / N3	B6 / B3			B6 / B3	N6 / N3	R6 / R3
R7 / R2	N7 / N2	B7 / B2			B7 / B2	N7 / N2	R7 / R2
R8 / R1	N8 / N1	B8 / B1			B8 / B1	N8 / N1	R8 / R1

WHITE

Condensed Symbols for Squares

The condensed symbols shown in the above diagram are used for squares on the Rook, Knight, and Bishop files when the description of a move and the position on the chessboard make it unnecessary to distinguish between the King-side and Queen-side files of the same name.

Although a square on one side of the board has exactly the same symbol as the corresponding square on the other side, there is no ambiguity when only one of the two squares may be occupied by a specified type of man, or when a check identifies the square.

The use of condensed symbols is illustrated in the positions diagramed on the next page.

White moves his King-Knight to the square KN5 (King-Knight 5). This square may be identified by the condensed symbol N5 (or Kt5) because it is impossible for a Knight to occupy the QN5 square.

Black moves his King-Knight to his KB3 square. In correct notation, the square is identified by the condensed symbol B3 because a Knight cannot move to the occupied QB3 square.

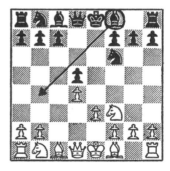

White moves his Bishop to the square QB4. To write this move, the square should be indicated by the condensed symbol B4. There is no ambiguity, for a white Bishop cannot move to the KB4 square.

Black checks the white King by moving his Bishop to the square QN5. The move is written *B-N5ch* (Bishop to Knight 5 check). The condensed symbol is sufficient because the check identifies the square.

NAMES AND SYMBOLS OF THE PIECES

The pieces are represented by the initials of their names. As illustrated in the diagram on page 75, the names and symbols are as follows:

King	K	Queen	Q
King-Rook	KR	Queen-Rook	QR
King-Knight	KN or KKt	Queen-Knight	QN or QKt
King-Bishop	KB	Queen-Bishop	QB

Basic Symbols for Pieces

When describing a move or capture, it is often unnecessary to use the full name of a King-side or Queen-side piece. The basic symbols *R* for Rook, *N* or *Kt* for Knight, and *B* for Bishop, are used when only one piece of the specified type can move (or be captured) in the manner described, or if a check identifies the move or capture.

In some positions, when a basic symbol would be ambiguous, it is specified that a King-side or Queen-side piece is moved or captured. However, after Rooks and Knights have moved from their original squares, it may be difficult or impossible for the reader to identify a Rook as the KR or QR, or a Knight as the KN or QN. In that case, ambiguity is removed by using a basic symbol for the piece and then adding in parentheses the number of the rank or the symbol of the square on which the piece stands. The number of the rank is counted from the player's side of the board.

The correct use of symbols for the chess pieces is illustrated in the following diagrams.

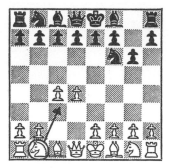

White moves his QN to the square QB3. Only one Knight can move to this square, so the move is written N-QB3. The full designation of the square shows the reader which Knight is moved.

White moves his QN to the square Q2. This move must be written QN-Q2 because either of White's Knights can move to Q2. The distinction is clear, for the QN has not moved from its original square.

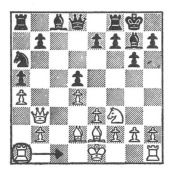

White moves his QR to the square QB1. Only one Rook can move to this square, so the move is written R-QB1. When the square is identified, a basic symbol is used for the only piece that can move to that square.

White moves his QR to the square QN1. This move is written QR-N1 because either of White's Rooks can move to the designated square; but the condensed N1 is sufficient to identify the square. The KN1 square is occupied.

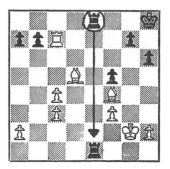

Black moves his Knight on the Queen-file to K7 and checks the white King. As either Knight can make this move, it is written N(Q5)-K7ch, showing that it is the Knight on Black's Q5 square that moves.

The Rook on Black's first rank (top of diagram) moves to K7 and checks the white King. Either Rook can make this move, so it is written R(1)-K7ch, showing that it is the Rook on Black's first rank that moves.

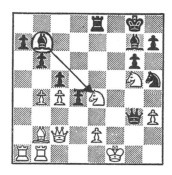

Black captures a Knight with a Bishop. Although there are two black Bishops and two white Knights, the move is written BxN, for only one Bishop can capture one Knight.

White's KB (on white square) captures the black Knight and checks. Although there are two possible BxN captures, the move is written BxNch, for the check identifies the capture.

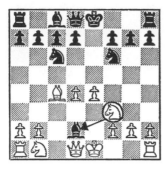

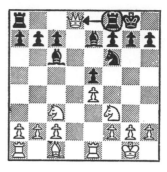

White's King-Knight (at right) captures the black Bishop. As either Knight can make this capture, it is written KNxB. White's KN has moved only once and the QN is still on its original square.

Black's King-Rook (right) captures the white Queen. Either Rook can make the capture, so the move is written KRxQ. As Black's QR is still on QR1, the reader can distinguish the KR from the QR.

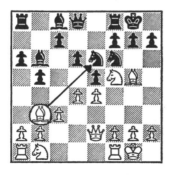

White's King-Bishop (left) captures the black Knight. There are two possible BxN captures, so the move is written KBxN. White's KB travels on white squares, his QB on black squares. The distinction is clear.

Black's Knight at his Q2 square captures the white Knight on the King-file. There are two possible NxN captures, so the move is written NxN(4) showing that it is the Knight on Black's 4th rank that is taken.

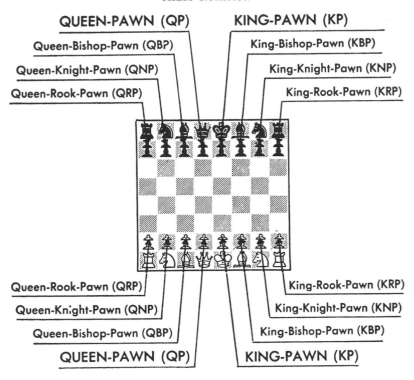

QUEEN-PAWN (QP)   KING-PAWN (KP)

Queen-Bishop-Pawn (QBP)   King-Bishop-Pawn (KBP)

Queen-Knight-Pawn (QNP)   King-Knight-Pawn (KNP)

Queen-Rook-Pawn (QRP)   King-Rook-Pawn (KRP)

Queen-Rook-Pawn (QRP)   King-Rook-Pawn (KRP)

Queen-Knight-Pawn (QNP)   King-Knight-Pawn (KNP)

Queen-Bishop-Pawn (QBP)   King-Bishop-Pawn (KBP)

QUEEN-PAWN (QP)   KING-PAWN (KP)

NAMES AND SYMBOLS OF THE PAWNS

Each Pawn is named after the file on which it stands. In the starting position of the game, as illustrated in the diagram above, each player's Pawns are named as follows:

Name of Pawn	Symbol
Queen-Rook Pawn (on QR-file)	QRP
Queen-Knight Pawn (on QN-file)	QNP or QKtP
Queen-Bishop Pawn (on QB-file)	QBP
Queen-Pawn (on Q-file)	QP
King-Pawn (on K-file)	KP
King-Bishop Pawn (on KB-file)	KBP
King-Knight Pawn (on KN-file)	KNP or KKtP
King-Rook Pawn (on KR file)	KRP

Unlike the pieces, a Pawn may change its name during a game by making a capture. For example, if a Queen-Pawn captures an enemy man on the King-file, the Pawn becomes a King-Pawn. If the same Pawn then makes a capture on the King-Bishop file, it becomes a King-Bishop Pawn, etc. At any stage of the game, a Pawn bears the name of the file on which it stands. A player may have two or more Pawns having the same name. For example, if a player has two Pawns on the Queen-file, each is called a Queen-Pawn.

Condensed Symbols for Pawns

The basic symbol *P* for Pawn is always sufficient to describe the move of a Pawn to a vacant square. Obviously, if the square is identified, only one Pawn can move to that square. However, when a Pawn captures (or is captured), it may be necessary to identify the Pawn. This may be done by using the full symbol for the Pawn, but one of the following semi-condensed symbols may be sufficient:

RP for King-Rook Pawn or Queen-Rook Pawn
NP (or *KtP*) for King-Knight Pawn or Queen-Knight Pawn
BP for King-Bishop Pawn or Queen-Bishop Pawn

Although a Pawn on the King's side has the same symbol as a Pawn on the Queen's side, there is no ambiguity if only one of the Pawns can capture (or be captured) in the manner described.

When either one of a player's two Pawns on the same file can be captured, and the identification of the capturing man does not clarify which Pawn is taken, it is necessary to specify the rank or square on which the captured Pawn stands. The basic symbol *P* is then used for the captured Pawn and the rank or square added in parentheses. When this method of identification is used, the number of the rank is always counted from the capturing player's side of the board.

The correct use of symbols for capturing and captured Pawns is illustrated on the next two pages.

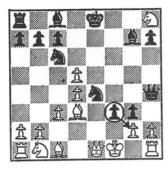

Black's KBP captures the KNP and checks the white King. Although Black has two Pawn captures, the move is written PxPch. Basic symbols are used because the check identifies the capture.

White's Rook captures the KP with check. The other white Rook can also capture a Pawn, but the check shows which Pawn is taken and the move is written RxPch. It is not necessary to use the full Pawn symbol.

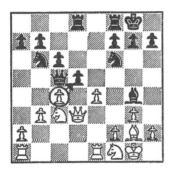

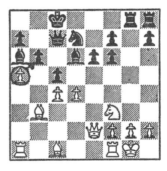

White captures the QP with his QBP. The description PxP would be ambiguous, for White's KP can also capture the QP. The move is written BPxP to show which Pawn captures. The condensed BP is sufficient.

White's QRP captures the QNP. As White's KP can also take a Pawn, the capture is written PxNP or RPxP. Semi-condensed symbols are clear because a similar capture cannot be made on the K-side.

White's Knight on KN3 captures the KRP with check. The
other Knight can capture the
KP with check, so the Pawn
taken must be identified. The
move is written NxRPch.

White's Knight captures the
KBP. As this Knight could take
the QBP, the Pawn must be
identified by a full symbol. The
capture is described as NxKBP,
not NxBP.

Black's Rook captures the
QNP on the file. As this Rook
could take the KNP on the
rank, a condensed symbol
would be ambiguous. The capture is written as RxQNP, not
RxNP.

White's Knight captures the
KBP on White's KB7. Black
has two Pawns on the KB-file
and either may be taken by
the Knight, so the square is
specified in the description
NxP(B7).

DESCRIPTIONS OF MOVES

To indicate that a man is moved to a vacant square, the symbol of the man and the designation of the square are linked by a hyphen or dash. Thus, "B-Q3" means "Bishop to Queen three."

To indicate that a capture is made, the symbols of the capturing and captured men are linked by an "x." Thus, "BxP" means "Bishop takes Pawn."

If the opponent's King is checked, the contraction "ch" (or †) is added to the description of the move or capture. Thus, "B-N5ch" means "Bishop to Knight five check" and "QxBPch" means "Queen takes Bishop-Pawn check."

If a Pawn captures *en passant* the capture is written "PxPep."

The Castling Moves

Castling on the King's side is indicated by the symbol "O–O" (or "Castles KR"), and castling on the Queen's side by the symbol "O–O–O" (or "Castles QR").

Pawn Promotion

When a Pawn is promoted, the symbol for the substituted piece is shown in parenthesis after the description of the move or capture.

White advances his Pawn to the 8th rank and substitutes a Queen. The move is written:
P-R8(Q)
This means "Pawn to Rook eight and Queens."

White captures the Queen with his Pawn and substitutes a Knight with check. The move is written:
PxQ(N)ch
This means "Pawn takes Queen and promotes to a Knight with check."

Quality of Moves

The player or an annotator may add to the description of a move or capture one of the following indications of the quality of the move:

Comment on Quality	Symbol
Best Move	!
Best and Spectacular Move	! !
Spectacular but possibly unsound or unnecessary	! ?
Unsound but trappy	? !
Inferior move	?
A blunder	? ?

Move Numbers

To enable the reader to follow the moves of a game in the correct sequence, each move is numbered. The number precedes the description of a White move and a Black reply. For example:

WHITE	BLACK
1 P–K4	P–K4
2 N–KB3	N–QB3
3 B–B4	N–B3

Here the moves are columnized. On each line, the move number is followed by White's move and Black's reply.

To save space in a book or periodical, the record of moves may be arranged as follows:

WHITE	BLACK	WHITE	BLACK
1 P-K4	P–K4	4 N–N5	P–Q4
2 N-KB3	N–QB3	5 PxP	P–N4
3 B-B4	N–B3	6 BxP	QxP

In this example the first three moves are columnized at the left, the next three moves at the right.

When moves are not columnized (as in annotations), White's move is followed by a comma, and Black's move by a semicolon. For example, the moves above would be written as follows:

1 P–K4, P–K4; 2 N–KB3, N–QB3; 3 B–B4, N–B3; 4 N–N5, P–Q4; 5 PxP, P–N4; 6 BxP, QxP.

A series of dots before the description of a move indicates that the move is made by Black. For example, 3 . . . N–B3 means that Black played N–B3 on his third move.

ILLUSTRATIVE GAME NO. 1

The use of descriptive notation to record moves is illustrated in the short games on the following pages.

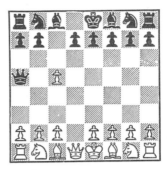

This position is reached after the opening moves:

    1 P-Q4   P-QB4

The full symbol for the square QB4 must be used to describe Black's move. The condensed symbol B4 would be ambiguous.

Position after 2nd moves:

    2 PxP   Q-R4ch

The description PxP is sufficient, for there is only one such capture on the board. Black's Queen goes to QR4 but the condensed R4 is enough.

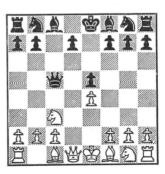

Position after 3rd moves:

    3 N-B3   QxBP

The notation N-B3 is right because N-KB3 would be illegal. The captured QBP is identified by the symbol BP. The Queen could capture KRP, but not KBP.

Position after 4th moves:

    4 P-K4   P-K4?

The basic P for Pawn is always used to describe a Pawn's move to a vacant square. The question-mark shows that Black's move was inferior.

Position after 5th moves:
  5 N-B3   P-Q3
For White's move it is bad
practice to write KN-B3 or
N-KB3. The QB3 square is
occupied by a Knight, so the
condensed N-B3 cannot be
misinterpreted.

Position after 6th moves:
  6 N-Q5   N-KB3?
Only one Knight can move to
Q5, so it is redundant to write
QN-Q5; but the Knight moved
by Black must be identified by
writing N-KB3, not the ambiguous N-B3.

Position after 7th moves:
  7 P-QN4!   Q-B3
The full symbol QN4 must be
used to show which NP is
moved; but Q-B3 describes
Black's move, for the Queen
could not go to KB3. The ex-
clamation means *best move.*

Position after 8 B-QN5! To
describe this move as B-N5
would be ambiguous, for this
could mean B-QN5 or B-KN5.
Now Black plays QxB and
resigns after White's 9 N-B7ch
winning the Queen.

ILLUSTRATIVE GAME NO. 2

Position after 1 P-K4, P-K4; 2 N-KB3. White's second move should not be written KN-B3. The piece moved is identified only if two of the same type can move to one square.

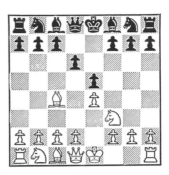

Position after 2 ... P-Q3; 3 B-B4. The condensed symbol B4 is used because the corresponding square on the King's side (KB4) cannot be occupied by a white Bishop.

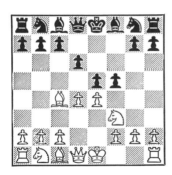

Position after 3 ... P-KB4; 4 P-Q4. The full symbol KB4 is necessary to show that Black moves the KBP, not the QBP. Now Black has two possible "PxP" captures.

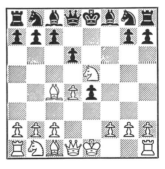

Position after 4 ... PxKP; 5 NxP. The Pawn captured by Black is identified as the KP. Basic symbols are used for White's capture since only one Knight can capture one Pawn.

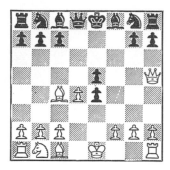

Position after 5...PxN; 6 Q-R5ch. Basic symbols describe Black's capture, for only one Pawn can capture one Knight. The condensed R5 identifies the KR5 square.

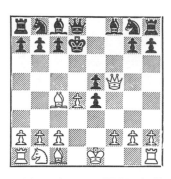

Position after 6...K-Q2; 7 Q-B5ch. The condensed symbol B5 cannot be misinterpreted. Note that Black has two King-Pawns and that White's Queen can capture either Pawn.

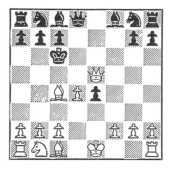

Position after 7...K-B3; 8 QxP(5). It is not advisable to write QxP, relying on the *omission* of check. QxP(5) shows that the Queen captures the Pawn on *White's* fifth rank.

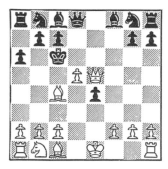

Position after 8...P-QR3; 9 P-Q5ch. Black's Pawn move must be clarified by the full symbol QR3. Concluding moves: 9...K-B4; 10 B-K3ch, KxB; 11 Q-Q4ch, K-N4; 12 N-B3ch, K-R4; 13 Q-R4 mate.

TOURNAMENT GAME SCORES

The Laws of Chess require every player in a tournament or match to record all the moves of his game on a "score sheet" provided for the purpose. The moves may be written in either descriptive or algebraic notation.

On the next page is reproduced the score sheet of U.S. Open Champion Larry Evans in which he records his game with Senior Master Max Pavey at the U.S. Championship tournament of 1954. Larry is one of the few players who write perfect descriptive notation. The moves of the game are repeated below:

U. S. Championship, New York, 1954

QUEEN'S GAMBIT DECLINED

WHITE: Max Pavey   BLACK: Larry Evans

WHITE	BLACK	WHITE	BLACK
1 P-QB4	N-KB3	14 NxP	N-K4
2 N-KB3	P-K3	15 B-B2	Q-N3
3 N-B3	P-Q4	16 B-K3	KR-Q1
4 P-Q4	P-B3	17 N-R5	B-B4
5 P-K3	QN-Q2	18 NxNch	PxN
6 B-Q3	PxP	19 Q-R5	BxN
7 BxBP	P-QN4	20 Q-R4	N-N3
8 B-N3	P-N5	21 Q-R6	Q-B4
9 N-K2	B-K2	22 B-N3	BxB
10 O-O	O-O	23 RxB	Q-KN4
11 N-N3	P-B4	24 Q-R3	Q-R5
12 P-K4	B-N2	25 Q-B3	P-B4
13 R-K1	PxP	26 Resigns	

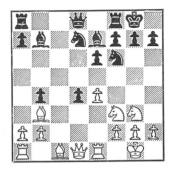

Position after Black's 13th move.

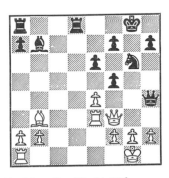

Position after Black's 25th move.

US Chmp. Q's Gambit Declined

DATE 6/19/54   ROUND 12

TIME ADJOURNED—WHITE   **TIME ADJOURNED— BLACK**

WHITE Pavey   BLACK Evans

White	Black		White	Black
1 P-QB4	N-KB3	31		
2 N-KB3	P-K3	32		
3 N-B3	P-Q4	33		
4 P-Q4	P-B3	34		
5 P-K3	QN-Q2	35		
6 B-Q3	PxP	36		
7 BxBP	P-QN4	37		
8 B-N3	P-N5	38		
9 N-K2	B-K2	39		
10 O-O	O-O	40		
11 N-N3	P-B4	41		
12 P-K4	B-N2	42		
13 R-K1	PxP	43		
14 NxP	N-K4	44		
15 B-Q2	Q-N3	45		
16 B-K3	KR-Q1	46		
17 N-R5	B-B4	47		
18 NxN ch	PxN	48		
19 Q-R5	BxN	49		
20 Q-R4	N-N3	50		
21 Q-R6	Q-B4	51		
22 B-N3	BxB	52		
23 RxB	Q-KN4	53		
24 Q-R3	Q-R5	54		
25 Q-B3	P-B4	55		
26 Resigns		56		
27		57		
28 Larry Evans		58		
29		59		
30		60		

RECORDING ADJOURNED POSITIONS

When a tournament or match game is adjourned, the Laws of Chess require the player having the move to record his move on his score sheet, then "seal" the move by inserting the score sheets of the game in an envelope. The adjourned position and other data must be recorded on the outside of the envelope.

The cover of an official USCF "sealed move" envelope is reproduced below. In this example, the adjourned position is recorded on the diagram blank by writing the initials of the chessmen on the squares they occupy, circling the initials of the black men.

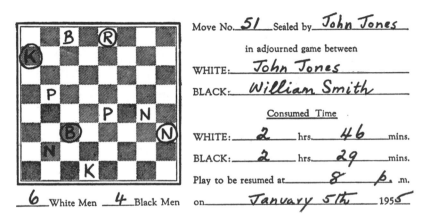

Move No. _51_ Sealed by _John Jones_

in adjourned game between

WHITE: _John Jones_

BLACK: _William Smith_

Consumed Time

WHITE: _2_ hrs. _46_ mins.

BLACK: _2_ hrs. _29_ mins.

Play to be resumed at _8_ _p._ .m.

_6_ White Men _4_ Black Men on _January 5th_ 1955

It is permissible, of course, to distinguish between the white and black men in other ways. A red pencil may be used to write the initials of the white men. Another method is to write the initials of the white men in capital letters, of the black men in lower case (as in Forsythe Notation). If a set of chess character rubber stamps is available, the symbols of the men may be stamped on the diagram, using red ink for the white men.

If an official envelope is not provided, an ordinary envelope may be used and the position recorded on the outside by Forsythe Notation.

BLACK

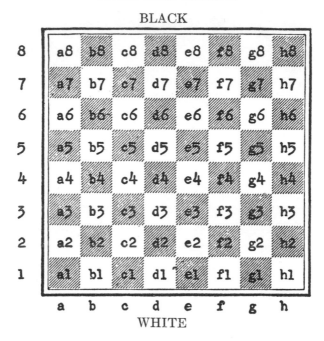

a   b   c   d   e   f   g   h

WHITE

ALGEBRAIC NOTATION

Algebraic notation is much easier to read and write than the descriptive system. As shown in the diagram above, the eight files (left to right from White's side of the board) are designated by the letters a to h. The eight ranks are numbered from 1 to 8, counting from White's first rank.

Each square is identified by a symbol comprising the letter of the file and the number of the rank, and each square has only one symbol for a move by White or a move by Black.

The chess pieces are designated by their initials, as in descriptive notation, but it is never necessary to distinguish between King-side and Queen-side pieces. The basic symbols are used invariably: K for King, Q for Queen, R for Rook, B for Bishop, and N or Kt for Knight. The Pawns are not specifically indicated.

Descriptions of Moves

A move by a piece is described by giving the initial of the piece, followed by the symbols of the squares of departure and arrival. If the move is to a vacant square, the symbols are linked by a hyphen or dash. If a man is captured on the square of arrival, the square symbols are linked by a colon or "x." For example, Rf1-d1 means "the Rook on f1 moves to d1." And Nf3:d4 means "the Knight on f3 captures on d4."

A move or capture by a Pawn is described in the same way but is *not* preceded by the initial *P* for Pawn. For example, e2-e4 means "the Pawn on e2 moves to e4." And h3:g4 means "the Pawn on h3 captures on g4." The omission of a preceding initial always indicates that a move or capture is made by a Pawn.

If the opponent's King is checked, the description of the move or capture is followed by a dagger (†) or plus sign (+) in many foreign-language publications. Mate may be indicated by a multiplication sign (×) or a double dagger (‡).

Castling on the King's side is indicated by the symbol "O-O" and on the Queen's side by "O-O-O."

When a Pawn is promoted, the initial of the substituted piece follows the symbol of the square of arrival. For example, h7-h8Q means "the Pawn on h7 moves to h8 and queens." Or h7:g8N + means "the Pawn on h7 captures on g8 and promotes to a Knight with check."

Illustrative Game

In the following game, the moves are recorded in algebraic notation at the left, in descriptive notation at the right:

	WHITE	BLACK		WHITE	BLACK
1	d2-d4	f7-f5	1	P-Q4	P-KB4
2	e2-e4	f5:e4	2	P-K4	PxP
3	Nb1-c3	Ng8-f6	3	N-QB3	N-KB3
4	f2-f3	e4:f3	4	P-B3	PxP
5	Ng1:f3	e7-e6	5	NxP	P-K3
6	Bf1-d3	Bf8-e7	6	B-Q3	B-K2
7	Qd1-e2	c7-c5	7	Q-K2	P-B4
8	d4:c5	Be7:c5	8	PxP	BxP
9	Bc1-g5	O-O	9	B-KN5	O-O
10	Nf3-e5	Nb8-c6	10	N-K5	N-B3
11	Rh1-f1	d7-d5	11	R-KB1	P-Q4
12	Ne5-g4	Bc5-e7	12	N-N4	B-K2
13	Ng4:f6 +	g7:f6	13	NxNch	PxN
14	Bd3:h7 +	Kg8-g7	14	BxPch	K-N2
15	Bg5-d2	Nc6-e5	15	B-Q2	N-K4
16	Qe2-h5	Rf8-h8	16	Q-R5	R-R1
17	Qh5-h6 +	Kg7-f7	17	Q-R6ch	K-B2

(Continued)

White	Black	White	Black
18 Bd2-f4	Kf7-e8	18 B-B4	K-K1
19 Bf4:e5	f6:e5	19 BxN	PxB
20 Qh6-g7	Ke8-d7	20 Q-N7	K-Q2
21 O-O-O	Kd7-c6	21 O-O-O	K-B3
22 Rf1-f7	Be7-d6	22 R-B7	B-Q3
23 g2-g4	Bc8-d7	23 P-KN4	B-Q2
24 g4-g5	Ra8-b8	24 P-N5	R-QN1
25 h2-h4	Resigns	25 P-KR4	Resigns

ABBREVIATED ALGEBRAIC NOTATION

In abridged notation, the description of a move omits the square of departure and gives only the square of arrival. For a move to a vacant square, the hyphen or dash is also omitted. For example: d4 means "a Pawn moves to the square d4." Re7 means "a Rook moves to the square e7." Qf3 means "the Queen moves to the square f3."

To indicate a capture by a piece, the initial of the piece and the symbol of the square on which it captures are linked by a colon or "x." For example: N:e8 (or N x e8) means "a Knight captures on e8." And B:g4 (or B x g4) means "a Bishop captures on g4."

To indicate a capture by a Pawn, the letter of the file on which the Pawn stands and the symbol of the square on which it captures are linked by a colon or "x." For example: c:d4 (or c x d4) means "the Pawn on file c captures on d4."

An optional method of showing a capture by a Pawn is to combine the letters designating the file of departure and the file of arrival. For example, "gh" means "the Pawn on file g captures on file h."

In German publications, the colon indicating a capture follows the symbol of the square on which the man captures. For instance, a Pawn capture may be written fg5: (instead of f:g5) meaning "the Pawn on file f captures on g5."

If the omission of the square of departure would result in ambiguity, the letter of the file or the number of the rank is added to the initial of the piece moved. For example: Nhf6 means "the Knight on file h moves to f6." And N3:e5 means "the Knight on rank 3 captures on e5."

As a rule, abbreviated notation is not columnized. It may be used to record all the moves of a game, or for the annotations to games in which the text moves are columnized in unabridged notation.

Illustrative Game

The moves of a short game are recorded below in abbreviated algebraic notation, following the style used in many publications:
1. e4 e6   2. d4 d5   3. Nd2 d:e4   4. N:e4 Nd7   5. Nf3 Be7
6. Bd3 Ngf6   7. Qe2 O-O   8. O-O N:e4   9. Q:e4 Nf6   10. Qh4 b6
11. Bg5 g6   12. c4 Bb7   13. d5 e:d5   14. Rfe1 h6   15. Q:h6 Ng4
16. Qh4 B:g5   17. N:g5 Nf6   18. Qh6 d4   19. Re6 Re8   20. B:g6 Resigns.

In descriptive notation, the above game would be recorded as follows:
1 P-K4, P-K3; 2 P-Q4, P-Q4; 3 N-Q2, PxP; 4 NxP, N-Q2; 5 N-KB3, B-K2; 6 B-Q3, KN-B3; 7 Q-K2, O-O; 8 O-O, NxN; 9 QxN, N-B3; 10 Q-R4, P-QN3; 11 B-KN5, P-N3; 12 P-B4, B-N2; 13 P-Q5, PxP; 14 KR-K1, P-KR3; 15 QxP, N-N5; 16 Q-R4, BxB; 17 NxB, N-B3; 18 Q-R6, P-Q5; 19 R-K6, R-K1; 20 BxP, Resigns.

INITIALS OF PIECES IN FOREIGN LANGUAGES

In foreign languages, the pieces are indicated by initials as listed below:

	King	*Queen*	*Rook*	*Bishop*	*Knight*
French	R	D	T	F	C
Italian	R	D	T	A	C
Spanish	R	D	T	A	C
Portuguese	R	D	T	B	C
German	K	D	T	L	S
Dutch	K	D	T	L	P
Swedish	K	D	T	L	S
Russian	Kp	Φ	Π	C	K
Yugoslav	K	D	T	L	S
Czech	K	D	V	S	J
Polish	K	H	W	G	S
Hungarian	K	V	B	F	H

Publications in French, Italian, Spanish, and Portuguese use descriptive notation. In these languages, the initial P for Pawn is the same as in English.

Publications in the other languages listed above use algebraic notation.

BLACK

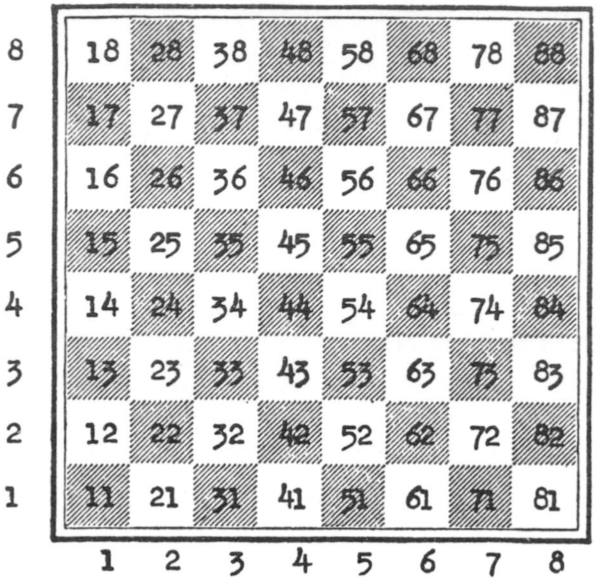

8	18	28	38	48	58	68	78	88
7	17	27	37	47	57	67	77	87
6	16	26	36	46	56	66	76	86
5	15	25	35	45	55	65	75	85
4	14	24	34	44	54	64	74	84
3	13	23	33	43	53	63	73	83
2	12	22	32	42	52	62	72	82
1	11	21	31	41	51	61	71	81

    1   2   3   4   5   6   7   8

WHITE

INTERNATIONAL POSTAL CHESS NOTATION

In the United States alone there are thousands of players who contest chess games by mail. Each move is sent on a postcard, sometimes accompanied by a diagram showing the position after the move. Descriptive notation is used almost exclusively, for the players are familiar with this system.

For postal games, it is important that each move be recorded correctly. If the notation of a move is misinterpreted by the recipient, a game may continue for a long time before the error is found. Clear, unambiguous notation is particularly necessary when games are conducted between players in different countries.

For games played by mail, the FIDE has authorized a system of recording moves which is, in fact, the only international chess notation. It can be used and understood by a player in any country of the world. The system is independent of language.

As shown in the diagram, the eight files (left to right from White's side of the board) are numbered from 1 to 8. The eight ranks are also numbered from 1 to 8, counting from White's first rank. Each square is identified by combining the number of the file and the number of the rank, thus forming a two-figure number. The square numbers are invariable, being used for moves by White and moves by Black.

Descriptions of Moves

A move, including a capture, is recorded by combining the number of the square of departure and the number of the square of arrival, thus forming a four-figure number. The initial of the man moved or captured is not included. For example: 6355 means "the man on square 63 moves to, or captures on, square 55."

A check need not be indicated. The recipient of a checking move knows that his King is attacked.

Castling is recorded as a move by the King. Thus, if White castles on the King's side, the move is written 5171; or if Black castles on the Queen's side, the move is written 5838.

It is only when a Pawn is promoted that it becomes necessary to use language. The name of the substituted piece, written in English, French, or any language understood by both players, is added to the record of the move. For example, "4748 (Queen)" records the queening of a Pawn on square 48.

Illustrative Game

In the following game, the moves are recorded in international postal chess notation at the left, in descriptive notation at the right:

White	Black	White	Black
1 4244	7866	1 P-Q4	N-KB3
2 3175	4745	2 B-N5	P-Q4
3 2142	2847	3 N-Q2	QN-Q2
4 7163	3735	4 KN-B3	P-B4
5 5253	4826	5 P-K3	Q-N3
6 1121	5756	6 R-QN1	P-K3
7 3233	6846	7 P-B3	B-Q3
8 6143	2637	8 B-Q3	Q-B2
9 5171	5878	9 O-O	O-O
10 4332	2726	10 B-B2	P-QN3
11 5354	3544	11 P-K4	PxQP
12 5445	4433	12 KPxP	PxBP
13 4556	6756	13 PxKP	PxKP
14 4254	6654	14 N-K4	NxN
15 3254	3816	15 BxN	B-R3
16 6151	1858	16 R-K1	QR-K1
17 2131	4766	17 R-QB1	N-B3

(Continued)

WHITE	BLACK	WHITE	BLACK
18 3133	3728	18 RxP	Q-N1
19 7566	7766	19 BxN	PxB
20 5487	7887	20 BxPch	KxB
21 6355	4655	21 N-K5	BxN
22 3383	8777	22 R-R3ch	K-N2
23 4174	7767	23 Q-N4ch	K-B2
24 8387		24 R-R7 mate	

BLACK

MA	NA	PA	RA	SA	TA	WA	ZA
ME	NE	PE	RE	SE	TE	WE	ZE
MI	NI	PI	RI	SI	TI	WI	ZI
MO	NO	PO	RO	SO	TO	WO	ZO
BO	GO	DO	FO	GO	HO	KO	LO
BI	CI	DI	FI	GI	HI	KI	LI
BE	CE	DE	FE	GE	HE	KE	LE
BA	CA	DA	FA	GA	HA	KA	LA

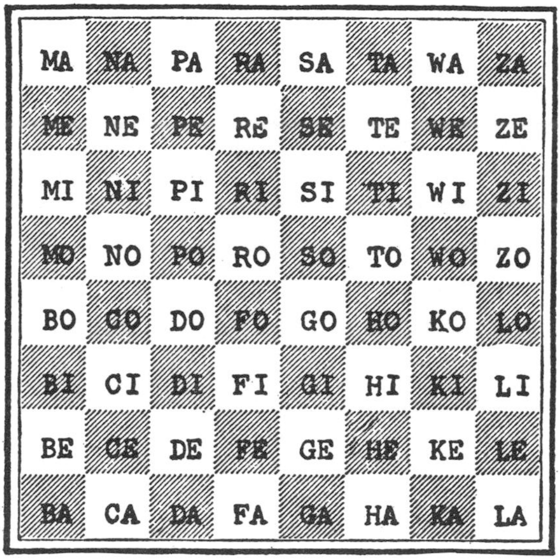

WHITE

THE UEDEMANN CODE

For matches in which the moves of games are transmitted by telegraph, cable, or radio, the FIDE has authorized the use of the Uedemann Code.

As shown in the above diagram, each square is identified by two letters of the alphabet. A move, including a capture, is transmitted as a four-letter code word which combines the two letters of the square of departure with the two letters of the square of arrival. The initial of the man moved or captured is not included. For example, the move P-Q4 for White would be transmitted by the code word FEFO.

As in postal chess notation, checks are not indicated, and castling is transmitted as a move by the King. Thus, if White castles on the King's side, the move is sent as GAKA.

If a match on two or more boards is in progress, each move message is usually preceded by the number of the board and an acknowledgment of the opponent's last move. For example, a message may be transmitted as follows:

ONE   GEGO   SESO   TWO   WATI   DEDO

Decoded, this means: "On Board No. 1, we acknowledge the move GEGO (P-K4) and reply SESO (P-K4). On Board No. 2, we acknowledge the move WATI (N-KB3 for Black) and make the move DEDO (P-QB4)."

FORSYTHE NOTATION

Forsythe Notation is a method of recording a chess position. It is a quick and easy way to jot down a position without using a diagram blank.

BLACK

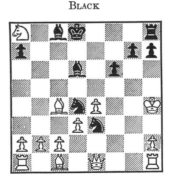

N	1	b	k	3	r
p	5	p	p		
3	b	1	p	2	
8					
2	B	n	P	2	K
3	P	n	3		
P	P	P	4	P	
R	1	B	1	Q	2	R

WHITE

The system can best be understood by examining an example, as illustrated above. The position on each rank, reading from left to right, is recorded by a series of initials and figures. The initials indicate the chessmen, capital letters being used for white men and lower case letters for black men. The figures represent the number of vacant squares. Thus, the first line records the position on White's 8th rank as follows:

N 1 b k 3 r

Decoded, this means: The first square at the left is occupied by a white Knight (capital N). Then there is one vacant square (figure 1). The next square is occupied by a black Bishop, and the next by the black King (lower case letters b and k). Then there are three vacant squares (figure 3) and a black Rook (lower case letter r).

The second line records the position on White's 7th rank as follows:

$$p \; 5 \; p \; p$$

Decoded, this means: The first square at the left is occupied by a black Pawn (lower case letter p). Then there are five vacant squares (figure 5) and two black Pawns.

The third line records the position on White's 6th rank as follows:

$$3 \; b \; 1 \; p \; 2$$

Decoded, this means: The first three squares from the left are vacant; the next square is occupied by a black Bishop (lower case letter b). Then there is one vacant square, and the next is occupied by a black Pawn. The last two squares are vacant.

The position on White's 5th rank is shown by the figure 8. This means that the rank is unoccupied, that there are 8 vacant squares on this rank.

The position on White's 4th rank is written:

$$2 \; B \; n \; P \; 2 \; K$$

This means: The first two squares are vacant. Then comes a white Bishop, a black Knight, and a white Pawn. The next two squares are vacant, and the last square is occupied by the white King.

The other three ranks are recorded in the same way. To save space, the notations for the ranks may follow each other, separated by slant-bars. Thus, the position of the example may be recorded as follows:

N 1 b k 3 r / p 5 p p / 3 b 1 p 2 / 8 /
2 B n P 2 K / 3 P n 3 / P P P 4 P / R 1 B 1 Q 2 R.

When written in this manner, the order is always from White's 8th rank down to his 1st rank.

CHAPTER IV

How to Run a Chess Tournament

The first international chess tournament, London 1851, was conducted under a modified knockout system. For the first round, the sixteen contestants were paired by lot, and each winner of two games out of three, not counting draws, qualified to play in the remaining rounds; the other eight players were eliminated. The eight qualifiers were paired by lot for the second round. The winners of these four matches (best of seven games, not counting draws) then played matches in the semi-final and final rounds to decide the winners of the first four prizes. The losers in the second round also played semi-final and final matches to determine the winners of the fifth to eighth prizes.

Similar knockout systems were used in other tournaments of that period. Thus, at the first American Chess Congress, New York 1857, eight of the sixteen contestants were knocked out in first-round matches, and four of the eight qualifiers were eliminated in the second round. The four survivors were then paired in the matches of the semi-final round. The two winners were matched in the finals to decide the first and second prize winners; the two losers played for the third and fourth prizes.

For most purposes, the knockout type of tournament is the least desirable form of chess competition, especially if the early round pairings are made by lot and if a contestant can be knocked out as a result of one or two games. At London in 1851, the haphazard pairing by lot resulted in matching two of the strongest entrants, Anderssen and Kieseritzky, for the first round. The latter was knocked out of the tournament after playing only three games. Mr. Lowenthal, who had come from the United States (a voyage of about two months in those days) to compete in this tournament, was also knocked out in three games of the first round.

The knockout system did not last long and is seldom used today. As it happens, however, it has been revived for the most important of all contests, the World Championship Candidates' Tournament, in which the winner earns the right to challenge the World Champion to a title match. But there is a special reason for this switch from a round robin to a knockout match-tournament; the change has been made to prevent possible collusion between contestants belonging to one country. This does not necessarily mean that chess ethics have deteriorated since the good old days. In fact, at London in 1851, Anderssen and Szen made a deal in the second round; they agreed that if either won first prize he would give one-third to the other. Unethical practices are not new and are probably not any worse today than they were in the past, but the ideological or chauvinistic type of collusion is a recent development and can best be met by a knockout contest.

Barring collusion, the fairest type of tournament is the round robin, known in England as the *all-play-all*. Each contestant meets all the other players, so the element of luck has a negligible effect on the result. If a double round is played, with colors reversed, the factor of luck is theoretically eliminated. This cannot be said of any other type of tournament.

When there are too many entrants to play a round robin, the choice lies between the Holland System and the Swiss System, but only the latter is capable of handling a huge number of players in a short tournament. The Holland System is named after Mr. Kirk D. Holland, an active promoter of the game and President of the American Chess Federation in 1937-38. His system was used to conduct the U. S. Open Championships prior to the adoption of the Swiss System in 1946. Under the Holland System, the entrants are seeded into preliminary groups of about the same size and approximately the same strength. Each preliminary group plays a round robin, and the players with the highest scores qualify for the championship finals; the others qualify for one or more "consolation" finals.

The Swiss System is by far the most popular type of tournament in the United States. It resembles the knockout type in that winners play one another, but no players are eliminated. In each round the players with equal scores are matched. When the scheduled number of rounds is completed, the player with the highest score wins. Cash prizes are divided among tied players, but ties may be broken to determine the champion and for other purposes.

Instructions for conducting round-robin and Swiss tournaments are given in this chapter. We do not include instructions on how to run a knockout tournament because the ordinary contest of this type has been supplanted by the Swiss System tournament. The World Championship Candidates' knockout match-tournament is described in Chapter VIII.

THE ROUND ROBIN TOURNAMENT

In most tournaments of this type each contestant plays one game with each of the other competitors. In a double round robin, he plays each opponent twice, once with white and once with black.

Each entrant is assigned a number, which may be chosen by lot. The pairings, order of rounds, and the first move in each game, for tournaments with from 3 to 24 players, are shown in the tables on pages 112-117. The player with the first number of each pairing has the white men. For example, a tournament with ten players is paired as shown in table D on page 112. In the first round, player No. 1 has white against No. 10; player No. 2 has white against No. 9, etc., as indicated on the first line of the table. The remaining lines show the pairings and colors for the subsequent rounds.

If there is an odd number of competitors, the player whose number appears in the first column is given a bye. Thus, a tournament with nine players is paired as shown in table D; but since there is no player No. 10, the contestant scheduled against No. 10 in each round has a bye. No. 1 has a bye in the first round, No. 6 in the second round, etc.

For a double round robin the applicable table is used to pair the competitors for play in the first leg of the contest in the manner described above. For the second leg the same table is used, but the colors are reversed. Thus, in the second leg of a ten-man tournament, players 10, 9, 8, 7, and 6 have white in the first round.

The players score one point for a win, half a point for a draw, zero for a lost or defaulted game. Cash prizes are divided among tied players. As a rule, ties for the title at stake are not broken. If there is some reason for breaking ties, the so-called Sonnenborn-Berger system should be used. For each player in the tie add up the scores of the opponents he has beaten and half the scores of the players with whom he drew, then arrange the tied players in the order of the sums so obtained. If a tie still remains, arrange the tied players in the order of their scores under the Kashdan system (win, 4 points; draw, 2 points; loss, 1 point; loss by default, zero). If a remaining tie must be dissolved, the order of finish will have to be decided by a toss-up.

An agreement on what to do about withdrawals should be reached before the contest begins. The fairest method is to cancel the score of a withdrawing player if he finished less than half of his scheduled games. If he played at least half, let his score stand for the games he finished and count the remaining unplayed games as won by the opponents he was supposed to play in these games.

The Holland System

This system was designed to handle a fairly large number of entrants in a tournament lasting at least ten rounds. It is usually restricted to a maximum of about fifty players; even such a large number may present difficulties in arranging the tournament to fit the time available.

The competitors are divided into preliminary qualifying groups with the same, or nearly the same, number of players in each group. The actual number of preliminary groups, and the number of players in each group, depends on the total number of entrants and the length of time available. For instance, if there are 30 entrants and there is time for not more than 14 rounds, the players may be divided into five groups of six, and a round robin played by each group. The top two players from each group qualify for the ten-man championship finals, the next two from each preliminary for the Class A "consolation" finals, and the last two for the Class B finals. Ties in the preliminaries should be broken as explained above.

When the preliminary sections are arranged, it is essential that the entrants he seeded into the groups so that the sections are about equal in playing strength. Thus, if there are five preliminary sections, and the top two from each group qualify to play in the championship finals, the ten strongest entrants should be divided equally among the five sections. The seeding is made simpler if the entrants have national ratings; otherwise, a committee should do the seeding. If desired, some highly rated players of recognized ability may be seeded directly into the championship finals without playing in the preliminaries.

Instead of dividing the entrants into preliminary groups, played as round robins, the Swiss System can be used to conduct the preliminary competition and classify the players for the final championship and consolation round-robin tournments.

Examples of Holland System round robins can be found in the last chapter of this book. The World Team Championships and Junior Championships are still conducted in this way. The early United States Championships were seeded competitions of this type.

Although the Holland System conducts the preliminaries and finals as round robins, this does not necessarily confer on the system the fairness and accuracy of the round robin. A player's fate is sealed by his performance in a short preliminary contest. He may have the bad luck to be seeded into a stronger section than the others; for no matter how the seeding is done, the sections are seldom equal in strength. If a player fails to qualify for the championship finals, he has no hope of winning the title. He may be as strong as several of the players who qualify from other sections, but he rates below them all in the finals.

In many cases, the Swiss System gives at least as good results as the Holland System and is fairer to the players. Every contestant has a chance to win the title and can recover from an early upset. Theoretically, to establish a single winner who has met some strong opposition, the minimum number of rounds of a Swiss System tournament should be equal to the square root of the number of players. To obtain fairly accurate placings below the winner, two rounds should be added for each place. For example, for about 50 players, seven rounds should suffice to produce an acceptable winner. If the second and third places must be fairly accurate, a minimum of 11 rounds would be required. Obviously, these conditions cannot be met in most weekend tournaments; but chess clubs should be able to schedule their championships to meet the minimum requirements of a Swiss System tournament.

Pairing Tables for Round Robins

On the following pages are pairing tables for round-robin tournaments with from 3 to 24 players.

TABLE A
3 or 4 Players

Round	Pairings	
1	1:4	2:3
2	4:3	1:2
3	2:4	3:1

TABLE B
5 or 6 Players

Round	Pairings		
1	1:6	2:5	3:4
2	6:4	5:3	1:2
3	2:6	3:1	4:5
4	6:5	1:4	2:3
5	3:6	4:2	5:1

TABLE C—7 or 8 Players

Round	Pairings			
1	1:8	2:7	3:6	4:5
2	8:5	6:4	7:3	1:2
3	2:8	3:1	4:7	5:6
4	8:6	7:5	1:4	2:3
5	3:8	4:2	5:1	6:7
6	8:7	1:6	2:5	3:4
7	4:8	5:3	6:2	7:1

TABLE D—9 or 10 Players

Round	Pairings				
1	1:10	2:9	3:8	4:7	5:6
2	10:6	7:5	8:4	9:3	1:2
3	2:10	3:1	4:9	5:8	6:7
4	10:7	8:6	9:5	1:4	2:3
5	3:10	4:2	5:1	6:9	7:8
6	10:8	9:7	1:6	2:5	3:4
7	4:10	5:3	6:2	7:1	8:9
8	10:9	1:8	2:7	3:6	4:5
9	5:10	6:4	7:3	8:2	9:1

TABLE E—11 or 12 Players

Round	Pairings					
1	1:12	2:11	3:10	4:9	5:8	6:7
2	12:7	8:6	9:5	10:4	11:3	1:2
3	2:12	3:1	4:11	5:10	6:9	7:8
4	12:8	9:7	10:6	11:5	1:4	2:3
5	3:12	4:2	5:1	6:11	7:10	8:9
6	12:9	10:8	11:7	1:6	2:5	3:4
7	4:12	5:3	6:2	7:1	8:11	9:10
8	12:10	11:9	1:8	2:7	3:6	4:5
9	5:12	6:4	7:3	8:2	9:1	10:11
10	12:11	1:10	2:9	3:8	4:7	5:6
11	6:12	7:5	8:4	9:3	10:2	11:1

TABLE F—13 or 14 Players

Round	Pairings						
1	1:14	2:13	3:12	4:11	5:10	6:9	7:8
2	14:8	9:7	10:6	11:5	12:4	13:3	1:2
3	2:14	3:1	4:13	5:12	6:11	7:10	8:9
4	14:9	10:8	11:7	12:6	13:5	1:4	2:3
5	3:14	4:2	5:1	6:13	7:12	8:11	9:10
6	14:10	11:9	12:8	13:7	1:6	2:5	3:4
7	4:14	5:3	6:2	7:1	8:13	9:12	10:11
8	14:11	12:10	13:9	1:8	2:7	3:6	4:5
9	5:14	6:4	7:3	8:2	9:1	10:13	11:12
10	14:12	13:11	1:10	2:9	3:8	4:7	5:6
11	6:14	7:5	8:4	9:3	10:2	11:1	12:13
12	14:13	1:12	2:11	3:10	4:9	5:8	6:7
13	7:14	8:6	9:5	10:4	11:3	12:2	13:1

TABLE G—15 or 16 Players

Round	Pairings							
1	1:16	2:15	3:14	4:13	5:12	6:11	7:10	8:9
2	16:9	10:8	11:7	12:6	13:5	14:4	15:3	1:2
3	2:16	3:1	4:15	5:14	6:13	7:12	8:11	9:10
4	16:10	11:9	12:8	13:7	14:6	15:5	1:4	2:3
5	3:16	4:2	5:1	6:15	7:14	8:13	9:12	10:11
6	16:11	12:10	13:9	14:8	15:7	1:6	2:5	3:4
7	4:16	5:3	6:2	7:1	8:15	9:14	10:13	11:12
8	16:12	13:11	14:10	15:9	1:8	2:7	3:6	4:5
9	5:16	6:4	7:3	8:2	9:1	10:15	11:14	12:13
10	16:13	14:12	15:11	1:10	2:9	3:8	4:7	5:6
11	6:16	7:5	8:4	9:3	10:2	11:1	12:15	13:14
12	16:14	15:13	1:12	2:11	3:10	4:9	5:8	6:7
13	7:16	8:6	9:5	10:4	11:3	12:2	13:1	14:15
14	16:15	1:14	2:13	3:12	4:11	5:10	6:9	7:8
15	8:16	9:7	10:6	11:5	12:4	13:3	14:2	15:1

TABLE H—17 or 18 Players

Round	Pairings								
1	1:18	2:17	3:16	4:15	5:14	6:13	7:12	8:11	9:10
2	18:10	11:9	12:8	13:7	14:6	15:5	16:4	17:3	1:2
3	2:18	3:1	4:17	5:16	6:15	7:14	8:13	9:12	10:11
4	18:11	12:10	13:9	14:8	15:7	16:6	17:5	1:4	2:3
5	3:18	4:2	5:1	6:17	7:16	8:15	9:14	10:13	11:12
6	18:12	13:11	14:10	15:9	16:8	17:7	1:6	2:5	3:4
7	4:18	5:3	6:2	7:1	8:17	9:16	10:15	11:14	12:13
8	18:13	14:12	15:11	16:10	17:9	1:8	2:7	3:6	4:5
9	5:18	6:4	7:3	8:2	9:1	10:17	11:16	12:15	13:14
10	18:14	15:13	16:12	17:11	1:10	2:9	3:8	4:7	5:6
11	6:18	7:5	8:4	9:3	10:2	11:1	12:17	13:16	14:15
12	18:15	16:14	17:13	1:12	2:11	3:10	4:9	5:8	6:7
13	7:18	8:6	9:5	10:4	11:3	12:2	13:1	14:17	15:16
14	18:16	17:15	1:14	2:13	3:12	4:11	5:10	6:9	7:8
15	8:18	9:7	10:6	11:5	12:4	13:3	14:2	15:1	16:17
16	18:17	1:16	2:15	3:14	4:13	5:12	6:11	7:10	8:9
17	9:18	10:8	11:7	12:6	13:5	14:4	15:3	16:2	17:1

TABLE I—19 or 20 Players

Round	Pairings									
1	1:20	2:19	3:18	4:17	5:16	6:15	7:14	8:13	9:12	10:11
2	20:11	12:10	13:9	14:8	15:7	16:6	17:5	18:4	19:3	1:2
3	2:20	3:1	4:19	5:18	6:17	7:16	8:15	9:14	10:13	11:12
4	20:12	13:11	14:10	15:9	16:8	17:7	18:6	19:5	1:4	2:3
5	3:20	4:2	5:1	6:19	7:18	8:17	9:16	10:15	11:14	12:13
6	20:13	14:12	15:11	16:10	17:9	18:8	19:7	1:6	2:5	3:4
7	4:20	5:3	6:2	7:1	8:19	9:18	10:17	11:16	12:15	13:14
8	20:14	15:13	16:12	17:11	18:10	19:9	1:8	2:7	3:6	4:5
9	5:20	6:4	7:3	8:2	9:1	10:19	11:18	12:17	13:16	14:15
10	20:15	16:14	17:13	18:12	19:11	1:10	2:9	3:8	4:7	5:6
11	6:20	7:5	8:4	9:3	10:2	11:1	12:19	13:18	14:17	15:16
12	20:16	17:15	18:14	19:13	1:12	2:11	3:10	4:9	5:8	6:7
13	7:20	8:6	9:5	10:4	11:3	12:2	13:1	14:19	15:18	16:17
14	20:17	18:16	19:15	1:14	2:13	3:12	4:11	5:10	6:9	7:8
15	8:20	9:7	10:6	11:5	12:4	13:3	14:2	15:1	16:19	17:18
16	20:18	19:17	1:16	2:15	3:14	4:13	5:12	6:11	7:10	8:9
17	9:20	10:8	11:7	12:6	13:5	14:4	15:3	16:2	17:1	18:19
18	20:19	1:18	2:17	3:16	4:15	5:14	6:13	7:12	8:11	9:10
19	10:20	11:9	12:8	13:7	14:6	15:5	16:4	17:3	18:2	19:1

TABLE J—21 or 22 Players

Round	Pairings										
1	1:22	2:21	3:20	4:19	5:18	6:17	7:16	8:15	9:14	10:13	11:12
2	22:12	13:11	14:10	15:9	16:8	17:7	18:6	19:5	20:4	21:3	1:2
3	2:22	3:1	4:21	5:20	6:19	7:18	8:17	9:16	10:15	11:14	12:13
4	22:13	14:12	15:11	16:10	17:9	18:8	19:7	20:6	21:5	1:4	2:3
5	3:22	4:2	5:1	6:21	7:20	8:19	9:18	10:17	11:16	12:15	13:14
6	22:14	15:13	16:12	17:11	18:10	19:9	20:8	21:7	1:6	2:5	3:4
7	4:22	5:3	6:2	7:1	8:21	9:20	10:19	11:18	12:17	13:16	14:15
8	22:15	16:14	17:13	18:12	19:11	20:10	21:9	1:8	2:7	3:6	4:5
9	5:22	6:4	7:3	8:2	9:1	10:21	11:20	12:19	13:18	14:17	15:16
10	22:16	17:15	18:14	19:13	20:12	21:11	1:10	2:9	3:8	4:7	5:6
11	6:22	7:5	8:4	9:3	10:2	11:1	12:21	13:20	14:19	15:18	16:17
12	22:17	18:16	19:15	20:14	21:13	1:12	2:11	3:10	4:9	5:8	6:7
13	7:22	8:6	9:5	10:4	11:3	12:2	13:1	14:21	15:20	16:19	17:18
14	22:18	19:17	20:16	21:15	1:14	2:13	3:12	4:11	5:10	6:9	7:8
15	8:22	9:7	10:6	11:5	12:4	13:3	14:2	15:1	16:21	17:20	18:19
16	22:19	20:18	21:17	1:16	2:15	3:14	4:13	5:12	6:11	7:10	8:9
17	9:22	10:8	11:7	12:6	13:5	14:4	15:3	16:2	17:1	18:21	19:20
18	22:20	21:19	1:18	2:17	3:16	4:15	5:14	6:13	7:12	8:11	9:10
19	10:22	11:9	12:8	13:7	14:6	15:5	16:4	17:3	18:2	19:1	20:21
20	22:21	1:20	2:19	3:18	4:17	5:16	6:15	7:14	8:13	9:12	10:11
21	11:22	12:10	13:9	14:8	15:7	16:6	17:5	18:4	19:3	20:2	21:1

TABLE K—23 or 24 Players

Round	Pairings										
1	1:24	2:23	3:22	4:21	5:20	6:19	7:18	8:17	9:16	10:15	11:14	12:13
2	24:13	14:12	15:11	16:10	17:9	18:8	19:7	20:6	21:5	22:4	23:3	1:2
3	2:24	3:1	4:23	5:22	6:21	7:20	8:19	9:18	10:17	11:16	12:15	13:14
4	24:14	15:13	16:12	17:11	18:10	19:9	20:8	21:7	22:6	23:5	1:4	2:3
5	3:24	4:2	5:1	6:23	7:22	8:21	9:20	10:19	11:18	12:17	13:16	14:15
6	24:15	16:14	17:13	18:12	19:11	20:10	21:9	22:8	23:7	1:6	2:5	3:4
7	4:24	5:3	6:2	7:1	8:23	9:22	10:21	11:20	12:19	13:18	14:17	15:16
8	24:16	17:15	18:14	19:13	20:12	21:11	22:10	23:9	1:8	2:7	3:6	4:5
9	5:24	6:4	7:3	8:2	9:1	10:23	11:22	12:21	13:20	14:19	15:18	16:17
10	24:17	18:16	19:15	20:14	21:13	22:12	23:11	1:10	2:9	3:8	4:7	5:6
11	6:24	7:5	8:4	9:3	10:2	11:1	12:23	13:22	14:21	15:20	16:19	17:18
12	24:18	19:17	20:16	21:15	22:14	23:13	1:12	2:11	3:10	4:9	5:8	6:7
13	7:24	8:6	9:5	10:4	11:3	12:2	13:1	14:23	15:22	16:21	17:20	18:19
14	24:19	20:18	21:17	22:16	23:15	1:14	2:13	3:12	4:11	5:10	6:9	7:8
15	8:24	9:7	10:6	11:5	12:4	13:3	14:2	15:1	16:23	17:22	18:21	19:20
16	24:20	21:19	22:18	23:17	1:16	2:15	3:14	4:13	5:12	6:11	7:10	8:9
17	9:24	10:8	11:7	12:6	13:5	14:4	15:3	16:2	17:1	18:23	19:22	20:21
18	24:21	22:20	23:19	1:18	2:17	3:16	4:15	5:14	6:13	7:12	8:11	9:10
19	10:24	11:9	12:8	13:7	14:6	15:5	16:4	17:3	18:2	19:1	20:23	21:22
20	24:22	23:21	1:20	2:19	3:18	4:17	5:16	6:15	7:14	8:13	9:12	10:11
21	11:24	12:10	13:9	14:8	15:7	16:6	17:5	18:4	19:3	20:2	21:1	22:23
22	24:23	1:22	2:21	3:20	4:19	5:18	6:17	7:16	8:15	9:14	10:13	11:12
23	12:24	13:11	14:10	15:9	16:8	17:7	18:6	19:5	20:4	21:3	22:2	23:1

THE SWISS SYSTEM TOURNAMENT

The tremendous increase in chess competition that has taken place in the United States during the past two decades can be credited, to a large extent, to the introduction and continued use of the Swiss System. Contests that formerly attracted a handful of entrants are now attended by large numbers of players. Instead of just a few tournaments being held each year, there are now hundreds. Most events are open to all comers.

The Swiss System has made the "weekend" tournament the most popular of all competitive events. Hundreds of players flock to national, state, and regional championships held over holiday weekends. Six or seven rounds are played in three days, the title is won, prizes are distributed, and everybody goes home after having spent an enjoyable weekend.

These brief tournaments have popularized chess competition, raised the level of chess skill in this country, aroused the interest of the public in the game itself. Only a few players can afford the time and expense to attend a tournament that lasts two weeks. The weekend tournament has enabled players by the hundreds to take part in competitive chess.

Even the staunchest advocates of the Swiss System do not claim that accurate results are obtained when about 100 contestants play seven rounds over a weekend. Only an optimist expects the Swiss System to accomplish miracles and produce a champion who has met all the strongest contenders under these conditions. It is sometimes forgotten, however, that accuracy of results is by no means the most important consideration in a great many tournaments. In fact, it is the sporting element of luck that attracts large fields. Any strong player might win the title. A player who "gets the breaks" in the pairings may shoot ahead and win a prize. Even a weak contestant may place ahead of an expert. A single lost game may tumble one of the leaders ten or more places in the standings. In the early rounds, when the master players meet the amateurs, brief and brilliant games are played. One of the amateurs may get the thrill of a lifetime if he defeats a master, or even draws with him. All these possibilities produce tension, suspense, and excitement, with the factor of luck ever present. So far as we know, the element of chance has never diminished interest in any sport.

History of the Swiss System

Believe it or not, the Swiss System originated in Switzerland! Ranneforth's *Schachkalender* for the year 1933 credits the invention of the system to Dr. J. Muller of Brugg, and states that the first tourney run under this method was held at Zurich in 1895—so the system is much older than most chess players realize.

Other historical sources confirm the fact that the Swiss System was being used at the turn of the century. Early issues of the *Schweizerische Schachzeitung* (Swiss Chess Magazine), first published in 1900, report the results of tournaments in Switzerland held under the basic rules of the system. In the first round, the players were paired by lot. In the subsequent rounds, the players were paired "in such a way that, so far as possible, those contestants who show an equal number of won games have to fight with each other." This is a translation of one of the earliest Swiss Systems rules to appear in print.

These original Swiss tournaments usually ran for four or five rounds, were played off in two days, and averaged about ten participants. By the year 1904, the number of entries had greatly increased and the system was being attacked by contributors to the Swiss Chess Magazine who claimed that the method was too dependent on chance factors. This all sounds very familiar.

The system did not achieve much popularity outside its native land until its introduction into the United States in the 1940's. Occasionally, some unimportant Central European tournament was conducted under the method. Brief descriptions of the system were sometimes included in the German Yearbooks. One year it would be mentioned, but the next year no details at all would be given. Apparently not much importance was attached to the system.

International Master George Koltanowski, the famous blindfold expert and one of America's leading chess promoters and writers, is given credit for introducing the Swiss System into this country and strenuously advocating its widespread use. Koltanowski directed the first Swiss System tournament in the United States, the Pennsylvania Championship of 1943.

The organizers of chess contests were quick to recognize the advantages of the system. It answered the problem that had long seemed unsolvable—how to handle a large number of participants in a limited time. In the years 1944 and 1945, many state and regional tournaments adopted the system. The U. S. Intercollegiate Championship of 1945 was the first national tournament to be conducted along these lines, and its success influenced the USCF to investigate the possibility of running the U. S. Open Championship and the U. S. Junior Championship by the same method.

The first step toward adoption of the system was taken at the U. S. Open Championship in Pittsburgh, 1946. With 58 entrants to accommodate, it was decided to run an 8-round Swiss System preliminary tournament instead of following the usual practice of dividing the players into small preliminary sections conducted as Round Robins. The top ten from the Swiss preliminary qualified for the championship finals, the next ten for the "Masters Reserve" tournament, etc. The finals were conducted under the traditional Round Robin system, but with the preliminary scores carried over into the finals.

The U. S. Junior Championship at Cleveland in 1947 used the same method—Swiss System preliminary and Round Robin finals. But the U. S. Open at Corpus Christi that year brought 86 entrants, and it was realized that a short Swiss preliminary would have little meaning with such a large field. For the first time in its long history, the U. S. Open Championship was then conducted as a straight Swiss System tournament for the entire 13 rounds of this classic event.

Since 1947, every U. S. Open has been conducted under the Swiss System. At Milwaukee in 1953, 181 players took part in the contest for the Open title. At San Francisco in 1961, there were 198 contestants. The 1963 Open at Chicago, with 266 players, was the largest chess tournament ever held in the United States up to that time. This large number could never be handled without the Swiss System.

Today, the U. S. Chess Federation uses the Swiss System for all its tournaments with the exception of the United States Chess Championship, the U.S. Women's Chess Championship, and the invitational U. S. Junior Championship. The system is also used extensively in Canada, Germany, and Great Britain. Even in the USSR, where the round robin reigns supreme, a few Swiss events are believed to have been held recently.

Swiss System Rules

The vast majority of Swiss System tournaments in the United States are governed by the following basic rules:

1. All participants may play together without classification of any kind.

Ordinarily, there is no division into groups of players seeded on the basis of skill, previous record, or any other qualification. The absence of such restrictions is considered by many to be one of the main attractions of a Swiss System contest. However, this is not a principle of the system itself; it can be used in preliminary or final sections of a tournament if the sponsors decide that it is more practical or desirable to divide the entrants into groups. In fact, the popularity of Swiss tournaments (and of chess itself) has so greatly increased in recent years that the number of rounds in many events is inadequate for the number of players. To improve the conditions, the organizers of some tournaments conduct separate sections restricted to players with approximately the same USCF ratings— usually those rated below Class A. (See pages 131-132.)

2. Pairings for the first round are determined by the USCF ratings of the contestants.

In the early days of the Swiss System, before the national rating system was fully established, first-round pairings were drawn by lot; but this is a most inefficient method and tends to destroy the purpose of Swiss pairings. The "Harkness" pairing system, based on the USCF ratings of the players, is now used in most tournaments. This method is described later.

3. If there is an odd number of players in any round, one contestant is given the bye.

In the first round, the bye is issued to the player with the lowest last-published USCF rating, in the second and third rounds to the player with the lowest score and the lowest USCF rating. In the fourth round, and in subsequent rounds, the bye is given to the player with the lowest score or to a player chosen by lot from among the contestants tied with the lowest score.

In any round, a bye is issued *only* when there is an odd number of contestants, and then only to one player. All other contestants, except those who have withdrawn, must be paired.

A player who has been given a bye must not be given a second bye in a later round.

A bye is not an award for arriving late at a tournament. If a late entrant has not been paired, he defaults the first round if it is inconvenient or too late for the entrant to be paired in accordance with the pairing system.

4. In the second round, and in each subsequent round, players with equal scores who have not previously met are matched against each other.

The all-important law of the Swiss System is that a player must not be matched with any other player more than once.

The second basic law, subject to the above, is that contestants with equal scores must be paired if possible.

These fundamental concepts of the Swiss System override all other considerations when pairings are being made. The allocation of color, and ranking or seeding systems, must give way to the absolute priority of these basic laws.

Thus, in the second round, the players who won their games in the first round are paired against each other; and players who drew their games are matched with other players who drew; and players who lost are paired.

In the later rounds, the same system is followed. For example, in the fourth round, those who tallied 3-0 in the first three rounds are paired; those who scored 2½-½ are paired; those who scored 2-1 are paired, and so on, down to the group that scored 0-3. In each group, no two players are matched if they met in a previous round. The most efficient method of matching players within each group will be explained later.

5. If it is impossible to pair a player with another player whose score is equal to his, he is paired with one of the players he has not previously met whose scores are most nearly equal to his.

Sometimes all the players in an equal-score group cannot be matched against each other. There may be an odd number of players, or one may have met all the others, or the "group" may comprise only one player, or two who have already met.

A player who cannot be paired in his own group must be matched with one of the players he has not met whose scores are most nearly equal to his. For example:

After the 8th round, one player leads the field with a score of 7½-½. For the 9th round, he cannot be paired with a player having the same score, for no other contestant has this score. There are two players who have scored 7-1, but the leader has met both in previous rounds. Therefore the leader is paired with a player he has not met in the 6½-1½ group. The two players with a score of 7-1 must be matched if they have not played each other; but if they have met in a previous round, they must also be paired with players they have not met in the 6½-1½ group. These pairings must be made before matching the remaining players in the 6½-1½ group itself. The players with higher scores must be given priority.

6. *If a player withdraws from the tournament, his name is removed from the pairing lists, and his remaining games are scored as losses.*

A contestant should not be given a free point by pairing him with a player who has withdrawn, and then scoring the game as won by default. This may be unavoidable if the withdrawing player fails to notify the Director in advance; but a player who defaults should not be paired for the next round unless he informs the Director he wishes to play and the latter accepts the player's explanation of his failure to show up for the previous round. In any case, any player who defaults two games during the course of the tournament should be debarred from further play.

7. *To allocate scores for pairing purposes, unfinished games may be temporarily adjudicated. If necessary, they are adjudicated permanently.*

If games are to be played to a finish, adjourned games should be adjudicated temporarily, but not conclusively, so that the Director may proceed with the pairing for the next round. If the adjudication presents difficult problems, the Director may, for pairing purposes only, call the game a draw. In tournaments where two or three rounds are played in one day, unfinished games are usually adjudicated permanently. In some contests of this type, however, games are played to a finish without adjournment but at an increasing rate of play (e.g., 50 moves in the first two hours, 15 moves in the next half hour, 20 moves in the following half hour).

8. *Colors are assigned by the Director as equitably as possible in all rounds.*

The Director attempts to pair contestants so that each player receives the white and black men in alternate games. If this is not possible, he tries to equalize the number of times that each player gets the white men. The allocation of color must not conflict with the basic pairing laws of section No. 4 above.

9. The scoring is one point for a win, half a point for a draw, zero for a loss. The unplayed game of a contestant who is given a bye is scored as a win.

The final positions are determined by the number of points scored. Though a single winner may be developed, ties are an inherent part of the Swiss System. Cash prizes should be divided equally among tied players. If desired, ties may be broken to decide the winner of a title or for any other purpose except the distribution of cash prizes. The recommended method of breaking ties is explained in a later section.

Harkness Pairing System for Swiss Tournaments

In an article in *Chess Life* (September 20, 1952) the writer suggested that his system of rating chessplayers, which had been adopted by the U.S. Chess Federation in 1950, could be used to rank and pair the contestants in a Swiss tournament. The sponsors of many tournaments adopted the idea with enthusiasm. Although the article in *Chess Life* gave no name to the method, tournament players quickly labeled it the "Harkness" pairing system. Full details were given in the *Blue Book*, published in 1956, and the system has since been used in practically all Swiss tournaments held in the United States.

HOW TO RANK THE PLAYERS

Pairing cards must be used. The USCF pairing card, designed for conducting a tournament under this system, is reproduced on the next page in condensed form.

Make out a card for each entrant with his name and address at the top. Enter each player's last-published USCF rating in the space provided. To find the rating, consult the most recent ranking list in *Chess Life*, then previous lists, if necessary. An entrant without a USCF rating should be given an estimated rating. The local committee, or friends of the player, or even the player himself, can usually provide information which will enable the Director to judge the player's strength and issue an approximate rating. If no information can be obtained, let the player remain unrated until his strength can be judged by his performance in the early rounds of the tournament. If he draws with a rated player, he can be given the latter's rating; if he defeats a rated player, he can be given the latter's rat-

Rating _____

PLAYER: _____ Starting Rank No. _____

ADDRESS: _____ Final Rank No. _____

Rd. No.	Color	GAME SCORE		OPPONENTS		TIE-BREAK POINTS	
		Round *	Total	Rank	Name	Median	Solkoff
1							
2							
3							
4							
5							
6							
7							
8							
9							
10							
11							
12							
13							

* Circle if won or lost without play.

ADJUSTED SCORE _____

ing plus 50 points. Any estimated rating can be modified later if the contestant's performance indicates that the estimate was too high or too low.

Now arrange the cards in the order of the players' ratings and enter each competitor's starting rank number on his card. The player with the highest rating is No. 1, the next highest is No. 2, etc. Place the cards of unrated players at the bottom of the heap, in alphabetical order. When an unrated player is given an approximate rating later, change his rank number to its new position. For instance, if an unrated player's starting rank number is 42, and he is later issued an estimated rating just below that of player No. 30, give the former rank number 30A.

If there is an odd number of entrants, issue the bye to *the player with the lowest USCF rating*. Take out this player's card, record the one-point score for the bye and circle this figure to show that the score is for an unplayed game. Write the word "bye" in the opponent's name column. Keep this card separate from the others.

FIRST-ROUND PAIRINGS AND COLORS

For the first round the players in the upper one-half division of the ranked field are paired in consecutive order with the players in the lower half. Thus, if there are 100 entrants, player No. 1 is paired with No. 51; player No. 2 is paired with 52, etc.

The color assigned to the No. 1 player is chosen by lot. The color so determined is given to all the odd-numbered players in the upper division of the field, and the opposite color to all the even-numbered players in the same division.

To accomplish the above, the simplest way is to divide the cards into two equal piles, one containing the top half of the field, the other the bottom half. Make sure the cards are ranked correctly, from the top down.

Toss a coin to decide whether the No. 1 player gets white or black; then give the selected color to all the odd-numbered players in the top-half pile, the opposite color to all the even-numbered players in this pile. E.g., if the toss decides that No. 1 gets white, write "W" in the color column of his card for round one. Then go down the entire pile, writing "B" for black on the No. 2 player's card, "W" for white on the No. 3 player's card, etc.

To make the pairings, take the top card from each ranked pile and match these two players. On each card, enter the opponent's name and rank number. On the card from the low-half pile, also enter the color of men this player gets—the opposite color to the one issued to his opponent.

Then take the second card from each pile and match these two players, making the entries described above. Continue pairing, in consecutive order from the piles, until all players have been matched.

SECOND-ROUND PAIRINGS

As the games of the first round are finished, enter the results on the player's cards in the "Game Score" columns. When all scores have been entered, divide the cards into three piles containing the cards of the players who won, drew, and lost, respectively. If a player received a bye in the first round, his card is included in the one-point stack.

To make the pairings, first arrange the cards in the one-point pile in the order of the players' rank numbers.* If there is an odd number of cards, one will have to be transferred to the half-point pile, but do not make this transfer immediately. Hold the card of the lowest-ranking player until you decide whether it is needed to equalize color allocation.

Divide the one-point stack into two piles, one containing the "top-half" of the group, as determined by their ratings, and the other the "bottom-half." If possible, match the players in the top half in consecutive order against the players in the bottom half. However, it is nearly always necessary to transpose or re-arrange slightly in order that the colors may be alternated. For example:

Top Half	Bottom Half
1—W	11—W
2—B	12—B
3—W	14—B
5—W	16—B
8—B	17—W
9—W	19—W

According to the system, Player No. 1 is supposed to be paired with No. 11, and No. 2 with No. 12. However, if these pairings are made, the colors cannot be alternated. Therefore they are transposed. No. 1 is paired with No. 12, and No. 2 with No. 11. All the others except Players 9 and 19 can be paired in order and colors alternated.

If there was an odd number of cards in this one-point group and

---

* In the *Blue Book* of 1956 a method of adjusting the players' ratings after each round was recommended. Experience has shown that this is an unnecessary refinement. The pairing system is greatly simplified, and may be just as efficient, if the rankings of the first round (amended only by changes in the rank of unrated entrants) are used to make the pairings throughout the entire tournament.

the player whose card was held back (the lowest-ranking player) had black in the first round, or was given a bye, his card can be substituted for No. 19's card and the latter transferred to the half-point pile. But if the player whose card was held back had white, this card will be transferred to the half-point pile and Nos. 9 and 19 will have to be matched, the colors for these two players being chosen by lot. This would also be true if this group originally had an even number of cards.

When pairing groups, make the simplest transpositions and rearrangements possible to maintain equalization of color. Unless it is absolutely unavoidable, do not pair two players in the same upper or lower division. Always try to pair a player in the top half against a player in the bottom half.

When the two piles of one-point players' cards have been arranged in the proper order for pairing, take a card from each pile in consecutive order, entering the names of the opponents, their rank numbers, and the colors for the second round.

Next arrange the cards of the players who lost in the first round, in the order of their rank numbers. If a bye has to be issued, the total number of all players being uneven, give it to the player with the lowest USCF rating and remove his card, making the necessary entries as explained on page 126.

If there is an odd number of cards in the zero-score group (after removing the card of the player who gets the bye, if any), transfer the card of the player with the highest rating to the half-point stack, unless this produces color complications, in which case transfer the card of a player with a lower rating. Then divide into two piles, top-half and bottom-half, and pair in the same way as the one-pointers.

Finally, pair the half-pointers (and the transferred cards, if any). Arrange in order of rank, divide into two piles, and pair in the same way as the other two groups. However, be careful when making these pairings to avoid breaking the fundamental pairing rules of the Swiss System. Players who met and drew in the first round *must not be matched*.

PAIRING LATER ROUNDS

For each subsequent round, the procedure is essentially the same as for the second round; but it becomes more complicated as the equal-score groups increase in number and diminish in size. Instead of three stacks of cards, you may have five stacks for the third round, seven for the fourth round, nine for the fifth, etc. Before making any pairing, examine the names and rank numbers of opponents to make sure the players have not met in a previous round.

The order of pairing the groups is important. After you have divided the cards into equal-score groups, start by pairing the group with the highest score, then work down to the group above the middle pile or piles. Next pair the lowest-score group and work up to the group below the middle. Finally, pair the middle group or groups. Adjustments and transfers up and down may have to be made when the central groups are paired.

When making transfers, remember that a transferred player has priority when pairing the group to which he is moved. He must not be transferred again unless it is *impossible* to pair him in the new group. If two or more players are transferred to the same group, and it is impossible to pair both or all in the new group, priority is decided by the scores. Thus, if a player with a score of 6 points, and another with 5½ points, are transferred to the 5-point group, and it is impossible to pair both, the player with the 6-point score has priority; the 5½-point player must go down to the 4½-point group. When pairing from the bottom up, it is the opposite way around; the player with the *lower* score has priority.

A tournament with a large number of players is easier to pair than a small tournament. There is less juggling needed to avoid matching players who have met, allocate colors equitably, and at the same time observe the basic idea of the pairing system—the matching of the top half of each group against the bottom half. Sometimes the fundamental laws of the Swiss System or equitable color allocation make it necessary to pair two players in the top half of a group, but this should be avoided if possible.

OPTIONAL METHOD OF PAIRING LATE ROUNDS

If the pairing becomes very difficult in the late rounds of a tournament, especially a contest with a small number of players, the following method of pairing may be used.

After giving the bye, if any, arrange all the cards in the order of the players' scores and within each equal-score group by the rank numbers. Then start pairing from the top down. Match the top man with the next available opponent, a player he has not met in a previous round; but if this pairing will cause inequitable color allocation, try to match him with another player in the same scoring group; if this is not possible, he will have to be matched with the first choice. Do not go down to a group with a lower score. Color allocation must give way to the fundamental pairing rules.

After the top player has been matched, repeat the process with the second-highest player, then the third player, and so on, until all the players above the middle group or groups have been matched. Then start at the bottom of the pile. Pair the player at the bottom with the first above him he has not met (or a player in the same group to avoid color trouble). Work upward in the same way with each player until all, or practically all, with minus scores have been paired. Finally, pair the middle group or groups. If all cannot be matched, the pairings already made in the adjacent groups must be revised to the extent that may be necessary.

MODIFICATION OF PAIRING SYSTEM

The primary objective of a pairing system is to produce a single winner who has met strong opposition so that he may be recognized as a worthy champion who has proved his right to the title at stake. Provided the number of rounds is not wholly inadequate, this objective can often be achieved by the use of the Harkness pairing system. Even if two or more players tie for first place, they usually have played against each other and a good tie-breaking system can often decide which player is entitled to the championship.

In some tournaments, however, the ratio of the number of players to the number of rounds is so large that it becomes possible for two or more contestants to finish with perfect scores without having played against each other. No pairing system will produce really efficient results if the players-to-rounds ratio is too large (see page 111). However, it has been found that tied winners with perfect scores càn often be avoided by modifying the pairing system for the first two rounds. The procedure is as follows:

In the first round, after ranking the players as explained on page

124, divide the cards into *four* piles and pair the top quarter of the field against the second quarter, then the third quarter against the fourth quarter.

In the second round, divide the cards into three piles containing the cards of the players who won, drew, and lost, respectively. Arrange each pile in the order of the players' rank. Then, starting with the one-pointers, divide this pile into four groups, pairing the first quarter against the second quarter, and the third quarter against the fourth quarter. Then pair the zero-score pile and finally the drawn-game pile in the same way as the one-pointers. Transfers and color allocation follow the methods described in connection with the regular pairing system.

For the remaining rounds of the tournament, use the standard Harkness system, pairing the top half against the bottom half of each equal-score group.

This modification is based on the pairing system originally proposed by the writer in 1952. At that time we suggested that the ranked players be divided into small groups in the early rounds, the top group to be paired with the second group, the third with the fourth, and so on. This method was changed to the more efficient "top half against bottom half" system published in the Blue Book of 1956. In the present volume we again recommend the "standard" system of 1956 with slight revisions.

By reverting to the original system of 1952, the modification described above deliberately reduces the efficiency of the standard system in order to produce more drawn games and make it less likely that two contestants will finish with perfect scores. In our opinion, it would be preferable, when possible, to provide special sections for weaker players in addition to the main event. The players-to-rounds ratio would then be reduced and the more effective standard pairing system could probably be used.

For example, we recently directed the five-round Gold Coast Championship at Palm Beach, Fla., which attracted 68 entrants and would have resulted in an excessive players-to-rounds ratio if all the contestants had played together in one section. However, in addition to the main open championship, the organizers provided an "amateur" section for players with USCF ratings of 1800 or lower, and a "reserve" section for entrants with USCF ratings of 1600 or lower. Unrated players were allowed to enter the section of their choice. In this way, the 68 entrants were divided into three sections and the standard Harkness pairing system worked effectively, producing a single winner in each division.

If the 68 entrants of this event had played in one open tournament, and the modified pairing system had been used, there would probably have been some ties for first place. Such a result puts too much reliance on tie-breaking systems. Incidentally, the weaker players in this event obviously preferred to enter the "amateur" and "reserve" sections in order to compete with other players of approximately their own strength.

EXPERIMENTAL MODIFICATION

Phil G. Haley, of Sarnia, Ont., suggests a method of pairing early rounds which some organizers may wish to test. Before doing so, however, the modification should be fully explained in the tournament announcements, so that the entrants will know what to expect. This is essential because the pairing method breaks the fundamental laws of the Swiss System (Rule 4, page 122).

We are not recommending or endorsing this modification. In fact, it is our impression that it may give too much weight to the players' ratings; but it is worth trying out in a few tournaments in which practically all the players have established USCF ratings. In brief, the modification is as follows:

Rank all entrants in the order of their USCF ratings. For pairing purposes only, credit each player in the top quarter of the field with 2 "rank-points," and each player in the middle half of the field with one "rank-point." The players in the bottom quarter get no such points. Then, for the first half of the tournament, add the "rank-points" to the actual game scores and use the *totals* as the basis for pairing in accordance with the Harkness system. For the second half of the contest, cancel the added points and pair in the regular way. Of course, the "rank-points" are never included in the final tournament scores.

For example, if there are 80 entrants, the top 20 are given 2 "rank-points" each, and are paired 1–10 vs. 11–20 for the first round; the players ranked 21 to 60 (the middle half) are given one "rank-point" each and are paired 21–40 vs. 41–60; the remaining players, in the bottom quarter, are paired 61–70 vs. 71–80. In the remaining rounds of the first half of the tournament, the "rank-points" are added to the actual game scores and the totals used to pair the players. In some cases, this will mean that players with unequal game scores are paired.

This modification is based on the belief that the results of the first two rounds of a regular Harkness-paired tournament are a foregone conclusion, and that these two rounds can be omitted to advantage. The pairings of the modified first round would be the pairings of the *third* round of a regular tournament in which all the higher-rated players defeated their opponents in the first and second rounds, with no drawn games and no upsets. According to Mr. Haley, "the top players will meet strong opposition from the first and the winner will have met a higher percentage of stronger opponents than is possible at present."

Allocation of Colors

The standard Harkness pairing system simplifies the equitable allocation of colors. When the contestants are ranked and paired by this method, experience has proved conclusively that nearly all the players in the top half of the field win their first-round games. There may be some draws, and possibly one or two upsets, but a large majority of the higher-rated players defeat their opponents.

Since the colors for the first round are alternated in the top division, it follows that about half of the players who win their games had white; the others had black. Consequently, it is usually easy to alternate most of the players' colors for the second round. Thus, when pairing the winners of the first round, the players who had white are matched with those who had black, and the colors are reversed for the second round. In the same way, the Director can alternate colors when pairing most of the players in the groups who drew and lost, respectively, in the first round. For a few pairings it may be impossible to alternate colors, in which case the color allocation must be made by lot.

COLOR RULE FOR LATER ROUNDS

In the subsequent rounds, the Director should continue to give contestants the white and black men in alternate games whenever this is possible. However, after two or three rounds have been played, the pairings will bring together contestants who have not received white and black in alternate games. To avoid making mistakes, the Director should observe the following rule when allocating colors:

Count the number of times that each player has been given the white men. If there is a difference, give black to the player who has received white oftener than his opponent. If there is no difference, allocate the move by lot.

Two contestants may have played the same color in the previous round, but it does not follow that the move must be allocated by lot. For example:

	Player A	Player B
1st Round	Black	White
2nd Round	Black	Black
3rd Round	White	White
4th Round	?	?

Although both of the above players had white in the third round, colors for the fourth round must not be chosen by lot. Player "A" has been given white once, whereas Player "B" has received white twice. Therefore "A" gets white and "B" gets black.

It should never be taken for granted that "the colors are reversed for the next round." The fact that one player had white and the other black in the previous round does not necessarily mean that the colors are to be reversed. For example:

	Player A	Player B
1st Round	Black	White
2nd Round	White	White
3rd Round	Black	Black
4th Round	Black	White
5th Round	White	Black
6th Round	?	?

Player "A" has been given white twice, and Player "B" has received white three times. Therefore "A" gets white and "B" gets black for the 6th round.

If the counting rule is followed, the Director will not make the mistake of automatically giving the opposite color to a player who has had one color in the two previous rounds. For example:

	Player A	Player B
1st Round	Black	White
2nd Round	Black	White
3rd Round	White	Black
4th Round	White	White
5th Round	?	?

Some directors, without thinking, would give Player "A" black because he played white in the 3rd and 4th rounds. Actually, it makes no difference which color "A" gets because he has had black twice and white twice. But the count shows that Player "B" has received white three times. Therefore "A" gets white and "B" gets black.

If the counting rule shows that two paired players have been given the white men the same number of times, the move is allocated by lot. For example:

	Player A	Player B
1st Round	White	Black
2nd Round	Black	White
3rd Round	Black	White
4th Round	White	Black
5th Round	?	?

Each of the players has received the white men twice. Therefore the colors for the 5th round are allocated by lot, despite the fact that the players had opposite colors in the 4th round.

Unless it cannot possibly be avoided, a contestant who has played two more games with one color than he has played with the opposite color should not be given the color that will increase this difference. For example:

	Player A	Player B
1st Round	White	White
2nd Round	Black	White
3rd Round	White	Black
4th Round	White	White

These two players should not be paired for the 5th round if there is any other way of arranging the pairings without violating the basic rules. Each of these contestants has played two more games with white than he has played with black. If they are paired, one of the players will get white for the fourth time.

If these rules and principles are followed carefully from the first round on, the color distribution should be as equitable as possible. In a tournament with an even number of rounds, a few players may receive white (or black) twice oftener than the opposite color—but the difference should seldom be greater than this. There will be fewer protests from the players, of course, if the tournament has an odd number of rounds, for it is then impossible for any player to have white (or black) the same number of times as he receives the opposite color.

It is again emphasized that the basic pairing rules must be given priority over the allocation of colors. Two players who have met must not be matched again, and players with the same score must be paired if possible. The pairing system should be followed as closely as possible, but pairings should be transposed or re-arranged within the same score group to prevent inequitable allocation of colors.

Breaking Ties

The organization conducting a Swiss tournament should announce in advance whether or not ties for any titles at stake are to be broken, and if so, what tie-breaking system will be used. Occasionally it may be necessary to break ties in order to award merchandise prizes, or to qualify players into another tournament; but ties for cash prizes should not be broken. The total amount of cash prizes announced for any final positions should be divided equally among players who tie with the same game scores for those positions.

For the final positions of the players it is customary to break all ties so that the names can be arranged in a table when the results are published without having to fall back on the use of the alphabet. Although some tie-breaking systems are better than others, minor differences in tie-breaking points should not be taken too seriously.

THE SONNENBORN-BERGER SYSTEM

Before the publication of our *Blue Book* in 1956, many sponsors of Swiss tournaments used the so-called Sonnenborn-Berger system to break ties. Each player in the tie is credited with the final scores of all the opponents he defeated, and half the scores of the opponents with whom he drew. These totals are called "S-B points."

This system is a hangover from the past, having been developed and used for Round Robin tournaments. It is also misnamed, since it was not invented by either Sonnenborn or Berger. Incidentally, it was not intended originally to break ties at all.

Just to get the record straight (for it is too late to change the name) the method we call the "Sonnenborn-Berger" system was invented about 1873 by Oscar Gelbfuhs of Vienna. There were, of course, no Swiss tournaments in existence at that time, and the method was intended for Round Robins. However, its purpose was not to break ties. It was proposed as a system of producing weighted scores. Gelbfuhs recommended that what we call "S-B points" be used as the players' scores, with positions and prizes to be decided by these scores instead of the game point scores.

In an article in the *Chess Monthly* of 1886 (Vol. 7, p. 165), W. Sonnenborn of London criticized the Gelbfuhs system and suggested an improvement which would produce a better weighted score, giving more emphasis to each player's own game points. His improvement: Give each player a weighted score consisting of his own score squared plus the points suggested by Gelbfuhs.

Sonnenborn's article did not attract much attention. However, in the *Deutsche Schachzeitung* for 1887 and 1888, J. Berger of Graz made a critical study of the Gelbfuhs system and discussed the improvement suggested by Sonnenborn. As a result of the publicity given to the subject by Berger, this improvement became known as the Sonnenborn-Berger system.

Sonnenborn's improvement was not needed when the Gelbfuhs system was used only to break ties and not to weight all scores. The method has been employed frequently to break Round Robin ties, so that prizes might be awarded without play-off matches. However, the name of the method's originator has long since been forgotten. It is known as the Sonnenborn-Berger tie-breaking system.

When used to break ties in a Swiss System tournament, the S-B method has glaring defects. In a Round Robin, all the players meet each other, so that the S-B points do not favor one player over another in a tie—but this is not true in a Swiss tournament, for each player has a different set of opponents.

In the first round of a Swiss, and to a lesser extent in the second and third rounds of a large tournament, the strong competitors are paired with much weaker players and usually win their games. When the final scores of these weak players are used to break ties among the strong players who finish in the high-score groups, some of the latter are placed below others because they happened to be paired with slightly weaker players in the early rounds. For instance, in the first round one strong player may have beaten an opponent who finished with a score of 2 points; another strong player in the same high-scoring group may have beaten an opponent who finished with 1½ points. This difference of ½ point in the S-B tie-breaking score may be sufficient to place one of these two strong players below the other in the final lineup. This is obviously unfair.

The S-B system's failure to evaluate losses sustained by tied players favors some players and penalizes others. One player may have been beaten by a competitor who finished near the top; another player may have lost to a contestant who finished near the bottom, but the system makes no distinction. Losses are not counted.

THE TOTAL SCORE OR SOLKOFF SYSTEM

In an effort to remedy the defects of the S-B method, Ephraim Solkoff of Raleigh, N. C., made some headway in popularizing a system that bears his name in the United States. The method was introduced here in 1950, but Mr. Solkoff did not originate the system; it was used in England prior to 1950 and is still employed there.

The system credits each player in a tie with the final scores of all his opponents. Win, lose, or draw, each tied player gets the full score of every opponent he met. The totals of the points so obtained are used to determine the standings of the tied players.

The total scores of a player's opponents are used as a means of evaluating the overall strength of the opposition he encountered. What the player accomplished against this opposition is indicated by his own score. The same yardstick is used for each player in the tie, and if the yardstick is accurate, the system will differentiate equitably between the performances of the tied players.

In our opinion, the yardstick is not accurate enough. Too much weight is given to losses to the players with the highest final scores, and the system fails to remedy the major defect of the S-B system —the inclusion of the scores of the weakest opponents.

THE HARKNESS MEDIAN SYSTEM

The Median tie-breaking system, proposed by the writer of this book, has been adopted by the USCF for its Swiss tournaments. By this method, each player in a tie is credited with the total of the "median" scores of his opponents. These totals are used to determine the players' standings.

The "median" scores of a player's opponents are as follows:

(a) In a tournament of 8 rounds or less, all the opponents' scores except the highest and lowest.

(b) In a tournament of 9, 10, 11, or 12 rounds, all the opponents' scores except the two highest and the two lowest.

(c) In a tournament of 13 rounds or more, all the opponents' scores except the three highest and the three lowest.

The "extremes" are omitted and only the scores in the median or middle range are taken into account. In the same way as the Solkoff system, no attention is paid to the results of the games.

The Median system is similar to the Solkoff, but the yardstick it provides gives a more representative measurement of the strength of the opponents. The extremes at the upper and lower end of the scale are removed and cannot distort the valuation. The two systems differ from each other in the same way as a mean or arithmetical average differs from a median average.

The following example illustrates the differences between the S-B, Solkoff, and Median systems. In the Southwestern Open Championship of 1953, John A. Hudson and Leon Poliakoff tied with four other players for 4th to 9th places. On S-B points, Hudson was placed 4th and Poliakoff 5th. The tables below compare the performances of these two players and show how their S-B points were computed:

HUDSON'S GAMES		POLIAKOFF'S GAMES	
	S-B Pts.		*S-B Pts.*
Drew No. 5	2½	Drew No. 1	3
Drew No. 7	2½	Beat No. 2	6
Beat No. 8	5	Lost to No. 3	0
Beat No. 9	5	Drew No. 4	2½
Beat No. 10	4½	Beat No. 10	4½
Lost to No. 17	0	Beat No. 22	3½
Beat No. 30	3	Beat No. 43	1
Total	22½	Total	20½

To simplify the comparison, we have arranged each player's opponents in the order they finished. Even a casual inspection shows that there is no justification for placing Hudson ahead of Poliakoff. In fact, the latter met stronger opponents and made the same score as

Hudson. If the tie is to be broken, it would seem that Poliakoff should be placed ahead of Hudson.

Note that Poliakoff met opponents who finished in the first, second, and third places and made an even score against these three (1½-1½). He drew with Hudson (who was placed 4th) and defeated the three other opponents with whom he was matched—the players who finished 10th, 22nd, and 43rd. On the other hand, Hudson did not meet any of the top three players, and lost to No. 17.

The S-B system fails to evaluate correctly the performances of these players, for two reasons:

1. The scores made by the weakest opponents give an unmerited advantage to Hudson. In the first round of the tournament, Hudson was paired with the player who finished in 30th place and scored 3 points. Poliakoff was paired with the player who finished in 43rd place and scored only 1 point. Since Poliakoff defeated the players who placed in the 10th and 22nd positions (with scores of 4½ and 3½ respectively), it is reasonable to assume that he would have beaten a player who scored only 3 points. If he had been so paired in the first round, his S-B points would have been the same as Hudson's. Poliakoff happened to draw a weaker player than Hudson in the first-round pairings. For this bit of hard luck he is penalized by the S-B system.

2. No discrimination is made between the strength of the contestants to whom the players lost. Whereas Poliakoff lost to No. 3 in the final standings, Hudson lost to No. 17 (a presumably weaker player, in this tournament at least). No evaluation is placed on these losses, although there is a distinct difference between the apparent strength of the two opponents.

The table below shows how the Median system corrects the defects of the S-B method in the above example:

HUDSON		POLIAKOFF	
Scores of Opponents	*Median Points*	*Scores of Opponents*	*Median Points*
5	—	6	—
5	5	6	6
5	5	5½	5½
5	5	5	5
4½	4½	4½	4½
4	4	3½	3½
3	—	1	—
	Total 23½		Total 24½

By omitting the highest and lowest scores in each case, the tie is broken in favor of Poliakoff by 24½ points to 23½. This reverses the obviously unfair result obtained by the S-B method. If the Solkoff system were used, the tie would not be broken. Each player would be given 31½ points, the total of his opponents' scores.

ADJUSTMENTS FOR UNPLAYED GAMES

To break ties by the Median system (or any other system, for that matter), best results are obtained by adjusting the scores of opponents who won or lost points as a result of unplayed games (byes and games won or lost by default). When entering a player's game score on his pairing card, all such results should be circled. For the tournament score, a bye or a win from a withdrawn player counts as one point; a loss by a withdrawn player counts as zero. For tie-breaking purposes, however, each score for an unplayed game should be counted as ½ point and the revised total entered at the bottom of the card as the player's adjusted score. This score is used only to break ties among *other* contestants and has no effect on the player's own tournament score.

The following examples from the 1954 U. S. Open show how scores are adjusted to break ties in which one or more of a player's *opponents* are involved:

PLAYER No. 84	Tourney Score	Adjusted Score		PLAYER No. 104	Tourney Score	Adjusted Score
W97	1	1		L64	0	0
W103	1	1		Bye *	1*	½
D12	½	½		L81	0	0
W22	1	1		L76	0	0
W28	1	1		L91	0	0
L4	0	0		L92	0	0
L18	0	0		L90	0	0
L6	0	0		L107	0	0
L33 *	0*	½		W97 *	1*	½
Withdrew	0*	½		W98	1	1
	0*	½		L93 *	0*	½
	0*	½		L106	0	0
Totals	4½	6½		Totals	3	2½

* Unplayed games   * Unplayed games

Player No. 84, at the left, scored 4½ points in the first five rounds, then lost three in a row, defaulted his 9th round game, and withdrew. His remaining three games were scored as zeros, giving him a final tournament score of 4½ points. For tie-breaking purposes, he is given an adjusted score of 6½ points, comprising his tournament score of 4½ plus 2 points for the four unplayed games.

Player No. 104, at the right, made a tournament score of 3 points, including a bye and a win by default. He also lost one game by default. Half a point is deducted for the bye, another ½ point for the win by default, but ½ point is added for the loss by default, giving him a net adjusted score of 2½ points.

After scores have been adjusted, where necessary, you can proceed with the job of breaking ties. Assemble the cards of a group of players with the same total game scores. Then enter on each card (in the median points column) the scores of all the player's opponents, using their adjusted scores when tournament scores have been changed for tie-breaking purposes. However, if any of the games with these opponents were not played (won or lost by default), or if the player himself had a bye, the "opponent's" score is entered as zero. Then cancel the high and low opponent's scores, the number of cancelled scores depending on the length of the tournament. Finally, add up the remaining median points to get the player's tie-breaking score.

For example, at the 1954 U. S. Open, W. Keith Hastings scored 7 points and tied with twelve other players. His median tie-breaking points are computed as shown in the table below.

	Scores of Opponents	Median Points
Lost to No. 16	8	—
Lost to No. 19	7½	—
Drew with No. 20	7½	7½
Lost to No. 25	7	7
Defeated No. 35	7	7
Defeated No. 58	6	6
Defeated No. 72	5	5
Defeated No. 80	5	5
Defeated No. 81	5	5
Defeated No. 86	4½	4½
Lost to No. 96	4	—
Won by default from No. 84	0	—
	Total Median Points	47

Since it was a 12-round tournament, the two highest and the two lowest scores of this player's opponents are not included in the Median tie-breaking column. Note, however, that the score of player

No. 84 is counted as zero because Hastings won from this opponent by default. The fact that Hastings did not play this opponent makes the latter's actual tournament score valueless for tie-breaking purposes; therefore this opponent's score is counted as zero. For the same reason, if Hastings had been given a bye, or if he had lost a game by default, the opponent's score in each case would have been counted as zero.

If it is necessary to compute the tie-breaking points of a player who withdraws, all his unplayed games are listed as played against "opponents" with zero scores. For example, in a recent 7-round tournament, one of the players withdrew after playing four rounds. His score at withdrawal was 2½ points, placing him in a tie with four other players. His tie-breaking points should be computed as follows:

	Scores of Opponents	Median Points
Lost to No. 20	4	—
Drew with No. 21	4	4
Defeated No. 38	3½	3½
Defeated No. 59	1½	1½
Forfeited 5th round	0	0
Forfeited 6th round	0	0
Forfeited 7th round	0	—
	Total Median Points	9

SECONDARY TIE-BREAKS

If the Median system does not break a tie, the players have probably met equal opposition, and there is no reason for believing that one should be placed above the other. However, some tournament organizers like to have all the ties broken, perhaps to announce a single winner and award trophies or merchandise prizes. Since the factor of chance is always present in a Swiss tournament, Lady Luck need not be denied the privilege of breaking a tie that should remain unbroken. If a tie is not dissolved by the Median system, other methods can be tried in the following order:

(a) Arrange the tied players in the order of their scores under the Kashdan scoring system.*

(b) Break remaining ties by the Solkoff system.

(c) If there is still a tie, use the S-B system.

(d) If all else fails, toss up for position.

* As explained on page 110, a win is counted as 4 points, a draw as 2 points, a loss as 1 point, a loss by default as zero. For tie-breaking purposes, a win by default should also be counted as zero.

CHAPTER V

The Chess Club

Chess clubs form the foundation of organized chess. It is in the chess club that the master develops his skill, and the average player improves his game. The club makes it possible for members to play in tournaments, team matches, and in various other types of competition. The club player enjoys chess to the full, develops an understanding and mastery of the game that cannot be equaled by the home player.

Some of the larger clubs have their own quarters and are open daily. In the metropolitan centers there are a few clubs with hundreds of members. But the big clubs are outnumbered ten to one by the small groups of players who meet once or twice a week in YMCA's, community centers, and other free or rented quarters in towns and cities all over the country.

In this chapter we describe how the chess clubs of the United States conduct their affairs.

ORGANIZING A CLUB

The desire to form a club usually originates among a few friends who play at their school, college, factory, or place of business, or in their homes. The friends decide to organize their activities and start a club.

If there is no intention of inviting other players into the group, or if plans for expansion are to be postponed until after the club has been formed, it is not necessary to make the elaborate preparations for a preliminary meeting described below. Instead of presenting resolutions at a preliminary meeting, the Constitution of the club can be prepared and adopted, the officers elected, and all business completed in a single organizational meeting.

If the group decides to expand immediately and get as many players as possible to join the new club, it is usually necessary to hold a preliminary meeting to discuss and adopt resolutions covering the details that will be included in the club's Constitution. At a second meeting, the Constitution is adopted, the officers elected, and the business of organization completed.

Planning the Preliminary Meeting

Arrangements should be made to hold the preliminary meeting at a suitable time and place. It can be held in a private home, but strangers are more inclined to attend such a gathering if it is held in a YMCA, Community Center, or similar place.

The promoters should discuss the proposals they intend to submit to prospective members. Agreement should be reached on such important matters as the following:

1. Is membership to be restricted in any way, or is it to be open to anybody who pays the dues? A college club restricts its membership to students and faculty, an industrial or commercial club to employees. Some clubs specify that the name of an applicant must be posted, and the application refused if any member objects to his admittance. Others rule that an application must be approved by the Board of Directors, or by three-fourths of the membership. Many clubs have no restrictions at all, but provide for the revoking of a membership under stated conditions.

2. Where will the club meet, and how often? If less than ten members are expected, the promoters may decide to suggest that the meetings be held at the members' homes in rotation. For a small club, this system has distinct advantages, for it makes a social occasion out of each meeting—and it is sociability that holds clubs together. If the expected membership is too large to make home meetings practical, inquiries should be made to determine the availability and rental of a meeting place.

About 47 per cent of the chess clubs in the United States meet at YMCA's. Others meet in community centers, recreation centers, park club houses, hotels, churches, restaurants, civic centers, libraries, V. F. W. halls, American Legion Posts, Elks Clubs, town halls, office buildings, etc. About 13 per cent of the clubs rent quarters permanently and are open daily, but most of these clubs have fifty or more members. The other clubs rent, or obtain free of charge, the use of quarters for their regular meetings.

3. What amount will be charged for annual dues? A rough estimate should be made of the anticipated annual expenses, including such items as rent, chess sets and boards, chess clocks, score sheets, tournament prizes, stationery and postage, affiliation dues, subscriptions to periodicals, chess books, etc. Some of these items are nonrecurring capital expenditures, but it is safer to include them in the estimate of expenses for the first year. Then the estimate is divided by the minimum number of players who are expected to join the club. If the resulting figure is too high for annual dues, the proposed expenses for the first year will have to be cut, or a special fund raised for purchases of equipment.

The dues charged by existing clubs are surprisingly low. In the writer's opinion, they are far too low. A club needs income to prosper and grow, but it is obvious that a great many clubs are not getting the income they need from the dues paid by members.

Our recommendation to promoters of new clubs is to propose dues of at least $5.00 per annum, even if this produces more income than is actually needed for operating expenses. The surplus, if any, can be used to buy clocks and other equipment, or spent on advertising to gain new members. It may be necessary, or course, to charge a great deal more than $5.00—but this amount should be considered an absolute minimum. An additional amount should be charged each member for his USCF dues. In this way, every member will have a USCF rating, which will help enormously in arousing interest in the club's tournaments, as will be explained later.

Special, low dues should be proposed for junior members under twenty-one years of age. Young players must be encouraged to join the club. Special rates should also be proposed for married couples. If the annual dues are $5.00, a married couple should be allowed to join for $7.50, with an additional charge for USCF dues at the "family" rate. Lower dues for women members is also a good idea. A club with plenty of women members is always more successful than an all-male club.

When the main proposals have been agreed upon, the promoters should plan the conduct of the preliminary meeting. Without guidance, the meeting may languish in discussion and never get down to the business of formal organization.

It is essential that each promoter should know his duties and be prepared to execute them. It should be decided that Mr. "A" will call the meeting to order and nominate Mr. "B" as chairman, and that Mr. "C" will then be nominated as secretary. One of the group—the best speaker—should be selected to make the opening explanation of the club's objectives. This person should prepare notes for his speech. Resolutions should be written, covering the name and purposes of the club, the membership qualifications, the meeting place, the days and times of meetings, the membership dues. Each member of the group should be assigned the duty of offering one or more of these resolutions.

Although these plans are laid with the intention of adjourning the preliminary meeting and holding a second meeting later, there is always the possibility that the resolutions may be adopted quickly, without much discussion. In that case, the promoters should be prepared to complete the organization of the club without adjourning. Therefore a Constitution should be drafted and arrangements made to nominate the permanent officers of the new club.

Word-of-mouth advertising may be sufficient to bring together enough players to start a small club, but more effective results can be obtained by paid advertising and publicity in the local newspaper. Here is an example of suitable copy for an advertisement:

CHESS If you play chess and would like to meet other players who are forming a chess club, you are cordially invited to attend a meeting at the YMCA, Main St., on Friday, October 15, at 8 p.m.

A brief, factual publicity release should also be sent to the editor of the newspaper and the local radio station. For example:

A meeting of chess players will be held at the Main Street YMCA on Friday, October 15, at 8 p.m., to discuss plans for organizing a chess club. All who are interested are invited to attend this meeting.

Many newspapers will print such an item in their society or neighborhood news columns.

If there is a chess column in a local paper, or in one of the metropolitan dailies with circulation in the town, the editor of the column should be given all the details.

If the names and addresses of chess players in the vicinity are known, or can be obtained, a letter should be sent to each player, inviting him to attend the meeting.

The Preliminary Meeting

The meeting should be conducted on a semi-formal basis. Avoid stiffness, but observe the basic rules of parliamentary procedure. For information on how to conduct such a meeting, buy or borrow a copy of *Robert's Rules of Order* or a similar book.

When the time arrives to start the meeting, one of the promoters calls it to order, and moves that Mr. Blank act as temporary chairman. When the motion is seconded, voted on, and adopted, Mr. Blank takes the chair. Then a secretary is nominated and elected. He should make careful notes of all the business discussed and the decisions reached.

The chairman, or one of the other promoters, explains the object of the meeting and outlines the activities planned for the club when it is organized. The explanation must arouse the interest of the newcomers and make them want to join the club. Suggested material is contained in the remaining sections of this chapter, in which the social and competitive activities of a club are described.

Then a resolution is offered giving the name and purposes of the club. For example:

Resolved, that an organization to be known as the Blanktown Chess Club shall be formed, and that the purposes of this organization shall be to enable its members to play chess, to conduct tournaments and matches, and to provide instruction, entertainment, and social life in chess for the members.

The resolution is seconded, and the chairman asks the meeting if it is ready to vote. Questions are answered, and suggested amendments voted on. When all discussion is over, the chairman asks the meeting to vote on the resolution (as amended, if any changes have been adopted). If the majority votes "aye," the first and most important objective of the promoters has been achieved.

Then a resolution is offered giving the qualifications for membership. For example:

Resolved, that any person may become a member of the Blanktown Chess Club upon payment of the annual dues.

If this is adopted, with or without amendments, a resolution on membership dues is submitted. For example:

Resolved, that the annual membership dues of the Blanktown Chess Club, including the cost of a one-year membership in the United States Chess Federation, shall be $15.00 for a man, $12.50 for a woman, $20.00 for a married couple, $10.00 for any person under twenty-one years of age.

If this resolution is adopted, and if the proceedings up to this point have gone smoothly and rapidly, it may be possible to complete the organization of the club without holding a second meeting. If so, a recess should be taken, so that minor changes may be made in the prepared draft of the Constitution. When the meeting is resumed, a motion is made to adopt this Constitution and the procedure outlined for the second meeting is followed.

However, if a good many changes have been made in the original plans, or if there is not enough time left to complete the organization, one of the promoters should make a motion to this effect:

"I move that the chairman appoint a committee of three to draft a Constitution and report at an adjourned meeting."

If seconded and adopted, the chairman appoints the committee, then asks if there is any further business. If nothing else comes up, a motion is made to adjourn to meet at a certain time and place. If seconded and adopted, the meeting adjourns.

The Club's Constitution

Before the second meeting is held, the club's Constitution is drafted (or re-drafted). The contents of the articles should conform to the decisions reached at the preliminary meeting. However, the article on the meeting-place and times of meetings should be indefinite, so that changes may be made later without amending the Constitution.

Each club must decide on the details of its Constitution, but the following example may serve as a guide:

CONSTITUTION

OF THE

BLANKTOWN CHESS CLUB

ARTICLE I

Name. The name of this organization shall be the "Blanktown Chess Club."

ARTICLE II

Purpose. The purposes of the club are:

(A) To enable its members to play the game of chess;

(B) To conduct tournaments, matches, and other forms of chess competition;

(C) To play matches with other clubs;

(D) To provide instruction, entertainment and social life in chess for the members;

(E) To promote the popularity of the game of chess.

ARTICLE III

Membership.

(1) Any person may become a member of the Club upon payment of the annual dues.

(2) In the event that any member of the Club should be guilty of conduct which in the judgment of three-fourths of the membership shall tend to bring the game of chess into disrepute, his membership may be revoked.

ARTICLE IV

Organization.

(1) The officers of the Club shall be a President, Vice President, Secretary, Treasurer, Tournament Director, and Team Captain, to be elected for a term of one year by majority approval of the members present at the first regular meeting of the club during the month of ——.

(2) The President, Vice President, Secretary, and Treasurer shall be the members of the Board of Directors.

(3) Should a vacancy occur between elections, it shall be filled by the majority vote of the members at a meeting held within one month after the vacancy has occurred.

(4) The Club shall be affiliated with the United States Chess Federation in accordance with the conditions specified by the said Federation.

ARTICLE V

Duties of Officers and Directors.

(1) The President shall:

    (a) Preside at all business meetings of the Club;

    (b) Preside at all meetings of the Board of Directors;

    (c) Appoint a Publicity Director, a Librarian, and any other administrative officer the Board of Directors may deem necessary;

    (d) Appoint all committees.

(2) The Vice President shall:

    (a) Assist the President;

    (b) Preside at all meetings in the absence of the President.

(3) The Secretary shall:
   (a) Keep the minutes of all meetings;
   (b) Carry on the correspondence of the Club;
   (c) Send notices of meetings to members.
(4) The Treasurer shall:
   (a) Collect all authorized dues;
   (b) Deposit all funds received by him with a bank designated by the Board of Directors;
   (c) Make disbursements as authorized by the Board of Directors;
   (d) Furnish a financial statement to the Board of Directors when requested by the said Board;
   (e) Prepare a financial statement for the first regular meeting of the Club during the month of ——;
   (f) Give a surety bond for the faithful performance of his duties in an amount set by the Board of Directors, the premium of which shall be paid by the Club.
(5) The Tournament Director shall:
   (a) Arrange and direct tournaments conducted by the Club;
   (b) Report the results of tournaments to the United States Chess Federation.
(6) The Team Captain shall:
   (a) Arrange and supervise all intra-club and inter-club team matches;
   (b) Prepare and send notices to team members for all inter-club matches.
(7) The Board of Directors shall:
   (a) Formulate a program of activities for the club;
   (b) Supervise the work of all committees.

Article VI

Dues.

(1) The annual dues for membership in the Club, including the cost of a one-year membership in the United States Chess Federation, shall be as follows:
   (a) $15.00 for a man;
   (b) $12.50 for a woman;
   (c) $20.00 for a married couple;
   (d) $10.00 for any person under twenty-one years of age.

(2) If a new member of the Club has previously paid his dues for membership in the United States Chess Federation, the club dues for the said new member shall be reduced by the amount representing the unexpired portion of his United States Chess Federation dues.

ARTICLE VII

Meetings. Regular meetings of the members shall be held throughout each year on such day and at such place as shall be decided upon by the membership. Meetings may be adjourned immediately upon call to order if there is no business of importance.

The Board of Directors may meet at any time and any place upon call of the President.

ARTICLE VIII

Amendments. This Constitution may be changed or amended by a two-thirds vote of the entire membership.

The Second Meeting

At the second meeting, the chairman and secretary serve until the permanent officers are elected. After the chairman has called the meeting to order, the secretary reads the minutes of the first meeting. Then the chairman of the Committee on the Constitution reads the draft that has been prepared and moves its adoption. It is advisable to distribute carbon or mimeographed copies of the Constitution.

The standard procedure of adopting a Constitution is to have each paragraph read aloud and any proposed amendments voted on. Then the entire Constitution is open for amendment, at which time amendments may be offered to any paragraph, and additional paragraphs may be inserted. Then a vote is taken on adopting the Constitution as amended. It requires only a majority vote to adopt the Constitution, or to amend it before it is adopted.

When the Constitution has been adopted, all who wish to become members should sign it. If some are unprepared to pay their dues, the payment may be deferred until the next meeting.

The secretary reads the roll of members. Only those who have signed the Constitution and joined the club are now eligible to vote. Then the permanent officers are elected. In a large organization, the Constitution usually specifies that a nominating committee be appointed, and the election may be by ballot. In most chess clubs, the nominations are made from the floor and the election is by voice vote.

After the election, the new President takes the chair. A resolution should be offered, seconded, and adopted, specifying the time and place of the regular meetings of the club. For example:

Resolved, That the meetings of this Club shall be held on Friday of each week, beginning at 8 P.M., at the Main Street YMCA.

Unless there is any other business, the meeting may then adjourn. The new club is organized.

The resolution above is an example of what is called a "standing rule." Such rules may be adopted by a majority vote at any business meeting. The secretary should keep a list of the standing rules in the minute book. Standing rules may be suspended by a majority vote, or they may be amended or rescinded by a two-thirds vote. If previous notice has been given to the members, they may be amended or rescinded by a majority vote.

THE CLUB LADDER CONTEST

A successful chess club does more than provide the members with a place to play chess. A program of activities is arranged to stimulate the interest of members and make them want to attend the sessions. Something new and different may be planned for each meeting, or special events may be scheduled once a month.

Most important are the competitive activities of the club. Every member must be given abundant opportunity to play in various kinds of tournaments, matches, and other contests.

Ladder play gets its name from the device used originally—and still used in many clubs—to indicate the rank of the contestants. The names of the players are put on movable plates or cards and suspended by hooks on the rungs of a miniature ladder—a metal or wooden stand or rack resembling a ladder. Some clubs use a rack with slots into which small name-cards can be inserted.

A player's position on the ladder indicates his rank. The player whose plate or card is on the highest rung is "at the top of the ladder." He is the No. 1 player. The name plates are moved up and down the ladder as the players win and lose (and sometimes draw) individual games or matches, depending on what rules are followed.

Another type of ladder arranges the contestants in the form of a triangle, as shown in the following example:

```
First Rung:                    1
Second Rung:                2      3
Third Rung:             4      5      6
Fourth Rung:        7      8      9      10
Fifth Rung:     11     12     13     14     15
```

The Challenge System

The original method of conducting a ladder contest, which is still used in many clubs, may be called the "challenge" system. A contestant challenges a player of higher rank to fight for his position on the ladder. If the challenger wins the duel, he moves up to the position occupied by his vanquished opponent, who then ranks immediately below the winner. If the bout ends in a draw, the challenger moves to (or remains in) the position immediately below his opponent. If the challenger loses the battle, there is no change in the standings.

As a good example of a ladder competition conducted under the Challenge System, we quote below the rules governing ladder play at the Lansing Chess Club, Lansing, Mich.

LADDER COMPETITION

The names of all contestants are placed on a bulletin board in the club. Play is conducted under the following rules:

1. A player may challenge only the next *available* player above him on the board.

2. A player is not available to be challenged:
    (a) If he already has a match for that evening, in which case the schedule sheet showing his match should be signed;
    (b) If he has not arrived at the club by 7:30 P.M. (He would, of course, be available for later matches if he arrived later.)
    (c) If he does not want to play a match. (But he cannot refuse a match to the committee, then later accept another that night.)

3. A player seeking a match determines through the committee the nearest available player above him to be approved for the match; then both players sign the match schedule on the bulletin board before starting play.

4. If a challenger wins his match, he takes his opponent's position on the ladder, and the opponent drops one place.

If a match is drawn, the challenger moves to one place below his opponent.

If a challenger loses his match, his position on the ladder remains unchanged.

5. A match consists of two games. However, if a challenger loses one game to an opponent ranked immediately above him, a second game is unnecessary.

6. The challenger has black in the first game, white in the second.

7. Except by permission or by order of the committee, the two contestants of a match are not paired again until after a period of two months has elapsed.

8. A newcomer is ranked according to the judgment of the committee, or, if no information is available, he is placed at the bottom of the ladder.

9. Unless specified otherwise by the committee, a match is played with clocks at the time limit of thirty moves per hour for each player; and each player records the moves of the games.

The Rating Point System

A more modern method of conducting a ladder competition uses rating points to rank the contestants. The publication of tables showing how postal chess ratings are adjusted caused chess clubs to adopt the system for their ladder play. For this reason, many of the club ladder ratings have about the same values as the ratings issued to postal players.

It has occurred to the writer that it would be more interesting to club players if their ladders used the values of the national rating system instead of postal chess systems. The procedure would be exactly the same, but the ladder ratings of the players would be closely related to the USCF ratings they obtain by playing in club, state, regional, and national tournaments.

To assist clubs that may wish to conduct their ladder competition with national rating-point values, we have prepared the following outline of suggested rules.

RATING POINT LADDER RULES

1. Any member of the club may take part in this contest by filing his entry with the Ladder Director at any time.

2. Each entrant is ranked in accordance with his last-published USCF rating. An unrated entrant is given an estimated rating.

3. A contestant's rating is adjusted at the conclusion of each ladder game as shown in the accompanying chart, using the values of the formula currently employed by the USCF.

4. A contestant may not play more than two ladder games in succession with the same opponent.

5. A game won or lost by default is not rated as a ladder game.

6. A game is counted as a ladder game (a) if the players agree that the game is to be rated; or (b) if the game is played in a tournament or match in which all games are to be rated by order of the Board of Directors.

7. With the exception of tournament and match games, the colors for a ladder game are chosen by lot. If two games are played in succession, the colors are reversed for the second game.

8. A ladder game must be played with clocks and the time limit must not exceed thirty moves per hour for each player.

ADJUSTMENT TABLE FOR RATING POINT LADDER

DIFFERENCE BETWEEN LAST RATINGS	IF HIGH WINS *Add to Winner and Deduct from Loser*	IF LOW WINS *Add to Winner and Deduct from Loser*	IF A DRAW *Add to Low and Deduct from High*
0 to 24	16	16	0
25 to 49	15	17	1
50 to 74	14	18	2
75 to 99	13	19	3
100 to 124	12	20	4
125 to 149	11	21	5
150 to 174	10	22	6
175 to 199	9	23	7
200 to 224	8	24	8
225 to 249	7	25	9
250 to 274	6	26	10
275 to 299	5	27	11
300 to 324	4	28	12
325 to 349	3	29	13
350 or more	2	30	14

REPORT CARDS

It simplifies the Director's job, and maintains a complete record of ladder play, if each contestant is given a Ladder Report Card and changes his own rating *after each game.* The rules and adjustment table should be posted prominently so that players know how to change their ratings.

Before starting a ladder game, the contestants show each other their cards and record the opponent's rating. When the game is finished, each player records his own rating for the next game. On the next page is an example of a player's Ladder Report Card after he has completed three games.

LADDER REPORT CARD

PLAYER'S NAME: John H. Doe

Game No.	Player's		Opponent's Name	Opponent's RATING
	SCORE	RATING		
1	½	1942	J. Jones	2056
2	1	1946	W. Smith	1772
3	0	1956	A. Anderssen	2082
4		1945		
5				
6				
7				
8				
9				
0				

As shown in the illustration, John H. Doe has completed three ladder games. In the first, he had a rating of 1942 points, and his opponent had 2056 points—a difference of 114. The game was drawn, so John Doe gained 4 points (see table) and his rating for the next game became 1946 points. Then he won from Smith, who had 1772 points. The difference being 174 points, Doe gained 10 points, and his rating for the third game became 1956. Then Doe was defeated by Anderssen (2082) and lost 11 points, giving him a rating of 1945 for the fourth game.

Once a week, the players submit their report cards to the Director, who checks the rating changes and transfers the results to his own records, so that the ladder standings may be posted. Then he returns the cards to the players. When a card is filled (ten games), it is turned in to the Director and a new card issued. The first game on the new card becomes No. 11, the second No. 12, etc.

To increase participation and add incentive, monthly prizes should be awarded—perhaps one to the player at the top of the ladder, one to the contestant who gained the most points during the month, and one to the contestant who played the largest number of games. The prize-winners should be featured in the club's bulletin.

If the treasury cannot afford prizes, the cost should be met by fees for participating in the Ladder Contest. A simple and fair plan is to charge a nominal fee for each Report Card. For the amount of the fee, the contestant is entitled to play ten ladder games—no matter when he plays them.

TEAM MATCHES AND LEAGUES

Developing a team spirit is one of the best ways to hold a chess club together. A member who gets on the team represents his club. He plays for the club, not just for himself. The team members help each other, study openings together, do all they possibly can to strengthen the team. The other members of the club have the satisfaction of rooting for the home team when it plays other clubs.

Inter-Club Matches

Inter-club matches are extremely popular. The players like to visit other clubs, meet new players, try to win the match for their own club. When pairing the teams, the strongest players are put at the top boards, the weaker players at the lower boards. The Team Captains announce their line-ups in advance, and each agrees to arrange his team in order of strength. As club members like to play on teams, matches made by special arrangement between clubs should have as many boards as possible.

If convenient, the club should join a Chess League. A League is an organization created to arrange an annual team tournament among clubs in a city, county, or area. As a rule, the teams play a Round Robin. Each team plays every other team. If the number of teams makes a Round Robin impractical, the League may be divided into sections. The strongest teams play in the Class A division, the weaker teams in the Class B division, etc. A club may have one team in Class A, and one or more in Class B. Another method is to divide into sections and play preliminaries and finals, the teams winning the preliminary sections going into the Class A finals, the runner-up teams into the Class B finals, etc. Still another method is to play a Swiss System team tournament. The teams all play in one section and are paired in the same way as an individual Swiss tournament. This method is used in the U. S. Intercollegiate Team Championship.

Team tournaments are scored by match points or by game points. Under match point scoring, a team wins one point when it defeats another team, no matter what the margin of victory may be. Thus, a four-man team wins one match point if it defeats another team by 4-0 or if it wins by 2½-1½. If two teams draw, each gets one-half match point. The team with the largest number of match points wins the tournament. Under game point scoring, each game won by a team member counts 1 point and each draw one-half point for the team. The team with the greatest number of game points wins the tournament. At the Chess Olympics conducted by the FIDE, the world team championship is now decided by game points. A great many of the Chess Leagues in the United States still use match-point scoring, breaking ties by game points.

Most Leagues require each club to announce in advance the names of its members who are eligible to play on the club's team or teams. A player who agrees to play for one club is not allowed to appear on the line-up of any other club during the tournament of the League.

As there is usually no restriction on substitutes, each club submits a list of all the members who are willing to play for the club. However, if the League has two or more divisions, and a club enters two or more teams, a player is not allowed to serve on more than one team. Therefore each club divides its players into groups. Those eligible to play on the Class A team are listed separately from those eligible to play on the Class B team, etc.

To avoid friction, hard and fast rules should be laid down to decide the ranking of team members. The larger clubs may have a great many players who are anxious to get on the teams. Therefore each club should rank its eligible players and select the teams on the basis of the players' rank.

Intra-Club Matches

Matches should be arranged between teams composed of members of the club itself. These are always popular events, especially if refreshments are served. It is remarkable how many members will show up to enjoy the sociability of an intra-club match accompanied by sandwiches and coffee! Be sure to give the teams fancy names: The Blanktown Rooks vs. the Blanktown Knights, or the Blanktown Giants vs. the Blanktown Cubs, etc.

Occasionally it adds interest to require all boards of an intra-club match to play the same opening. A Gambit match makes for lively play.

MATCH LADDER

At the Jamestown YMCA Chess Club, Jamestown, N. Y., the members play a series of matches with a novel scoring system and re-arrangement of teams after each match. Here is how Mr. William Wilcock describes the procedure:

"Two of our leading players choose up sides to form two teams. We usually give a grandiose name to each team, such as 'Laskers' and 'Capablancas' or 'Marshalls' and 'Pillsburys.'

"At the end of the match, each player on the winning team, and each player on the losing team, gets credit for the total points scored *by his team.*

"The next week, two new teams are formed, each containing half of the previous week's winning team, and half of the previous week's losing team. Any new players are placed at the lowest boards of the two teams. Again each man gets his team's score, which is added to his score from the previous week.

"The third week, the teams are split up again. The players with the highest scores play at the top boards of the opposing teams, and so on, down the line. The player with the highest total score wins the contest."

ROULETTE CHESS

In the 1940's, N. P. Wigginton of Washington, D. C., made the Washington Chess Divan famous by staging novel events. One of his ideas was called "Roulette Chess." It was written up in *Chess Life* (July 5, 1948) by the late Gene Collett as follows:

Roulette Chess is played by teams, with at least six members on each team. During the first round, one team plays White on all boards, and in the concluding round, the same team plays Black on all boards.

Players of the white pieces make their moves at the sound of a chime and then go immediately to the next higher numbered board, except that the White player at the last board moves to the No. 1 board.

Thirty seconds after the White players make their first moves, opening the match, the chime sounds again and the Black players, who remain stationary throughout the play, make their moves immediately. In another fifteen seconds the chime sounds again and the white moves are made, after which the White players shift to the next boards as previously explained. This process is repeated throughout the match.

When a game is completed, the two players at the board remove the pieces, or otherwise indicate that the board is "dead" and retire from play. This board is then skipped by the remaining players. The winner of a game reports to the timekeeper, or to a separate scorekeeper. In the case of a draw, the player with the white men reports. The team with the best score at the end of two rounds wins the match.

To make the contest exactly fair, players must not make their moves before the chime sounds and must remain at their boards until it is time to go to the next board. Kibitzing at adjourning boards is forbidden.

It is recommended that two score sheets (one for White and one for Black) be provided at each board, with both players being required to record their moves. Some of the "composite" games should be interesting to review.

As an alternative, players at White boards may move in one direction, those at the Black boards in the other. The time interval in this case should be equalized, allowing the same amount of time, say thirty seconds, regardless of whether the player is Black or White.

CLUB TOURNAMENTS

Tournament play is the mainstay of competitive chess. Practically every club holds an annual tournament for the championship of the club. A great many stage Junior Championships, Class Tournaments, Rating-Point Tournaments, 30-30 Tournaments, and other special events. A popular contest at large and small clubs is the "Rapid Transit" or Speed Tournament. The successful chess club offers a wide selection of tournaments, so that every member may play in the type of contest he likes best.

The Club Championship

The tournament for the championship of the club should be conducted under formal conditions, and supervised by a Director. Prizes should be awarded, and the champion should get a trophy.

It is important that every member of the club be given the opportunity to compete for the title. Bad feeling is created if any members are barred from entering the championship tournament. However, it is unwise to extend a tournament over too long a period of time. Even in the largest and most important clubs, the championship is usually restricted to about sixteen players who compete in a single Round Robin. When there is a large number of players, or when a long-winded double Round Robin is played, the contestants get bored, default games, and drop out before the schedule is finished. Experience has shown that it is better to limit the number of rounds in order to maintain interest, and to prevent defaults and withdrawals.

When a large number of entrants must be accommodated, the tournament may be conducted under the Swiss System, or the Holland System described in Chapter 4.

Junior Championship

If the club has several junior members, an annual Round Robin tournament should be arranged, and the winner awarded the title of Junior Club Champion. The tournament should be open only to members under 21 years of age on the starting day of the contest.

Young players are the lifeblood of a chess club. Every effort should be made to stimulate and encourage their ambitions. If the club can afford it, the Junior Champion should be given financial assistance, if necessary, to enable him to compete in the annual U. S. Open Junior Chess Championship.

Class Tournaments

To provide competition among players who are approximately equal in strength, the larger clubs conduct Class Tournaments. There is a Class A contest for strong players, Class B contests for weaker players, and special tournaments for beginners. Each tournament is restricted to about ten entries, and a Round Robin is played with chess clocks under formal conditions. An entry fee is charged, and prizes awarded. In this way, players are given the opportunity to meet each other, play with competitors who are not too strong or too weak, and gain experience in tournament play.

Novice Tournaments

One of the best ways to attract new members to the club is to advertise tournaments for novices only. A contest of this type is open to players who have never competed in a chess tournament before. Depending on the number of entrants, conduct the event as a Round Robin or under the Swiss System. Charge a small entry fee —fifty cents or so—and award prizes.

Rating-Point Tournaments

With the possible exception of the Novice Tournaments, the contests described above can all be rated by the USCF. However, special tournaments should be held to enable members to obtain or improve national chess ratings. For an event of this type, seven rounds can be played over a weekend, using the Swiss System. Entry fees are charged and prizes awarded. A special "handicap" prize may be given to the player who gains the most rating points. The results are submitted to the USCF so that the performances of the players may be rated.

The Chess Tornado

To the Minnesota Chess Association goes the credit for originating a rating-point tournament aptly called the Chess Tornado. Four rounds are played in one day at a time limit of 30 moves for the first hour and 15 moves for each half-hour thereafter. This is the fastest rate at which games can be rated by the USCF.

30-30 Tournaments

As the name suggests, 30-30 chess is played at the time limit of 30 moves in 30 minutes. Dr. Ariel Mengarini of New York was the originator of this type of chess and gave it the name by which it is known. At a Marshall Chess Club intra-club match in 1952, Mengarini and Jimmy Sherwin played the first thirty-thirty match instead of a regular clock game. By arranging various contests, Dr. Mengarini created a great deal of interest among New York players. In 1953, the Metropolitan Masters Invitation 30-30 Tournament was held. Since then, many tournaments of this type have been promoted, including state championships.

As Dr. Mengarini has pointed out, at this time limit a three-game match can be played in about the same length of time as a regular tournament game. He suggests that it is ideal for Swiss System contests. Each round can consist of two games between each pair of players, changing colors, thus avoiding the difficulties of color allocation and adjournments. Best of all, the number of games is doubled, which produces better results in the final scores. And, if you lose, you can always blame the time limit!

Mandatory Opening Tournaments

Some clubs conduct informal Round Robins in which all the players are required to play the same opening moves. This is a good way to learn an opening. The club champion, or some other strong player, may give a lecture on the opening, explaining the objectives and describing the most important variations. After the tournament is finished, he may select a few of the score sheets and explain how the competitors played correctly or went astray.

Rapid Tournaments

One of the most popular of all contests is the tournament played at the rate of ten seconds per move. Around New York, where the big clubs hold weekly tournaments of this type, the contest is called a "Rapid Transit" or a "Rapid." It is also known as a Speed Tournament, or a Lightning Tournament.

The contest is conducted as a Round Robin and it is all over in one evening. A bell or buzzer sounds every ten seconds and the players are supposed to make their moves immediately or be forfeited. When there are no official referees, players tear their hair and protest loudly but unavailingly when their opponents take two or three "bells" to make moves. As it is more or less a social event, forfeits are seldom imposed unless a player is a habitual offender.

A game may last about ten minutes, so it is possible to play five or six rounds an hour, or about twenty rounds in one evening. If there are more than twenty entrants, it is better to split up into sections and let the section winners play off for the prizes.

The timing bell or buzzer is actuated by an electric clock. Most of the clubs have special clocks made to order, for they are not manufactured in this country. They can be imported from Europe.

As the players file their entries, their names are written down on a Round Robin crosstable form, as shown in the illustration. Each player bears the number on the line on which his name is written.

PLAYERS' NAMES	1	2	3	4	5	6	7	8	9	10	SCORE
1 A. Anderssen	✕	1			½						
2 B. Bird		✕	0						1		
3 C. Chekhover	0		✕		½						
4 D. Deschapelles		1		✕				½			
5 E. Evans			½		✕				0		
6 F. Falkbeer	½					✕	1				
7 G. Greco						0	✕	1			
8 H. Harrwitz				½			0	✕			
9 J. Jaenisch			0						✕	1	
10 K. Kieseritsky					1				0	✕	

In an attempt to save time, and to maintain an informal atmosphere, some clubs do not play the rounds in order. When play begins, the contestants pair up arbitrarily. Then, when a game is finished, the contestants find two more players who are free and start other games. As each game is concluded, one of the players records the result on the crosstable. Thus, in the illustration, each player has finished two games, but in no particular order.

RULE FOR COLORS

To avoid continually referring to a Round Robin pairing table, the club displays a sign giving the rule for colors:

Odd vs. Odd, or Even vs. Even: Higher Number has White.
Odd vs. Even: Lower Number has White.

This means that if two contestants have odd numbers, or if two contestants have even numbers, the player with the higher number has the white men. For example, when No. 3 plays No. 5, it is No. 5 who has white. Similarly, when No. 2 plays No. 4, it is No. 4 who has white. But when one contestant has an even number and his opponent has an odd number, it is the player with the lower number who has the white men. For example, when No. 2 meets No. 5, it is No. 2 who has white.

This color rule applies at all times when there is an odd number of players in the tournament. However, if there is an even number of players, it does not apply to the player with the highest number. This contestant plays black against all the players with low numbers, up to and including the player whose number is half the total number in the field, and he plays white against all the players with higher numbers. For example, in a ten-man tournament, the No. 10 player has black against Nos. 1, 2, 3, 4, and 5, white against Nos. 6, 7, 8, and 9. Similarly, in a fourteen-man tournament, the No. 14 player has black against 1, 2, 3, 4, 5, 6, and 7, white against the others.

Chess for Fun Nights

Another popular type of tournament can be advertised as Chess for Fun. It is a kind of rapid contest, but not at the rate of ten seconds a move. Played with clocks, each player is allowed half an hour to make all his moves. The rules are the same as those for Five-Minute Chess described on page 168. Since each player is allowed 30 minutes, games are finished in one hour or less. Game scores need not be kept.

GAMES BETWEEN MEMBERS

When players are not competing in ladders, team matches, and tournaments, or playing skittles (off-hand games), the Directors of live-wire clubs help the members to enjoy all the different ways in which the greatest two-handed game in the world can be played. Some of the activities promoted by successful clubs are described in this section.

Individual Matches

A match of four, six, eight, or any other even number of games is arranged between two members. The games are played with clocks. The player who makes the higher score wins the match. The contestants may put up a small stake to add incentive.

Consultation Games

Two or more players (but not too many) play a single game against another group. Although there is only one game in progress, two boards are used—one for each group. The opposing sides are separated from each other so that conversation is not overheard. The "allies" discuss the positions and agree on the selection of each move for their side, announcing the move to the opposing side. The discussion is mutually helpful to the players on each side, but the contest is mainly intended for entertainment.

Alternating Partnership Chess

Two players take one side of a board against two opponents. Without consulting, the two players on each side make alternate moves. One player on each side makes the first, third, fifth, seventh moves, etc., and his partner makes the second, fourth, sixth, eighth moves, etc. The game is interesting because each player attempts to read his partner's mind, tries to discover the purpose of his last move. Some combinations go astray when the partner fails to follow through. To be entertaining, a player is not allowed to think too long over a move. Sometimes the game is played at the rate of ten seconds a move.

Blitz Chess

This is the ultimate in fast chess. It is played at the rate of no-seconds-per-move. As each player moves, the opponent must reply instantaneously. No thinking is allowed. It is reflex chess, pure and simple. As can be imagined, it is a mad scramble, but good fun. Young players love it. A player loses if he leaves his King in check or makes any other illegal move—provided the opponent sees it. Kings have been known to remain in check for several moves.

Pots

Playing "pots" is one of the favorite sports at some of the leading clubs. There may be three or four contestants, and each antes a small stake into the pot. The man who beats the other contestants wins the pot—and a new pot begins. Play is at ten seconds a move, and there are always lots of kibitzers to see that the moves are made on time.

The first two opponents are chosen by lot. If they draw, they may play a second game, or they may toss to decide which remains. The winner of any game has a "leg" on the pot and the loser is replaced by the third (or fourth) contestant. A player is also replaced if he draws with an opponent who has a leg on the pot.

The kibitzers are essential. No pot game is complete without a running fire of comments and advice. Between the players, anything goes. If you can talk your opponent out of the game, you are a good pot player.

Five-Minute Chess

In Sweden, club players have abandoned ten-seconds-a-move chess and play "five-minute chess" in individual games and in lightning tournaments. The game must be played with clocks equipped with flags. Each player's clock is set at 11:55, allowing him five minutes to make all his moves. Only one hand may be used to make a move and punch the clock.

The game can be won by mating the opponent, or by winning on a time forfeit. A player may have a lost game but he wins on time if his opponent's flag drops before his own time limit expires. However, a game cannot be won on a time forfeit if it would be *impossible* (not just improbable) for the game to be won otherwise. The game is a draw if there is not enough material left on the board to checkmate, even against bad defense. In such positions a player's flag may drop but he does not lose the game.

Games can be won by playing the opening moves quickly, then crowding the opponent when he gets into time trouble. Lost games are always played out in an effort to obtain a draw or win by time-forfeit. The same game can be played with a longer time limit. Some clubs feature "Chess for Fun" tournaments in which this type of chess is played with a time limit of 30 minutes for each player (see page 166).

Odds-Giving Chess

As in many sports, a handicap is often given in a chess game to equalize the winning chances. In this way, a game is made more interesting to two players of unequal skill. If odds were not given, the stronger player would lose interest quickly, and the weaker player would not enjoy losing game after game.

The following grades of handicap range in order from minimum to maximum:

Draw Odds. The weaker player "wins" in the case of a draw.

Pawn and Move. White goes to the weaker player and Black removes his King-Bishop Pawn.

Pawn and Two. The stronger player has the black men and removes his King-Bishop Pawn. White is allowed two moves before Black moves.

Knight-Odds. The stronger player has the white men but removes his Queen-Knight.

Rook-Odds. The stronger player has white but removes his Queen-Rook. Before moving, White is permitted to place his Queen-Rook Pawn at QR3 instead of QR2.

Rook and Knight Odds. White removes his Queen-Rook and King-Knight, places his Queen-Rook Pawn at QR3 before starting the game. These odds are given rarely. Ordinarily, the next jump after Rook-odds is to Queen-odds.

Queen-Odds. White removes his Queen.

Capped Pawn. Usually more difficult than Queen-odds. The stronger player has white and retains all his men. To win, he must mate with his King-Bishop Pawn, unpromoted. Thus, all Black has to do is to capture this "capped Pawn" to win the game. Another variation is "Capped Knight" odds. White must mate with his Queen-Knight.

Occasionally, a strong player gives the odds of "any number of moves." White is permitted to make as many moves as he likes before Black moves, provided White does not place any man beyond his fourth rank until Black moves. The strong player retains all his men. Actually, White can set up a mating position if given these odds, but it is assumed that the weaker player is not skillful enough to do this.

There are no official laws governing chess at odds, but it is customary to observe the following rules:

1. The player who receives odds of two or more moves must not place any man beyond his fourth rank until his opponent has made one move.

2. The player who gives the odds of a Rook may castle as though this Rook were on the board, on the side from which the Rook has been removed, subject to the condition that this Rook's square is not occupied by any other man, white or black.

3. If the odds consist of several moves, they count for that number of moves in all calculations of time limit. The first move of the player who gives the odds counts as the same number of moves as those made by the receiver of the odds.

Kriegspiel

The German name of this game means "war play." It is a popular variant of chess, and most amusing to spectators. The play is more closely related to military tactics and strategy than chess itself, for neither player knows the actual position of his opponent's men.

Three boards and three sets of chessmen are required. The two players sit back to back, each facing his own board; or they may face each other with a screen between the two boards. The referee sits at a third board and is posted between the two players so that he can see the moves made by each combatant. The referee's board must be screened, or the position he occupies must make it impossible for the players to see his board.

At the start of the game, the player with the white men sets up his men as for an ordinary game of chess. If he wishes, he may also line up the black men; or he may leave the black men at the side of the board, with the intention of placing some of his opponent's men on the squares he believes they are occupying. The player with the black men follows the same procedure, setting up his own men on the board, and placing the white men according to his choice. The referee places both white and black men on his board in the starting position.

Throughout the game, the referee repeats each move on his own board, so that the actual position is always set up on the referee's board. Even though each player does not have sight of his opponent's position, there are several ways in which information can be gained by inference. As the game progresses, each player may place his opponent's men wherever he thinks or guesses them to be.

When a player has moved, the referee announces to the opponent: "White (or Black) has moved." He reports captures, checks, and illegal moves as follows:

CAPTURES

The referee announces the square (e.g., Black's KR4) on which a capture occurs, but not which man was captured or the name of the capturing man. Thus, the player whose man has been captured knows which one it was, but he does not know which enemy unit performed the capture.

CHECKS

The referee announces each check, and the direction of the check: on the rank, on the file, on the long diagonal, on the short diagonal, or by a Knight. For example, "Black has moved, checking on the short diagonal" would describe a check by a Bishop or Queen, specifying the diagonal occupied by the checking piece. In this case, White would know that the checking piece is on the shorter of the two diagonals on which his King stands.

ILLEGAL MOVES

If a player attempts an illegal move, the referee says, "No!" or "Illegal!" and another move must be substituted. A deliberate attempt to convey a false impression to the opponent is not allowed. Thus, if a player "captures" one of his own men, the referee says, "Nonsense!"

PAWN TRIES

To save time, a player may ask the referee if there are any Pawn captures available to him. Without this information, time would be wasted as a player tries to move his Pawns diagonally. The player asks "Are there any?" or just "Any?" The referee answers "No" if there are no possible Pawn captures, or "Try!" if there is one or more available to the player.

If a player has asked if there are any Pawn captures and has been told to try, he must attempt at least one Pawn move in a capturing direction. If that proves to be the correct move for a capture, the move stands; if not, the player may try to capture with the same Pawn in the other diagonal direction, or he may try captures with other Pawns—but he is not obliged to make more than one "try."

The information given by the referee enables each player to deduce, to some extent, the location of his opponent's men. Thus, by trying long-range moves of Rook, Queen, or Bishop, a player may determine whether a rank, file or diagonal is open, or whether there are obstructions. If an attempted King move is called illegal, the player knows that an enemy man is attacking the square to which the King was moved illegally. If a player parries a check by interposing, then moves the interposed man later, he can discover whether or not the man is still pinned. A capture by the opponent locates the position of the capturing man and the player may be able to deduce the type of man that made the capture.

When a player makes a capture he should always remove one of his opponent's men from the board (or from one side of the table to the other). He may not remove the correct man, but he is able to keep an accurate count of the number of men the opponent has left on the board.

The foregoing "rules" are followed in most of the leading clubs of the United States. Since there are no official Kriegspiel Laws, players sometimes follow slightly different rules. For instance, in Holland (where the game is called "Can I?" from "Can I capture with a Pawn?") the referee announces the name of a captured man, but not the square on which it was captured; and the direction of a check is not announced.

The following short game is by no means typical of a Kriegspiel game but illustrates the procedure. The "annotations" are by Eliot Hearst.

WHITE   BLACK

1 P-K4

Referee announces "White has moved." All Black knows is that White has moved a Pawn or a Knight—not a very brilliant deduction!

1 ....   P-KB3

Referee reports, "Black has moved." White asks "Are there any?" and referee answers, "No." White thus deduces that Black's first move was neither P-Q4 nor P-KB4. Otherwise, White would have a Pawn capture available.

2 Q-R5

Referee says, "White has moved, checking on the short diagonal." The long diagonal, White's QR4 to K8 has five squares; the short diagonal, KR5 to K8, has only four squares. Actually, in this position there could be no check on the long diagonal; but if Black's Queen-Pawn had also been moved, specifying the diagonal would indicate the direction of the check.

White's second move was made without knowing that it would

give check. On learning that his Queen is attacking the King's square, he knows that Black's first move was P-KB3.

2 ....   P-N3

Referee: "Black has moved."

3 B-K2

Referee: "White has moved." White sets a little trap into which Black might fall—and does.

3 ....   PxQ

Black first asked "Are there any?" and the referee replied, "Try!" Knowing that a white piece had checked on his KR4, Black tried the capture with his KNP. The referee announces: "Black has captured on his King-Rook four."

4 BxP mate

Referee: "White captures on his King-Rook five and mates."

From the October, 1950, issue of the magazine *Chess* (Sutton Coldfield, England) we quote the following Kriegspiel brilliancy won by Mr. E. H. Shaw at the Gambit Chess Rooms, London:

WHITE	BLACK
1 P-K4	N-QB3
2 P-KB3	

Q.:"Are there any?" Ans.: "No."

2	P-K4
3 K-B2	B-B4ch

"Black checks on the long diagonal."

4 K-N3

Q.: "Are there any?" Ans.: "No." Now Black knows that White did not play P-Q4.

4 ....   Q-N4ch

"Black checks on the file." Black deduces that White's first move was P-K4. Otherwise he would have played P-K3 at his fourth move. The check locates the White King. If 4...QN4 had not been a check, White's previous move might have been P-K3, K-K1, or K-N1. White's next three moves are forced.

5 K-R3   Q-R3ch

"Check on the file."

6 K-N3   Q-B5ch

"Check on the long diagonal."

7 K-R3   P-KR4!

Now White tries every possible move with his King but finds they are illegal. So he tries to make a loophole.

8 P-KN3

"Are there any?" "No." This shows that White did not play P-Q4 or P-KN4. Having an almost positive knowledge of White's position, Black guesses that White played P-KN3.

8 ....   P-Q4ch

"Black checks on the long diagonal." As the referee does not announce mate, Black knows that White's last move was P-KN3.

9 K-N2

"Are there any?" "No." Therefore White played K-N2 and not P-N4.

9 ....   R-R3

Now White asks "Are there any?" "Try!" says the referee. From the previous moves, White has located the black Queen. So he tries the capture with his Knight-Pawn.

10 PxQ

"White has captured on his KB4."

10 ....   R-N3 mate.

Note that White's 3 K-B2 would be suicidal in an ordinary game of chess, but "prospecting" with the King in an attempt to locate enemy pieces is customary in Kriegspiel.

Vegas Fun Chess

Strictly speaking, this belongs in the category of unorthodox chess. We give it a section of its own for two reasons: its popularity is spreading rapidly, and in a sense it is the most orthodox of all chess games, for it goes back to the origin of chess itself. In India, hundreds of years ago, dice were thrown to decide which piece could be moved. This idea has been revived by the inventors of Vegas Fun Chess: Art Gamlin and Herman Estrada of the Las Vegas Chess Association. The rules were formulated by George Koltanowski.

The game combines skill with luck. It is played with a regular chess set and two dice, each cube having chess symbols on its six sides except that one side of one cube has an "optional" symbol. The chessmen are set up as usual, White is first to play, and the right to move alternates between the two contestants. When it is his turn, a player rolls the two dice and can then move any man represented by either of the two symbols rolled uppermost, provided the man he selects can be moved legally. If he cannot move either type of man, he passes his turn. However, if the "optional" symbol comes up he may make any legal move on the board.

There are other rules for a few special situations. If a player giving check wishes to follow up the attack with another check, he may do so without throwing the dice, and with any piece he has on the board, as in a regular game. He may continue to checkmate or until he runs out of checks. In the latter case, he may make one free legal move of any man on the board. The complete rules accompany the special equipment which may be purchased from the USCF Sales Department.

According to Bobby Fischer, Larry Evans, and other masters who enjoy the game, the stronger player wins the majority of games despite the factor of luck which is present in a big way.

If desired, tournaments can be played with this type of chess, but a word of warning is needed: it is noisy! A club that permits the game to be played, or encourages it, should set aside special nights for Vegas Chess and prohibit it on other nights.

Unorthodox Chess

There are countless variants of chess in which the standard rules are thrown out of the window. The games range from mildly interesting to wildly insane. We shall not attempt to give more than a few samples. Those who like this sort of thing should get a copy of *Les Jeux D'Échecs Non Orthodoxes* published in French by the author, Professor Joseph Boyer.

ROTATION CHESS

In the north of England, where it was once popular (and may still be, for all we know) it is called "Gumption Chess." Don't ask us why. After ten moves on each side, the board is turned around, White taking Black's position and *vice versa*. After twenty moves, if the game is still going, the positions are reversed again; and so on, every ten moves.

PAWN-SNATCHER'S DELIGHT

According to Russell Chauvenet in an old issue of *Chess*, this is a good one for players who like an "open" game. If Pawns give you a feeling of claustrophobia, place all the white Pawns on White's 4th rank, and all the black Pawns on Black's 4th rank. Then go ahead as in regular chess. Pawns move forward one square only, if you have any Pawns left.

SIXTEEN-PAWN CHESS

A Queen is supposed to be worth eight Pawns. Okay, prove it! Try playing without your Queen but with eight extra Pawns to take its place. Here is the opening line-up:

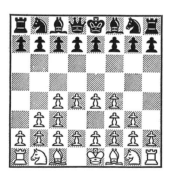

The eight extra Pawns move only one square forward. All other moves as in a regular game of chess.

GIVEAWAY CHESS

No Scotsman should play this game. In fact, this Scotsman shouldn't even be writing about it. The object of the game is to compel your opponent to capture all your men. The winner is the player who gets rid of all his men first. Captures are compulsory. If there is a choice of captures, the player may select the capture he wishes to make, without restriction. There are no checks, checkmates, or stalemates. The King is captured in the same way as any other man. If a Pawn reaches the 8th rank it must be promoted to a Queen. The game is drawn if the player having the move is unable to make a legal move. The starting position and all moves are the same as in regular chess, including *en passant* captures and castling.

Eliot Hearst gives us the following example:

	WHITE	BLACK
1	P-Q3	P-KN4
2	BxP	B-N2
3	BxP	BxP
4	BxQ	BxR
5	BxP	B-B6
6	BxN	RxB
7	NxB	P-Q4
8	NxP	N-B3
9	NxN	R-N1
10	NxK	. . . .

A strange move to record, but it is that kind of a game.

10	. . . .	RxP
11	BxR	P-B3
12	BxP	RxB
13	NxP	R-N1
14	NxP	R-N8
15	QxR	B-N2
16	QxB	P-R3

And White resigns, for 17 QxP is forced and Black has given away all his men.

SCOTCH CHESS

May be taken straight, or with soda. Starting line-up and moves of the men as in regular chess. The procedure: White makes one move, and Black makes two moves in a row; then White makes three moves in succession, and Black makes four in succession. Then

White plays five in a row, etc.—except that there aren't too many et ceteras. The game doesn't get that far. If a player checks the enemy King he loses the right to make any more moves in the series. A check must be parried immediately, and the King must not be exposed to check.

Combinations are made easy, because the opponent has to sit there and take it. A sample game by C. H. O'D. Alexander:

> White: 1 P-K4
> Black: 1 P-Q4 & PxP
>
> White: 2 B-B4, Q-R5, & QxPch
> Black: 2 K-Q2, N-KR3, NxQ, & N-KR3
>
> White: 3 P-QN3, B-R3, B-B7, N-KB3, & N-K5 mate.

PAWNS VS KNIGHTS

Try battling four Knights and a Pawn with eight Pawns. The opening position:

The Knights should win, but it isn't easy. Good practice in maneuvering Knights and defending against them.

DOUBLE-MOVE CHESS

This may seem tame after trying Scotch Chess, but it is a better game. Starting line-up and movement of the men as in regular chess. The only real difference is that each player is allowed to make two moves in a row at each turn. However, if a player checks on his first move, he is not allowed to make the second. Check must be parried immediately by the first reply. There are special rules on the *en passant* capture and on stalemate:

1. If a Pawn is moved forward two squares on a player's second of two moves, the opponent has the right to capture *en passant,* but only with his first reply.

2. If a Pawn is moved forward two squares on a player's first move, and another man is played on his second move, the opponent has the right to capture *en passant,* but only on his first reply.

3. If a Pawn is moved forward two squares on a player's first move, and the same Pawn is moved forward one more square on the player's second move, the opponent does not have the right to capture *en passant.*

4. A player can stalemate his King by making his first move with the King and producing a stalemate position for his second move. Since he cannot make a legal second move, the game is drawn.

A sample game:

WHITE	BLACK
1 P-K4 & P-K5	P-Q3 & PxP
2 Q-R5 & B-N5ch	B-Q2 & BxB
3 QxRP & QxR	Q-Q6 & Q-B8 mate

BUGHOUSE CHESS

Another name is "Putback Chess," but we prefer the first. More descriptive. In this crazy game no men are ever taken off the board. When a man is "captured" the player making the capture replaces the enemy man on a vacant square. However, captured Pawns must not be placed on the opponent's first rank, and a captured Bishop must be placed on a square of the same color as the Bishop's original square.

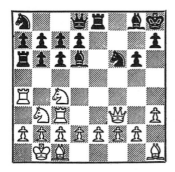

White mates in one bughouse move.

The starting position and the moves of the men are the same as in regular chess. The player's King must be out of check on completion of the player's move. Pawns are promoted to Queens only. A move with capture is completed only when the captured man has been placed on another square. Obviously, the only way to win is by checkmate.

A "bughouse" position, supplied to us by Eliot Hearst, is shown in the diagram at the bottom of page 179.

Under bughouse rules, White has a mate in one move. We won't keep you in suspense. The solution is 1 QxN, replacing the captured Knight on Black's K2.

ENTERTAINMENT AND PROMOTION

Tournaments and other contests bring the members together and develop friendly relationships, but the club's Directors should also arrange exhibitions, lectures, and social events in order to entertain the members. Some of these activities also publicize the club and help to obtain new members.

Simultaneous Exhibitions

An exhibition by a visiting chess master is always a popular form of entertainment. The club players meet the master, compete against him as he goes from table to table in his simultaneous exhibition, sometimes have the satisfaction of drawing their games, or even defeating the master. Some masters play blindfold games and give interesting lectures.

George Koltanowski of San Francisco is probably the most active exhibitor and always puts on a good show. Grandmasters Benko, Robert Byrne, Fischer, Lombardy, and Reshevsky also make tours from time to time. A few other masters give occasional exhibitions. Arrangements can be made to have one of these masters visit the club. The local newspapers will give space in their columns to stories describing the visit of a prominent master—especially if pictures are supplied to the papers. The occasion should be used to make the club known and to get the public to visit the club.

For the benefit of clubs that have not held simultaneous exhibitions, the customary procedure is as follows:

The tables are arranged so that it is convenient for the exhibitor to go from board to board without too much walking. A circular or quadrangular arrangement is satisfactory.

The exhibitor usually has the white men, although he may agree to take black on some boards.

The exhibitor goes from board to board in rotation. When the exhibitor reaches a board, the competitor (the opponent of the exhibitor) must make his move immediately and not delay the exhibition. However, the competitor must not make his move *before* the exhibitor reaches his board. The exhibitor must see the move being made.

While the exhibitor is away from a competitor's board, the men on the board *must not be touched*. It should be explained to each competitor that the position must remain absolutely undisturbed until the exhibitor reaches his board.

If a competitor wishes to reply instantly to the exhibitor's move, he may do so, and in this manner play as many moves against the exhibitor as the latter permits.

It is not considered good form to offer the exhibitor a draw. Any offer of a draw should come from the exhibitor.

Unless special arrangements have been made, each competitor plays only *one game* with the exhibitor. When the game is finished, the chessmen should be grouped in the center of the board, so that the exhibitor knows the board is "dead."

Near the end of the exhibition, when there are not more than four competitors still playing, each competitor is allowed two minutes to consider each move.

At the time fixed for the conclusion of play, any unfinished games are adjudicated. The exhibitor is awarded all games in which he has a slight but definite advantage. In doubtful positions, the exhibitor is given the benefit of the doubt.

Club Promotion

A club perishes unless there is a continual influx of new blood. By holding regular meetings, and by continually staging interesting competitive and social events, the old members can be retained—but it is also necessary to attract new members to the club.

A competent member should be appointed to handle advertising and publicity. With the approval of the Directors, he places occasional advertisements announcing "open house" nights at the club, simultaneous exhibitions, special tournaments, etc. He also submits regular news items to the local paper which will usually print such items if they are sent in promptly, are brief, have names in them, and give evidence of activity. Sometimes a phone call to the disc jockey at the local radio station will result in the broadcast of a club's announcement of a special event.

A mimeographed bulletin with news and announcements of the club's activities is one of the most effective means of publicizing the club. It should be devoted almost entirely to local news. Chess players can read about international and national events in regular chess periodicals, but only in the club bulletin can they learn the latest standings in the club championship, the ladder ratings, the results of inter-club and other matches, etc. The national periodicals have little space to devote to non-master games, but the club bulletin can feature the scores of games played in the club.

CHAPTER VI

Rating Chessplayers

A system of ranking chessplayers is one of the most important requirements of a national chess organization. In the absence of an accurate means of comparing the performances of contestants in tournaments and matches, there exists a wide divergence of opinion as to the strength of the players. The title of Master, being undefined, lacks prestige. The title is often abused, being applied to players who are by no means Masters.

Under a good rating system, the qualifications of a Grandmaster, Senior Master, Master, Expert, etc., are clearly defined, and the titles are conferred on players who meet the required playing standards. A high-ranking player's standing in the chess community becomes official. Attention is focused on the demonstrated ability and achievements of the strongest players in all sections of the country. The monetary rewards of chess competition may be small, but a ranking system provides the incentives of dignity and prestige.

In the lower categories, competitors in chess contests may be graded as Class A, Class B, and Class C players. In this way, a ladder to chess fame is set up. Players are eager and willing to climb such a ladder. Every contestant in a rated event knows that his performance is being recorded and recognized. He knows that each tournament success increases his rating, brings him closer to his goal —the ranking of Master.

Even if a player lacks the ability to rise to the top, the possession of a national rating is a valuable asset. He is able to compare his standing with other players in his own class. He is given the pride of achievement when he advances his rating or "crosses" another player who has been ahead of him in the past. If he goes down the scale, he is given the incentive to study and improve his play so that he will make a better showing in future contests.

Many problems are solved by a rating system. The selection of a team becomes a simple matter. A player's right to compete for the title of national champion is made plain for all to see. Entries in a tournament can be classified intelligently, for seeding is no longer a matter of guesswork or personal opinion. The ratings of players in a Swiss tournament enable the Director to pair systematically and thereby achieve the objectives of this type of contest.

In brief, a good ranking system creates contests, increases the number of entries in tournaments, develops strong players, improves standards of play in general, adds zest and interest to competitive chess.

Chronology of Rating Systems

1933: The Correspondence Chess League of America (CCLA), first national organization to adopt a numerical rating system, chooses the Short System, formerly employed by West Coast clubs to conduct their ladder contests. In 1934 the CCLA switched to the Walt James Percentage System. In 1940 they returned to a point system developed by Kenneth F. Williams.

1942: The magazine *Chess Review* initiates rating system produced by Kenneth Harkness. This improved and simplified adaptation of the Williams System is still being used in 1967.

1944: The CCLA changes to an improved version of the Williams System composed by William Wilcock. A slight revision was made in 1947. In 1949, all numerical values of the system's chart were proportionately reduced. Still used in 1967.

1946: The USSR Chess Federation, first national organization to employ a systematic but non-numerical method of classifying over-the-board players, describes its system in chess magazine. Presumably inaugurated after the end of World War II.

1948: The Ingo System is described in a Bavarian chess magazine and is subsequently employed by the West German Chess Federation. Still used in 1967.

1949: The World Chess Federation (FIDE) issues regulations governing the award of international titles. Revised in 1957, the rules were again modified in 1965.

1949: The Harkness System for rating over-the-board tournaments, developed during 1946 through 1949, is submitted to the U.S. Chess Federation. In 1950 it was approved as the first official USCF rating system. Subsequently the British Chess Federation and the Chess Federation of Canada adopted it. Still used by the BCF in 1967.

1959: The USCF names a professional committee, headed by Arpad E. Elo, to examine all rating systems, and to make appropriate recommendations.

1961: Professor Elo develops basic rating system theory (from probability and statistical theory) in algebraic formulae. The resulting rating procedures became the USCF Rating System, still in use in 1967.

THE HARKNESS-USCF RATING SYSTEM

During the years 1946 through 1949 this writer developed a system of rating the performances of chessplayers in tournaments. This was something that had not been done before by numerical means. In 1949, while still working on the construction of a list of players who had competed in U. S. tournaments from the year 1921 onward, we submitted a complete description of the system to Mr. William Byland, then Vice President of the United States Chess Federation, and offered to permit the USCF to use the system to rate American chessplayers, if it so desired. Mr. Byland, who had been appointed to evaluate different rating systems submitted to the USCF, considered our own the best and recommended it to the Federation. In 1950 it was accepted as the first official rating system of the USCF.

The first rating list appeared in the November 20, 1950, issue of *Chess Life*. It contained the ratings of about 2400 players as of July 31, 1950. An active player's rating in this list may have been his annual average for 1947, 1948, 1949, or the first seven months of 1950, whichever was highest.

Under the impression that the system had been developed by our good friend Bill Byland, the December 1950 issue of *Chess Review* editorialized: "... a herculean task ... the list of ratings is a splendid boost to chess. It will spur interest of chess fans and be an incentive to chess players.... We hail this system, therefore, as a fine accomplishment. The rating list is bound to be a better and better measure of chess players' abilities the longer the system is in operation."

During the ten-year period 1950 through 1960 when the Harkness System was used by the USCF, rating lists were published about twice a year and the membership of the Federation grew by leaps and bounds, especially after April 1958 when new regulations went into effect requiring USCF membership of all players in rated tournaments. From 1950 to 1960 the number of members rose from about 1000 to approximately 5000. The growth has continued to the present day, when the Federation has about 10,000 members. A great deal of this progress has been due to the interest created by the USCF rating systems and the requirement that a player must be a member to obtain a rating.

Classifications

After an initial trial of a different arrangement, players were classified at 200-point intervals and given the titles shown below:

Grandmaster	.... 2600 points and up
Senior Master	.... 2400 to 2599 points
Master	.... 2200 to 2399 points
Expert	.... 2000 to 2199 points
Class A	.... 1800 to 1999 points
Class B	.... 1600 to 1799 points
Class C	.... Below 1600 points

These titles and values are still used by the USCF today.

Formulae of the System

The various postal chess systems were designed to measure the performances of a player and his opponent in a single game played by mail, or to rate the results of several postal games during a given period of time. The Harkness-USCF system, however, was expressly designed to measure the performances of contestants in over-the-board chess tournaments.

The basic formula of the system may be stated as follows:

When a player competes in a rated contest, he is given a *performance rating* based on two factors:

(a) the player's *competition average,* which is the median average of his opponents' ratings, and

(b) the player's *percentage score* against his opponents.

A player who makes a 50 per cent score receives the competition average as his performance rating. A player who makes a score of more than 50 per cent receives the competition average plus 10 rating points for each percentage point of his score above 50 per cent. If he scores less than 50 per cent his performance rating is the competition average minus 10 rating points for each percentage point of his score below 50 per cent.

The difference between the competition average and the player's own rating constitutes what is known as the *handicap factor.* If a player's opponents are weaker than himself, the competition average is below his own rating and represents a handicap he must overcome by his game score in order to retain or increase his rating. On the other hand, if the competition average is higher than his own rating he is thereby given a handicap in his favor.

For example, a player with a 2000-point rating competes in a ten-round tournament and scores 8–2. The competition average of 1800 points is 200 below his own rating. To retain or increase his rating, the player's game score must earn enough points to overcome this handicap. His score of 8–2 is 30 per cent above an even score. For each percentage point above 50 he earns 10 rating points for a total of 300. Therefore his performance rating is the competition average of 1800 plus 300 = 2100 points. This is 100 points higher than his previous rating.

Another example: A player with a rating of 1600 scores 2½–8½ in eleven games. Translated into percentages, this is 27.3 per cent below an even score. The competition average of 1850 is 250 points above his own rating; so this player receives a handicap of 250 in his favor. His performance rating is the competition average of 1850 minus 273 (10 rating points for each percentage point below a 50 per cent score) for a total of 1577 points.

At first, the above formula was used for all Round Robins and, with a special weighting method to adjust the competition average, for all Swiss System tournaments. But this "straight percentage" type of formula tends to exgagerate the ratings achieved by the winners of short contests. With the increasing use of the Swiss System, the number of short tournaments grew rapidly. To correct the tendency toward inflated ratings we originated the following formula for tournaments of six to nine rounds:

A player's performance rating is his competition average plus or minus 100 rating points for each game point above or below a 50 per cent score, as the case may be.

With this formula a player's game score may gain or lose up to a maximum of 300 points in a six-round contest, up to 350 points in a seven-round tournament, up to 400 points in an eight-rounder, and up to 450 points in a nine-rounder. Then the basic "straight percentage" formula takes over and a player's score may gain or lose up to 500 points in a tournament of ten rounds or more.

Here is an example of the short-contest formula: A player with a rating of 2200 scores 7–1 in an eight-round tournament. This is 3 game points above an even score. The competition average is 1920 points, representing a handicap of 280. The player's performance rating is 1920 plus 300 (100 rating points for each game point above 50 per cent) for a total of 2220.

Safeguard Rules *

A few protective rules were adopted. The most important are as follows:

1. When computing a player's competition average, games won from opponents rated more than 350 points below the player's own rating are omitted from the calculation. Similarly, games lost to opponents more than 350 points above the player's own rating are omitted.

2. The performance rating of the winner of a contest (or a player who ties for first) is cancelled if a 100 per cent score would not have produced a high enough rating at least to duplicate his last average rating.

3. When a player scores zero game points in any contest, his performance rating is cancelled if it is higher than his last average.

4. If a player qualifies for any championship finals by playing in a preliminary tournament, his performance rating for the preliminary is cancelled if it is lower than his previous average rating.

Published Ratings

In the early days of the Harkness-USCF System, a player's published rating was the arithmetic average of his last-published rating and his subsequent performance ratings. This was changed in 1957 when rating lists were supposed to be published at intervals of three months. To avoid large fluctuations as a result of one or two good or bad performances, it was decided that a player's published rating would be the average of his last four performance ratings (see *Chess Life*, August 20, 1957).

---

* The British Chess Federation uses only the straight percentage formula. Hence Rule 1, mainly intended for the short-contest formula, is not employed. Ratings are adjusted annually. A player's new rating is determined by his total score in 30 or more games played in tournaments and matches during the twelve-month period prior to the closing date of the most recent "grading" list (but, if necessary, up to 20 games from the previous year may be included to make up the required minimum of 30). The BCF improved on rules 2 and 3 by specifying that a player is credited with his own rating for a game won from an opponent rated 500 or more points below him, or a game lost to an opponent 500 or more points above him.

THE ELO-USCF SYSTEM

In 1959, after the resignation of the writer as Business Manager and Rating Statistician of the United States Chess Federation, a committee was formed to make a study of rating systems. The committee was headed by Arpad E. Elo, Professor of Physics at Marquette University in Milwaukee, Wis. The committee's progress report was published in *Chess Life* during March, April, and May of 1960, and a comprehensive description of the Elo-USCF System was published in the June, 1961, issue. At that time Professor Elo privately published a full explanation of the mathematical procedure used to develop the rating formulae, together with the basic probability or "percentage expectancy" curve (see page 191). As a result of these reports, the USCF adopted the recommended changes; the new system, although titled "The USCF Rating System" in all the reports, continues to be known as "The Elo System."

Fundamentals of All Rating Systems

The committee's initial reports made it clear that there is an element of inaccuracy in ratings from any "closed" system, that is, a system in which one player gains points only at the expense of another. All the systems studied were discovered to be basically identical, even though they looked different, superficially. The general features of all rating systems were defined and clarified as follows:

A certain number of rating points is assigned to a game between two players. The winner gains these points and his opponent loses them. (If the game is drawn, these points are not won or lost by either player.) In addition, the stronger player, as measured by the respective ratings of the two contestants, gives a handicap to his weaker opponent. The handicap is the number of points represented by a fixed percentage of the difference between the ratings of the two players.* These handicap points are gained by the lower-rated player and lost by the higher-rated. However, a limitation must be placed on the handicap. If the handicap points amount to more than

---

* The early rating systems used variable amounts for the rating point value of a game or the handicap percentage. The Harkness–Chess Review System of 1942 was the first to use a fixed amount for the rating point value of a game and a fixed percentage of the difference in ratings for the handicap. In some systems, the handicap is the entire difference in ratings, not just a fraction of this difference.

the number of points assigned to the value of a game, the higher-rated player would lose points by defeating his opponent and the latter would gain points by losing the game.

To rate a player's performance in a tournament, the points he gains and loses in his individual encounters with the contestants are added up and his previous rating is changed by the amount of the resulting net gain or loss.

The stronger player gives an opponent odds in rating points. If he wins, he gains points; if he loses, he suffers the loss of more points than he would have gained by winning the game. If the game is drawn, he loses the handicap points. The important consideration is the relation between the number of points the stronger player can win and the number he stands to lose. For a rating system to be effective, this relation should be the same as or close to the relation between his chances of winning and losing the game.

The Probability Curve

Using the mathematics of statistical theory, Professor Elo and his committee determined the relationship that exists between the probability of a player defeating an opponent and the difference between their ratings.* This relationship is shown in the diagram on page 191 which visualizes a player's chances of defeating an opponent with a different rating.

Note that there are two "graphs" in this diagram. The solid line looks a little like a straggling letter S and is a standard type of curve in probability theory. (In statistical work it is called a "cumulative probability" or "standard sigmoid" curve.) The broken line is a linear approximation of the main curve. For the purposes of our simplified explanation of this subject we will refer to these two graphs as the "S-curve" and the "straight line" approximation.

The diagram illustrates the basic principles and operation of the Elo-USCF Rating System. The S-curve shows the percentage chance a player has of defeating an opponent with a different rating. The straight line indicates a close approximation of his winning chances. In a tournament, the percentage score a player may be expected to

---

* An explanation of the mathematics is beyond the scope of this book. Two papers by Professor Elo on the mathematical development of the theory of rating sytsems may be obtained for $1 from the U.S. Chess Federation. They are entitled "Theory of Rating Systems" and "The USCF Rating System."

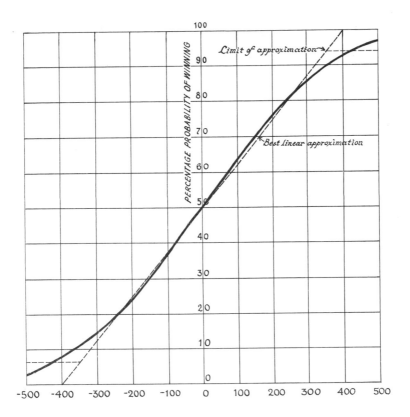

DIFFERENCE IN RATING

This "probability curve" visualizes a player's chances of defeating an opponent in a game. If there is no difference in their ratings (zero on the horizontal scale) the chances are even (50 per cent on the vertical axis). If the player has a lower rating than his opponent (to the left of zero) his chances of winning diminish as shown by the curve. Thus, if he is rated 200 points below his opponent his chances of winning are only about 25%. If the player has a higher rating than his opponent (to the right of zero) his chances of winning increase as indicated by the curve. The solid line is the standard "sigmoid curve" of probability theory, in this case for class intervals of 200 points. The broken line is a linear approximation of the solid curve.

make is the average of his percentage expectancies against his individual opponents.

The S-curve is precise and exact, according to mathematical theory, but its values cannot be expressed in a simple manner, other than graphically as in the diagram. On the other hand, the straight line approximation can be easily expressed by a simple equation. Except at the ends, where the two graphs are farthest apart, the results obtained with the straight line approximation are almost identical to those furnished by the S-curve.

Although inexact at the ends, the straight line approximation was chosen for rating purposes generally. In this way, the rating calculations were greatly simplified. However, as we shall see, this necessitated the adoption of some "safeguard rules."

Rating Adjustment Formula

From the straight line approximation of the probability curve and the principles described above, the formula below was developed for computing a player's new rating after competition in a match or tournament:

$$R_n = R_0 + 16 (W\text{--}L) + 4\% (\Sigma D) \tag{1} *$$

where

R_n = player's new rating
R_0 = player's old rating
W = game points won
L = game points lost
ΣD = algebraic sum of all the differences between the opponents' ratings and the player's rating.

The difference between any opponent's rating and the player's rating must be limited to 350 points. A draw counts $\frac{1}{2}W$ and $\frac{1}{2}L$.

The expression $16 (W - L)$ is the game score factor in which the coefficient 16 is the rating point value of a game. The expression $4\% (\Sigma D)$ is the handicap factor. (In algebra the Greek capital S, called sigma and written Σ, is used to indicate that terms are to be added up.) The sum of these two factors is added to the player's rating.

* In the first progress reports, the formula used 5% instead of 4%, the figure coming from empirically-developed data from several Western Open and North Central Open tournaments. However, the results continued to exhibit inconsistencies which were not completely eliminated until the application of formula (1) in 1961.

The handicap of any individual game cannot be more than 14 points because the maximum allowable difference in ratings is 350, and 4% of 350 is 14. Hence a player must gain at least two points when he defeats an opponent with a lower rating.

Safeguard Rules

As we have pointed out, formula (1) above is based on the values of the straight line approximation of the standard probability curve. If you will refer again to the diagram on page 191 you will observe that according to the straight line a player rated 350 points above his opponent has about a 94 per cent probability of winning, whereas the standard S-curve indicates that the chances are actually 88 per cent under these conditions. There is a similar difference at the bottom ends of the two lines. This means that formula (1) is not accurate for rating differences exceeding 350 points, nor for percentage scores below 15 per cent or above 85 per cent.

The limitations of the straight line approximation made it necessary to adopt certain safeguard rules when using formula (1). The most important is effectively the same as Rule 1 from the Harkness System, given on page 188. However, where the Harkness System omitted rating contests in which the players were over 350 points apart, the Elo System rates these games but uses 350 as the rating difference.

One or two additional safeguard rules were improvised by the rating statisticians, but it is not necessary here to go into details, as they are relatively unimportant and have been superseded by the use of a new formula, to be explained later.

The Concept of Odds

A fundamental concept of this system is that the relation between the number of rating points a player may gain and the number he may lose when playing an opponent with a different rating should be about the same as the odds for or against his winning the game as indicated by the probability curve.

To show how this works, let us assume that player A with a rating of 2000 points encounters player B who is rated 200 points lower at 1800. According to the probability curve, player A has a 75 per cent chance of winning. This means that his chances are 75 out of 100, or 3 out of 4. Again according to the curve, player B has a 25 per

194 OFFICIAL CHESS HANDBOOK

cent chance of winning, which means that his chances are 25 out of 100, or 1 out of 4. In other words, player A is a 3 to 1 favorite to win.

To be effective, the rating system should have about the same 3 to 1 odds. Player A should be required to risk three times as many rating points as the number he stands to gain by winning the game. Now let us see how the rating formula takes care of this situation. How many points does player A stand to win, and how many points does he stand to lose? First, what happens if he wins is indicated by substituting the given values in formula (1) as follows:

$$R_n = 2000 + 16 (1-0) + 4\% (-200)$$
$$= 2000 + 16 - 8$$
$$= 2000 + 8$$

If player A wins, he gains 8 points. Now, if he loses:

$$R_n = 2000 + 16 (0-1) + 4\% (-200)$$
$$= 2000 - 16 - 8$$
$$= 2000 - 24$$

Player A's loss is 24 points, which is three times as many points as he can gain by winning the game. This corresponds exactly with the 3 to 1 odds of the probability curve. Obviously, if the values for player B are substituted in the formulae above, it will be shown that the 3 to 1 underdog risks the loss of 8 points to gain 24.

Rating Formula Constants

It should be understood, of course, that the same proportionate results will be obtained by this formula with other coefficients having the same relationship as 16 and 4 per cent. Any combination with the same 400 to 1 (16 to .04) ratio will satisfy the requirements of this probability curve. The coefficients could be 8 and 2 per cent, or 20 and 5 per cent, or 40 and 10 per cent, or 200 and 50 per cent, or even 400 and 100 per cent. With any of these or other 400 to 1 combinations the number of rating points a player may gain and the number he may lose will be in the same ratio as the odds for and against his winning the game according to this probability curve. The only difference is that with larger constants the rating fluctuations are greater. For a given performance in a match or tournament a formula with large coefficients produces a greater change in a player's rating than the same formula with smaller constants. However, the average of a large number of performance ratings with either formula will be about the same.

When the constants are high, greater weight is given to more recent performances. High constants are therefore appropriate for players whose performance is changing rapidly, particularly young players whose playing strength is improving almost from tournament to tournament. On the other hand, low constants are appropriate for players whose rate of change has diminished, such as those in the Senior Master class. Accordingly, the coefficients for senior masters were set at 8 and 2 per cent (instead of 16 and 4 per cent) in formula (1). This reduces fluctuations and produces a more realistic rating. Incidentally, the lower coefficients reduce from 2 points to 1 point the amount a player in the Senior Master class gains when he defeats a player rated 350 or more points below him.

Examples from Tournaments

To illustrate the application of the Elo formula to the measurement of players' performances in tournaments, we present first the example of Bobby Fischer's outstanding success in retaining the U.S. Championship in 1963-64. At the start of the event Bobby had a rating of 2685 points. The champion's opponents are listed below in alphabetical order with the differences between their ratings and Fischer's rating.

Opponent	Rating	Difference
Addison	2462	−223
Benko	2566	−119
Bisguier	2507	−178
Donald Byrne	2500	−185
Robert Byrne	2545	−140
Evans	2559	−126
Mednis	2438	−247
Reshevsky	2611	− 74
Saidy	2512	−173
Steinmeyer	2451	−234
Weinstein	2434	−251
		−1950

All the opponents have lower ratings than Fischer, but in no case is the difference greater than 350 points, so there is no need for adjustment. The total of the differences is minus 1950. Fischer won this event with a perfect score of 11–0. Substituting the given values in the formula, we get:

$$R_n = 2685 + 8 \ (11\text{--}0) + 2\% \ (-1950)$$
$$= 2685 + 88 - 39$$
$$= 2685 + 49$$
$$= 2734$$

Fischer's new rating is 2734, a gain of 49 points. Note that the constants 8 and 2 per cent are used in this calculation instead of 16 and 4 per cent.

A second example: Robert Byrne scored 7–1 at the National Open of 1965. Although he had the same game score as the winner (Reshevsky), Robert was placed second on tie-breaking points. The runner-up had a rating of 2546 at the start of the eight-round struggle. Subtracting 350, we see that if any opponent has a rating of less than 2196 we must call the difference the maximum allowable figure of 350. Below we tabulate the actual difference and the adjusted difference between each opponent's rating and Byrne's rating of 2546.

Opponents' Ratings	Actual Difference	Adjusted Difference
1798	−748	−350
1990	−556	−350
2174	−372	−350
2196	−350	−350
2218	−328	−328
2361	−185	−185
2242	−304	−304
2261	−285	−285
		−2502

The total of the "adjusted difference" column is minus 2502. Substituting the given values in the formula, we get:

$$R_n = 2546 + 8 \ (7\text{--}1) + 2\% \ (-2502)$$
$$= 2546 + 48 - 50$$
$$= 2546 - 2$$
$$= 2544$$

Byrne's new rating is 2544, a loss of 2 points. Again the constants of 8 and 2 per cent are used, this player being in the Senior Master class.

Note that it is possible for a player to win a tournament (or tie for first) and lose rating points, as the Byrne example shows. This does not mean that the rating system is defective. On the contrary, the occasional losses by winning players are due to an essential feature of such systems. The relationship between the handicap and game score factors of the rating formula must require a player to make a high percentage score to gain rating points when he is competing against opponents far below his strength. With a different relationship, permitting the gain of points with a lower percentage score, a player could easily build up a false rating by just defeating weak opponents. However, as a result of this protective feature, it becomes possible occasionally for a player to win a tournament and lose rating points. Incidentally, this acts as an incentive for a player to put forth his best efforts at all times.

The following example shows how the rating of a Class A player is adjusted as a result of his performance in a seven-round tournament. The table below indicates the result of each game, the ratings of the opponents, the actual difference between each opponent's rating and the player's own rating of 1950, and the adjusted difference when the actual difference exceeds 350.

Opponents' Ratings	Actual Difference	Adjusted Difference	
W 1420	−530	−350	
W 1740	−210	−210	
W 1900	− 50	− 50	
L 2330	+380		+350
D 1920	− 30	− 30	
L 2160	+210		+210
W 1800	−150	−150	
		−790	+560

In the first round this player defeated an opponent rated 530 points below his own rating of 1950; this difference is reduced to minus 350. In the fourth round, the player lost to a master rated 380 points above his own rating; this is reduced to plus 350. The ratings of the other opponents are within the limitation of 350 points.

At the right, the minus difference column adds up to 790, the plus column to 560. The net total (or algebraic sum) of all the differences, therefore, is minus 230. The player's total score is $4\frac{1}{2}$–$2\frac{1}{2}$. Substituting the given values in the formula, we get:

$$R_n = 1950 + 16 \ (4\frac{1}{2}\text{–}2\frac{1}{2}) + 4\% \ (-230)$$
$$= 1950 + 32 - 9$$
$$= 1950 + 23$$
$$= 1973$$

The player's new rating is 1973, a gain of 23 points. As this player is not in the Senior Master class, the constants of 16 and 4 per cent are used, as shown in formula (1) on page 192.

The last example shows how the rating of a Class B player is changed by his performance in a seven-round tournament. The player's own rating is 1795 points.

Opponents' Ratings	Actual Difference	Adjusted Difference
L 2281	+486	+350
W 1481	−214	−214
D 1646	−149	−149
D 1601	−194	−194
L 2216	+421	+350
L 2064	+269	+269
W 1710	− 85	− 85
	−642	+969

The two masters this player met (in the first and fifth rounds) were rated more than 350 points above his own rating, so these differences are cut down to the maximum allowable difference of 350. The net total of the differences at the right is 969 minus 642 = 327. The player's total score is 3–4. Substituting the given values in the formula:

$$R_n = 1795 + 16\ (3\text{--}4) + 4\%\ (327)$$
$$= 1795 - 16 + 13$$
$$= 1795 - 3$$
$$= 1792$$

The player's new rating is 1792, a loss of 3 points.

How New Players Are Rated

The formula for issuing a provisional rating to a previously unrated player is as follows:

$$R_p = R_c + 400 \left(\frac{W\text{--}L}{N} \right) \tag{2}$$

where

R_p = provisional rating
R_c = competition average
W = game points won
L = game points lost
N = number of games played

The competition average is the arithmetic mean of the ratings of all the player's opponents. A draw counts ½W and ½L.

For example, a new player competes in a five-round tournament with the results listed below:

Opponents'
Ratings

L	1700
L	1400
W	1350
L	1600
D	1450

Total   7500

The total of the opponents' ratings is 7500 and the average is 1500. The player scored $1\frac{1}{2}$–$3\frac{1}{2}$. Substituting in the formula, we get:

$$R_p = 1500 + 400\left(\frac{1\frac{1}{2}-3\frac{1}{2}}{5}\right)$$
$$= 1500 + 400\left(\frac{-2}{5}\right)$$
$$= 1500 - 160$$
$$= 1340.$$

The player's provisional rating is 1340 points.

Practices and Regulations

1. A player is not given an established rating until he has played 25 or more games in rated events, including the event being rated. Formula (2) above is used to compute the new rating of a provisionally rated player when he competes in rated events. However, when using this formula, *all* the player's games, including those in previous contests, are used to make the calculations. For instance, if the player in the example above competes in a second rated event, a four-round tournament, the competition average for the new calculation becomes the average of all nine opponents, five from the first contest and four from the second. His total score is the number of points he won and lost against all nine opponents. In other words, the two contests are treated as though they were one event. This method of adjusting ratings continues until he has played a total of 25 games or more, including the event being rated. When the total is 25 or more, his rating is computed using formula (1) and he becomes an established player.

2. In all calculations the pre-event rating of an opponent is used, if he has previously played ten or more games. If an opponent is

unrated or has previously played less than ten games, his post-event rating is used. This rule also applies to the opponents of provisional and established players.

3. In formula (1) the coefficients are set at 16 and 4 per cent for all players rated below 2400. For players 2400 and over, these coefficients are 8 and 2 per cent.

4. All games played in USCF tournaments are rated for both players, including games won by time forfeit, games won by failure to appear after adjournment, and games played by a contestant who subsequently withdrew. Games in which the opponent made no move are considered unplayed games and are not rated.

5. Individual matches are rated only between established players, and only for ten games or less. Longer matches may be divided into ratable segments of ten games or less.

6. All competitions are supposed to be rated in chronological order. A player's published rating is the rating he obtained after the last competition reported before the closing date of the list.

7. In all computations by the rating statistician, the ratings used are the latest in the USCF files. These are more current than the last published ratings.

8. Ratings of all players who competed during the twelve months prior to the closing date of the list are published annually in *Chess Life*. Supplementary lists appear intermittently.

CURRENT REFINEMENTS OF ELO-USCF SYSTEM

At the FIDE Congress of 1965, the USCF was asked to make a full presentation of its rating system for consideration by the Congress at Havana in October, 1966. The British Chess Federation requested Professor Elo to make a similar presentation to its grading committee in London. As this book goes to press, both have been prepared. They include some minor modifications of the rules and a major simplification in method of presentation. Formulas (1) and (2), with their need for safeguard rules, are superseded by the simple formulas (3) and (4) and the new Tables, which will now be explained.

Fundamentally, the system is not changed, but the modifications improve accuracy. Formula (1), based on the straight line approximation of the probability curve in the diagram on page 191, has been used for the adjustment of ratings mainly because it simplifies the work of the rating statistician. However, electronic computers have now made it unnecessary to continue the use of the inexact straight line approximation. Calculations can now be based on the S-curve itself. When programmed for computers, the "safeguard" rules will no longer be required; regulations 1 and 2 (page 199) may be simplified; and regulation 3 may be significantly refined.

In this modified system, the fundamental probability curve is used to indicate a player's percentage expectancy of winning a game from an opponent with a different rating; but the curve is also used in the opposite way—to find the rating difference indicated by a player's percentage score in a match or tournament.

Table I (page 202) is used to find a player's percentage expectancy of winning a game from an opponent with a different rating. Table II (page 203) is used to convert a difference in ratings into the probability of winning.

How New Players Are Rated

The formula below is used to issue provisional ratings to players having less than 17 games experience against rated players:

$$R = R_c + D\,(P) \tag{3}$$

where

R   is the performance rating
R_c is the average competition rating
$D\,(P)$ is the rating difference, taken from Table I, for the percentage score achieved.

For example, an unrated or provisionally rated player scores 2–6 in an eight-round tournament. His percentage score is 2/8 or 25 per cent. The competition average is 1800. According to Table I, a 25 per cent score represents 193 points below average. Therefore the player's performance rating for this tournament is 1800 − 193 = 1607.

Another example: A new player competes in a seven-round tournament and scores 3 game points against opponents whose ratings average 1700. His percentage score is 3/7 or 43 per cent. As shown in Table I, a 43 per cent score is 50 rating points below average. Hence this new player's performance rating is 1700 − 50 = 1650.

TABLE I: RATING DIFFERENCES

P Percentage Score	D(P) Rating Point Difference	P Percentage Score	D(P) Rating Point Difference
.50	0	.50	0
.51	+7	.49	−7
.52	+14	.48	−14
.53	+21	.47	−21
.54	+29	.46	−29
.55	+36	.45	−36
.56	+43	.44	−43
.57	+50	.43	−50
.58	+57	.42	−57
.59	+65	.41	−65
.60	+72	.40	−72
.61	+80	.39	−80
.62	+87	.38	−87
.63	+95	.37	−95
.64	+102	.36	−102
.65	+110	.35	−110
.66	+117	.34	−117
.67	+125	.33	−125
.68	+133	.32	−133
.69	+141	.31	−141
.70	+149	.30	−149
.71	+158	.29	−158
.72	+166	.28	−166
.73	+175	.27	−175
.74	+184	.26	−184
.75	+193	.25	−193
.76	+202	.24	−202
.77	+211	.23	−211
.78	+220	.22	−220
.79	+230	.21	−230
.80	+240	.20	−240
.81	+251	.19	−251
.82	+262	.18	−262
.83	+273	.17	−273
.84	+284	.16	−284
.85	+296	.15	−296
.86	+309	.14	−309
.87	+322	.13	−322
.88	+336	.12	−336
.89	+351	.11	−351
.90	+366	.10	−366
.91	+383	.09	−383
.92	+401	.08	−401
.93	+422	.07	−422
.94	+444	.06	−444
.95	+470	.05	−470
.96	+501	.04	−501
.97	+538	.03	−538
.98	+589	.02	−589
.99	+677	.01	−677
1.00	*	.00	*

* Indicates an indeterminate value.

TABLE II: WINNING EXPECTANCIES

Difference in Ratings	Percentage Expectancy High *	Low †	Difference in Ratings	Percentage Expectancy High *	Low †
0–3	.50	.50	198–206	.76	.24
4–10	.51	.49	207–215	.77	.23
11–17	.52	.48	216–225	.78	.22
18–25	.53	.47	226–235	.79	.21
26–32	.54	.46	236–245	.80	.20
33–39	.55	.45	246–256	.81	.19
40–46	.56	.44	257–267	.82	.18
47–53	.57	.43	268–278	.83	.17
54–61	.58	.42	279–290	.84	.16
62–68	.59	.41	291–302	.85	.15
69–76	.60	.40	303–315	.86	.14
77–83	.61	.39	316–328	.87	.13
84–91	.62	.38	329–344	.88	.12
92–98	.63	.37	345–357	.89	.11
99–106	.64	.36	358–374	.90	.10
107–113	.65	.35	375–391	.91	.09
114–121	.66	.34	392–411	.92	.08
122–129	.67	.33	412–432	.93	.07
130–137	.68	.32	433–456	.94	.06
138–145	.69	.31	457–484	.95	.05
146–153	.70	.30	485–517	.96	.04
154–162	.71	.29	518–559	.97	.03
163–170	.72	.28	560–619	.98	.02
171–179	.73	.27	620–735	.99	.01
180–188	.74	.26	over 735	1.00	.00
189–197	.75	.25			

* The percentage expectancy of winning for the higher-rated player.
† The percentage expectancy of winning for the lower-rated player.

Rating Adjustment Formula

The formula below is used to determine an established player's new rating after competition in a match or tournament:

$$R_n = R_o + K (W - W_e) \qquad (4)$$

where

R_n is the player's rating after the event
R_o is the player's rating before the event
W is the number of wins, draws counting ½
W_e is the expected number of wins, taken from Table II, based on ratings prior to the event
K is the player's development coefficient.

This formula can be more easily understood by taking an example. Let us say that a player rated at 1760 competes in a seven-round tournament, meeting seven rated opponents. The table below analyzes his performance:

Opponent	Opponents' Rating	Rating Difference (Player's rating minus opponent's)	Player's % Expectancy (Table II)	Player's Actual Result
A	1645	115	.66	1
B	1680	80	.61	.5
C	1920	−160	.29	0
D	1720	40	.56	1
E	1980	−220	.22	.5
F	1905	−145	.31	1
G	2010	−250	.19	0
			2.84	4.0

We shall explain the coefficient K in a moment. Let us assume it is 45. The values can now be substituted in formula (4) as follows:

$$R_n = 1760 + 45 \ (4\text{--}2.84)$$
$$= 1760 + 45 \ (1.16)$$
$$= 1760 + 52$$
$$= 1812$$

The figure 2.84 is the sum of the individual expectancies against the seven opponents. The player performed better than this, for he scored 4 points. As a result, his new rating is 52 points higher than before.

Now as to the coefficient K. This is a variable figure to take care of the fact that a player improves rapidly during the earlier stages of his career, more slowly or not at all later on. When the rate of change is rapid, a high value of K is used. Later, as the rate of change slows down, the value of K declines. Furthermore, a high K gives greater weight to recent performances and a low K gives more weight to earlier performances. (See rule 3 below. With K at 30, formula (4) gives approximately the same results as formula (1) with coefficients of 16 and 4 per cent.)

New Practices and Regulations

The simplified rules 1, 2 and 3 are as follows:

1. For each new player entering the rating pool, the rating is computed by equation (3) for at least 16 games. These games may be from one or more events, but must be from rated tournaments, or

from league play, not from individual matches. During this period the player is considered provisionally rated. After this period, he is considered established, and the rating is computed by equation (4).

2. When rating an event, performance ratings using equation (3) are obtained, first for the unrated players and next for the provisionally rated players. After this, the new ratings of established players are calculated, using equation (4). Thus, when a game with a non-established opponent enters the rating of an established player, it enters on the basis of the opponent's performance *in that event only*. It follows that the established players *as a group* neither gain nor lose rating points. Individually, however, they may gain or lose, depending on their respective performances against the non-established player.

3. The coefficient K for each player is set at 45 for his first 100 rated games, at 30 for the next 200 such games, and at 20 thereafter. During his first 100 games if his rating exceeds 2200, K drops to 30. At any time, if his rating exceeds 2400, K drops to 20.

Rules 4 through 8 remain as on page 200.

The foregoing is a brief summary of the modified Elo-USCF System as explained in the paper entitled "The USCF Rating System" by Arpad E. Elo. The entire paper is available from the U. S. Chess Federation. See footnote, page 190.

THE INGO SYSTEM

This system is used by the West German Chess Federation. In one respect it is similar to the Harkness-USCF System, for ratings are computed by a straight percentage formula, although in other respects it differs. The formula is as follows:

$$R = R_c - (P\text{-}50)$$

where

R = performance rating
R_c = competition average
P = percentage score obtained, as a whole number

Note the minus sign between the competition average and the game score factor. This means that a plus score decreases the performance rating, and a minus score increases it. For example, a player competes in a ten-round tournament and scores 8–2 (80 per cent). The competition average is 120 points. Substituting these values:

$$R = 90$$
$$= 120 - 30$$
$$= 120 - (80-50)$$

If the player had made a minus score of 2–8 (20 per cent), his rating would have been 150.

The usual direction of a rating scale is reversed. The highest possible rating is zero. Shown below are the Ingo ratings corresponding to the ratings and classifications of the USCF:

USCF Ratings	Ingo Ratings
2600 to 2800	25 to 0
2400 to 2600	50 to 25
2200 to 2400	75 to 50
2000 to 2200	100 to 75
1800 to 2000	125 to 100
1600 to 1800	150 to 125
1400 to 1600	175 to 150
1200 to 1400	200 to 175

The Ingo ratings are lifetime averages, so they do not necessarily represent the current strength of the players.

CHESS RATINGS IN THE USSR

Since the end of World War II, chessplayers in the USSR have been given the national titles of Grandmaster, Master, Master Candidate, and classified in five lower categories, in accordance with a non-numerical rating system that was described in a Soviet chess magazine published in 1946.

It is not surprising that the Soviet Union has a tough qualification system that makes it extremely difficult for a player to reach the Master rank. There are probably more strong players in the USSR than in all the rest of the world combined. The Soviet chess authorities believe in making the minimum standards of Master rank considerably higher than those in effect in many other countries. Most of the Russian Master Candidates and many first-category players would qualify as Masters under more lenient ranking systems.

To become a Master, a Soviet player has to work his way up through five classes, make a good enough showing as a first-category player to be accepted as a Master Candidate, then turn in a 45 per cent score in an all-Master tournament, or up to 75 per cent in a tournament with only a few non-masters. Even then, his games have to be examined by a committee to make sure that the quality of his play justifies issuing the title of Master. A Candidate can also become a Master by winning a match with another Master. In other words, a Candidate has to be a stronger player than a good many established Masters to gain the title.

Soviet Grandmasters earn their titles in the USSR Championship Tournaments. A player who wins the national championship becomes a Grandmaster. Provision is also made for awarding the title to players who finish near the top in two or more championship tournaments.

Russian Master titles are not necessarily given for life. For example, if a Master fails to perform as a Master should, he may be called upon to confirm his title by playing a match with another Master, or by competing in a tournament and making the score required of Master Candidates to qualify for the title.

In the lower echelons, there are five categories of rated players. The strongest is the first, the weakest the fifth. Players are classified on the basis of their successes in qualifying tournaments or in match play. Qualifying matches are held only among players in adjacent categories, and not lower than for the second category.

A Round Robin tournament may become a qualifying event if it has at least eleven participants. Occasionally, a double Round Robin with six or more entrants is arranged. In team competitions, at least seven games must be played to be counted toward qualification.

In any qualifying event, a chessplayer can attain only the next higher category. An exception is made in the case of unclassified players who may be advanced at once to the third category upon fulfilling the requirements in a mixed tournament.

The qualification into each category is awarded for a three-year period. At the end of this period, the player must confirm his category. A player who fails to confirm his classification for three years is transferred to a lower category.

An exception is made in the confirmation of categories 1 and 2 for those who have attained them for the first time. In large cities, such as Moscow, Leningrad, Kiev, etc. (seventeen cities altogether), those who have attained categories 1 and 2 for the first time must be confirmed within one year—and in other places not later than two years from the date they attained their ratings.

Unclassified players participate in primary tournaments. All those who win 50 per cent of their games or more are classified in the fifth category.

Qualification Tournaments

In practice, the most widespread form of competition is a mixed tournament, with participants from various categories. To determine the score a player must make in any tournament to attain or retain classification in a given category, a tournament "coefficient" is computed, based on the number of players and their classifications. For example: A tournament is held with sixteen players. The number of players in each category is multiplied by the number of the category, and the resulting products are totaled, as follows:

Category		No. of Players		Total
1	×	2	=	2
2	×	5	=	10
3	×	3	=	9
4	×	6	=	24
		Grand Total		45

The total of 45 is then divided by the total number of players (16) resulting in an average tournament coefficient of 2.813.

It will be noted that a strong tournament has a lower coefficient than a weaker tournament. An all-Master tournament has a coefficient of zero. A tournament in which all the contestants belong in Category 5 (the weakest class) has a coefficient of 5.000.

The computation of a tournament coefficient is accurate to the third place beyond the decimal point. (If the fourth place equals five or more, increase the third place by one.) In the example given above, the average category of the participants (2.813) is between categories 2 and 3, but is nearer the latter. In this tournament, the players may attain or confirm categories 2, 3, and 4.

Qualification Tables

The following tables show the minimum percentage score a player must achieve in a tournament to attain or retain classification in the highest possible category into which the coefficient of the tournament allows the player to qualify. It also shows the percentage score he must achieve to attain or retain classification in the next lower category.

Thus, Table No. 1 lists tournaments with coefficients from zero (an all-Master event) to 1.000. In an all-Master tournament, a player must make a score of 45 per cent to attain or retain the title of Master. The last line of the table shows that a player in a tournament with a coefficient between 0.901 and 1.000 must make a score of 75 per cent to reach or retain Master rank, or a score of 45 per cent to attain or retain classification in category 1.

In each table, the scoring requirements for only two categories are indicated. If there are contestants belonging to the next lower category, they must achieve the lowest percentage score shown in the table to confirm their classification. For example, a category 2 player who competes in any of the tournaments listed in Table No. 1 must make a score of at least 27 per cent to confirm his classification in category 2. Similarly, a category 3 player who competes in any of the tournaments listed in Table No. 2 must make a score of at least 23 per cent to confirm his classification.

Qualification Table No. 1

Tournament Coefficient		% Score to attain or retain Master title	% Score to attain or retain category 1
From	To		
0.000 (All-master)		45	—
0.001	0.100	48	27
0.101	0.200	51	29
0.201	0.300	54	31
0.301	0.400	57	33
0.401	0.500	60	35
0.501	0.600	63	37
0.601	0.700	66	39
0.701	0.800	69	41
0.801	0.900	72	43
0.901	1.000	75	45

(Continued)

Qualification Table No. 2

Tournament Coefficient From	To	% Score to attain or retain category 1	% Score to attain or retain category 2
0.901	1.000	45	23
1.001	1.100	48	25
1.101	1.200	51	27
1.201	1.300	54	29
1.301	1.400	57	31
1.401	1.500	60	33
1.501	1.600	63	35
1.601	1.700	66	37
1.701	1.800	69	39
1.801	1.900	72	41
1.901	2.000	75	43

Qualification Table No. 3

Tournament Coefficient From	To	% Score to attain or retain category 2	% Score to attain or retain category 3
1.901	2.000	43	20
2.001	2.100	46	22
2.101	2.200	49	24
2.201	2.300	52	26
2.301	2.400	55	28
2.401	2.500	58	30
2.501	2.600	61	32
2.601	2.700	64	34
2.701	2.800	67	36
2.801	2.900	70	38
2.901	3.000	73	40

Qualification Table No. 4

Tournament Coefficient From	To	% Score to attain or retain category 3	% Score to attain or retain category 4
2.901	3.000	40	19
3.001	3.100	43	19
3.101	3.200	46	21
3.201	3.300	49	23
3.301	3.400	52	25
3.401	3.500	55	27
3.501	3.600	58	29
3.601	3.700	61	31
3.701	3.800	64	33
3.801	3.900	67	35
3.901	4.000	70	37

Qualification Table No. 5

Tournament Coefficient From	To	% Score to attain or retain category 4	% Score to attain or retain category 5
3.901	4.000	37	17
4.001	4.100	40	17
4.101	4.200	43	19
4.201	4.300	46	19
4.301	4.400	49	21
4.401	4.500	52	23
4.501	4.600	55	25
4.601	4.700	58	27
4.701	4.800	61	29
4.801	4.900	64	31
4.901	5.000	67	33

INTERNATIONAL RANKING SYSTEM

The World Chess Federation issues the following titles, valid for life:

International Grandmaster
International Master
International Woman Master

International Referee
International Master of Compositions
International Judge of Compositions

After World War II, when the World Federation (FIDE) was reorganized, regulations governing the award of international titles were formulated. Based on an applicant's record in international competition, titles were conferred by resolution of the FIDE General Assembly and the Qualification Committee. It was also decided that elderly players who had been recognized prior to 1949 as International Masters and Grandmasters would be given these titles without further qualification in competitive play. The latter method of awarding titles was discontinued in 1953, but provision was made later for the possibility that some elderly masters may have been overlooked. As a result of this provision, Edward Lasker of the United States and Carlos Torre of Mexico became International Masters in 1963.

New regulations were adopted by the Congress at Vienna, 1957. This marked the end of prolonged preparatory work started in 1953 when, following the suggestions of Italian Professor Giovanni Ferrantes, different committees studied the so-called FAV system for classification of tournaments and numerical evaluation of tournament results. It was called the FAV system in view of the work performed by Messrs. Ferrantes, Alexander, and Dal Verme in connection with its elaboration.

Some of the fundamental principles of the rules adopted in 1957 were based on the ideas of Yugoslav Master Voja Popovic, besides those of Prof. Ferrantes.

Titles Conferred Automatically

Under the 1957 regulations, the title of *International Grandmaster of the FIDE* is conferred automatically on the following:

(a) the world champion;

(b) a player whose performance in an Interzonal Tournament qualifies him to compete in a Candidates' Tournament, even if he does not play in the latter for any reason;

(c) a player whose performance in an Interzonal Tournament would have qualified him to compete in a Candidates' Tournament but who is excluded because a limitation was placed on the number of participants from his Federation;

(d) any other player who actually plays in a Candidates' Tournament and makes a score of at least 33⅓%.

The title of *International Master of the FIDE* is conferred automatically on the following:

(a) the woman champion of the world;

(b) the junior champion of the world, provided the number of players in the championship tourney was not less than ten;

(c) a player whose performance in a Zonal Tournament qualifies him to compete in an Interzonal Tournament, even though he does not play in the latter for any reason;

(d) a player who competes in a Zonal Tournament in which several Federations could be represented and whose performance would have qualified him to compete in an Interzonal Tournament but who is excluded from the latter because a limitation was placed on the number of participants from his Federation;

(e) any other player who actually plays in an Interzonal Tournament and scores at least 33⅓%.

The title of *International Woman Master of the FIDE* is conferred automatically on the following:

(a) a player whose performance in a Zonal Tournament qualifies her to compete in a Women Candidates' Tournament, even if she does not play in the latter for any reason;

(b) a player who competes in a Zonal Tournament in which several Federations could be represented and whose performance would qualify her to play in a Women Candidates' Tournament but who is excluded from the latter because a limitation was placed on the number of participants from her Federation;

(c) any other player who actually plays in a Women Candidates' Tournament and scores at least 33⅓%.

Titles Awarded by FIDE Congress

International titles may also be awarded by a FIDE Congress on the recommendation of the Qualification Committee. The regulations outline a system of classifying tournaments, depending mainly on the percentage of Grandmasters and International Masters playing in the contests. The regulations also specify the performances in such tournaments which require or justify the recommendation of the Qualification Committee that titles be given to applicants.

The title of *International Referee of the FIDE,* according to the regulations, is awarded to persons who, by their repeated activity as director or referee of competitions, have shown a profound knowledge of the laws of chess and other regulations prescribed by the FIDE for competitions and who have always shown absolute objectivity.

The title of *FIDE International Judge of Compositions* is awarded to persons who, by their repeated activity as director or referee of international chess composition competitions—problems, studies, etc.—have acquired great experience, showing always proof of absolute objectivity.

At the FIDE Congress of 1961, the late Grandmaster Milan Vidmar stated that the regulations adopted in 1957 "made it possible to award international titles to players without sufficient merit." In 1964, at Tel Aviv, a sub-committee was formed to recommend changes in the regulations. This committee believed that, in principle, the automatic award of titles should be abolished. It also criticized the methods used to qualify players for titles as a result of their performances in approved tournaments, and recommended that the composition of the Qualification Committee should be changed.

The committee's report was discussed at the Congress and received the strong support of several delegates, especially Grandmaster Miguel Najdorf, who felt that measures should be taken to put an end to the "inflation" of international titles. Other delegates were just as strongly opposed to the suggestion that the automatic awarding of titles in zonal tournaments be abolished.

At the 1965 Congress in Wiesbaden, the regulations covering the awarding of titles were revised to make it more difficult for a player to qualify from an international tournament. The percentages of Grandmasters and International Masters were increased and a new rule was adopted under which a Master or Grandmaster is not counted as such in evaluating the strength of a tournament if in the five-year period preceding the tournament he had not obtained a Master or Grandmaster result. The regulations covering the automatic award of titles were not changed.

Although the rules state that the title of International Referee is to be awarded only to persons who have repeatedly served as directors or referees and who have shown a profound knowledge of the laws of chess, this title has frequently been awarded to persons who have seldom or never directed a tournament and who know little or nothing about the laws of chess. In these cases it has been regarded as an honorary title. There are now so many "International Referees" that there has been considerable agitation in FIDE Congresses to form a corps of real referees who know what it is all about. So far, no definite action has been taken.

The holders of FIDE titles, up to and including the year 1965, are listed on the following pages. Our list of International Referees includes only those who are residents of the United States or Canada.

Any titles conferred or awarded at the 1966 Congress in Havana are not included, for the names of 1966 titleholders have not been made available to us up to the time of going to press.

International Grandmasters

ANTOCHIN, Vladimir (USSR)
AVERBACH, Yuri (USSR)
BARCZA, Gedeon (Hung.)
BENKO, Pal (U.S.A.)
BILEK, Istvan (Hung.)
BISGUIER, Arthur B. (U.S.A.)
BOBOTZOV, Milko G. (Bulg.)
BOLESLAVSKY, Isaac (USSR)
BONDAREVSKY, Igor (USSR)
BOTVINNIK, Mikhail (USSR)
BRONSTEIN, David (USSR)
BYRNE, Robert (U.S.A.)
CHAMKOVICH, Leonid (USSR)
CIRIC, Dragoljub (Yugo.)
DAMJANOVIC, Mato (Yugo.)
DARGA, Klaus (W. Ger.)
DONNER, Jan H. (Neth.)
ELISKASES, Erich (Arg.)
EUWE, Dr. Max (Neth.)
EVANS, Larry (U.S.A.)
FILIP, Dr. Miroslav (Czech.)
FINE, Dr. Reuben (U.S.A.)
FISCHER, Robert J. (U.S.A.)
FLOHR, Salo (USSR)
GELLER, Ewfim (USSR)
GHEORGHIU, Florin (Rum.)
GLIGORIC, Svetozar (Yugo.)
GUIMARD, Carlos E. (Arg.)
HORT, Vlastimil (Czech.)
IVKOV, Borislav (Yugo.)
JANOSEVIC, Dragoljub (Yugo.)
KASHDAN, Isaac (U.S.A.)
KERES, Paul (USSR)
KHOLMOV, Ratmir (USSR)
KORCHNOI, Victor (USSR)
KOSTIC, Bora (Yugo.)
KOTOV, Alexander (USSR)
KROGIUS, Nikolai (USSR)
LARSEN, Bent (Den.)
LENGYEL, Levente (Hung.)

LILIENTHAL, Andrei (USSR)
LOMBARDY, William (U.S.A.)
MATANOVIC, Alexander (Yugo.)
MATULOVIC, Milan (Yugo.)
NAJDORF, Miguel (Arg.)
O'KELLY DE GALWAY, Albéric (Belg.)
OLAFSSON, Fridrik (Iceland)
PACHMAN, Ludek (Czech.)
PADEVSKI, Nicolas B. (Bulg.)
PANNO, Oscar (Arg.)
PARMA, Bruno (Yugo.)
PETROSIAN, Tigran (USSR)
PILNIK, Herman (Arg.)
PIRC, Dr. Vasja (Yugo.)
POLUGAEVSKY, Lev (USSR)
POMAR, Arturo (Spain)
PORTISCH, Lajos (Hung.)
RESHEVSKY, Samuel (U.S.A.)
ROBATSCH, Karl (Austria)
ROSSETTO, Hector D. (Arg.)
ROSSOLIMO, Nicolas (U.S.A.)
SAEMISCH, Friedrich (W. Ger.)
SCHMID, Lothar (W. Ger.)
SIMAGIN, Vladimir (USSR)
SMYSLOV, Vassily (USSR)
SPASSKY, Boris (USSR)
STAHLBERG, Gideon (Sweden)
STEIN, Leonid (USSR)
SUETIN, Alexei (USSR)
SZABO, Laszlo (Hung.)
TAIMANOV, Mark (USSR)
TAL, Mikhail (USSR)
TOLUSH, Alexander (USSR)
TRIFUNOVIC, Dr. Petar (Yugo.)
TRINGOV, Gueorguy P. (Bulg.)
UDOVCIC, Mijo (Yugo.)
UHLMANN, Wolfgang (E. Ger.)
UNZICKER, Wolfgang (W. Ger.)
VASIUKOV, Eugeni (USSR)
YANOFSKY, Dan A. (Canada)

International Grandmasters (Deceased)

BERNSTEIN, Dr. Ossip (France) 1882–1962
BOGOLIUBOV, E. D. (W. Ger.) 1889–1952
DURAS, Oldrich (Czech.) 1882–1957
GRUENFELD, Ernst (Austria) 1893–1962
LEVENFISH, Grigory (USSR) 1889–1961
MAROCZY, Geza (Hung.) 1870–1951

MIESES, Jacques (Eng.) 1865–1954
RAGOZIN, Viacheslav (USSR) 1908–1962
RUBINSTEIN, Akiba (Belg.) 1882–1962
STOLTZ, Gosta (Sweden) 1904–1963
TARTAKOVER, Dr. Xavier (France) 1887–1956
VIDMAR, Dr. Milan (Yugo.) 1886–1962

International Masters

AARON, Manuel (India)
AHUES, Carl (W. Ger.)
ALATORTSEV, Vladimir (USSR)
ALEXANDER, C. H. O'D. (Gt. Brit.)
ANDERSEN, Borge (Den.)
ANDERSON, Frank R. (Canada)
ARONIN, Lev (USSR)
BAGIROV, Vladimir (USSR)
BALANEL, Ion (Rum.)
BARDA, Olaf (Norway)
BARENDREGT, J. T. (Neth.)
BECKER, Albert (Arg.)
BEDNARSKI, B. J. (Poland)
BELY, Miklos (Hung.)
BENI, A. (Austria)
BERGER, Bela (Austral.)
BERTOK, M. (Yugo.)
BHEND, Edwin (Switz.)
BIELICKI, Carlos (Arg.)
BLAU, Max (Switz.)
BOGDANOVIC, Rajko (Yugo.)
BOHATIRTCHUK, Dr. F. (Canada)
BOLBOCHAN, Jacobo (Arg.)
BOLBOCHAN, Julio (Arg.)
BOOK, Eero E. (Fin.)
BOUWMEESTER, Hans (Neth.)
BRINCKMANN, Alfred (W. Ger.)
BUKIC, Enveir (Yugo.)
BYKOVA, Elizaveta (USSR)
BYRNE, Donald (U.S.A.)
CANAL, Esteban (Peru)
CARDOSO, R. T. (Phil.)
CASTALDI, Vincenzo (Italy)
CHEKHOVER, Vitaly (USSR)
CHRISTOFFEL, Dr. M. (Switz.)
CIOCILTEA, Victor (Rum.)
CORTLEVER, Nicolaas (Neth.)
CUELLAR GACHARNA, Miguel (Colombia)
CZERNIAK, Miguel (Israel)

DAKE, Arthur W. (U.S.A.)
DE GREIFF, Boris (Colombia)
DELY, Peter (Hung.)
DENKER, Arnold S. (U.S.A.)
DODA, Zbigniew (Poland)
DRIMER, Dolfi (Rum.)
DUBININ, Peter (USSR)
DUCKSTEIN, Andreas (Austria)
DUNKELBLUM, Arthur (Belg.)
DURASEVIC, B. (Yugo.)
DUZ-KHOTIMIRSKY, F. J. (USSR)
EKSTROM, Folke (Sweden)
ENEVOLDSEN, Jens (Den.)
ERDELYI, Stefan (Rum.)
FAIRHURST, Wm. A. (Scot.)
FARRE MALLOFRE, Miguel (Spain)
FAZEKAS, Dr. S. (Gt. Brit.)
FICHTL, Jiri (Czech.)
FLESCH, Janos (Hung.)
FLORIAN, Dr. Tibor (Hung.)
FOGUELMAN, Alberto (Arg.)
FORINTOS, Gyozo (Hung.)
FRYDMAN, Paulino (Arg.)
FUCHS, Reinhardt (E. Ger.)
FUDERER, Andrija (Yugo.)
FURMAN, Semen (USSR)
GAPRINDASHVILI, Nona (USSR)
GARCIA, Raimundo (Arg.)
GEREBEN, Erno (Hung.)
GERMAN, Eugenio (Brazil)
GHITESCU, Teodor (Rum.)
GILG, Karl (W. Ger.)
GIPSLIS, Aivar (USSR)
GIUSTOLISI, Alberto (Italy)
GOGLIDZE, Viktor (USSR)
GOLOMBEK, Harry (Eng.)
GROB, Henry (Switz.)
GUFELD, Edward (USSR)
HAAG, Ervin (Hung.)
HEINECKE, Herbert (W. Ger.)

HENNEBERKE, F. W. (Neth.)
HONFI, Karoly (Hung.)
HOROWITZ, I. A. (Al) (U.S.A.)
ILIVITSKY, Georgy (USSR)
JANSA, Vlastimil (Czech.)
JIMINEZ ZERQUERA, E. (Cuba)
JOHANNESSEN, Svein (Norway)
JOHANSSON, Ingi R. (Iceland)
JOHNER, Hans (Switz.)
KAILA, Osmo (Fin.)
KAN, Ilya (USSR)
KARAKLAJIC, N. (Yugo.)
KASPARIAN, Genrikh (USSR)
KATETOV, Dr. M. (Czech.)
KAVALEK, Lubomir (Czech.)
KELLER, Dieter (Switz.)
KELLER, Rudolf (E. Ger.)
KHASSIN, Abram (USSR)
KIENINGER, Georg (W. Ger.)
KLUGER, Gyula (Hung.)
KMOCH, Hans (U.S.A.)
KOCH, Berthold (E. Ger.)
KOLAROV, Atanas S. (Bulg.)
KOLTANOWSKI, George (U.S.A.)
KONIG, Imre (U.S.A.)
KONSTANTINOPOLSKY, A. (USSR)
KOTTNAUER, Cenek (Czech.)
KOVACS, Laszlo (Hung.)
KOZMA, Julius (Czech.)
KOZOMARA, Vlado (Yugo.)
KRAIDMAN, Yoshe (Israel)
KRAMER, Haye (Neth.)
KUPPER, Josef (Switz.)
KURAJICA, Bojan (Yugo.)
KUYPERS, F. A. (Neth.)
LANGEWEG, K. (Neth.)
LASKER, Edward (U.S.A.)
LEHMANN, Heinz (W. Ger.)
LEIN, Anatolyi (USSR)
LETELIER MARTNER, R. (Chile)
LIBERSON, Vladimir (USSR)
LISITSYN, Georgy (USSR)
LOKVENC, Josef (Austria)
LUNDIN, Erik (Sweden)
MAKARCZYK, K. (Poland)
MAKOGONOV, Vladimir (USSR)
MALICH, Burkhard (E. Ger.)
MARIC, Rudolf (Yugo.)
MAROVIC, Drazen (Yugo.)
MEDINA GARCIA, A. (Venez.)
MICHEL, Pablo (Arg.)
MIHAILJCISHIN, M. (Yugo.)

MIKENAS, Vladas (USSR)
MILEV, Zdravko (Bulg.)
MILIC, Borislav (Yugo.)
MINEV, Nicolay N. (Bulg.)
MINIC, Dragoljub (Yugo.)
MONTICELLI, Mario (Italy)
MUELLER, Hans (Austria)
MUFFANG, André (France)
MUHRING, Willem J. (Neth.)
NAVAROVSZKY, Laszlo (Hung.)
NEDELJKOVIC, Dr. S. (Yugo.)
NEIKIRCH, Oleg N. (Bulg.)
NEJMETDINOV, Rachid (USSR)
NEY, Ivo (USSR)
NOVOTELNOV, Nikolai (USSR)
OJANEN, Kaarlo S. (Fin.)
OPOCENSKY, Karel (Czech.)
OSNOS, Viacheslav (USSR)
PALAU, Luis (Arg.)
PANOV, Vassily (USSR)
PAOLI, Dr. Enrico (Italy)
PELIKAN, Jiri (Arg.)
PENROSE, Jonathan (Eng.)
PEREZ PEREZ, Francisco J. (Spain)
PFEIFFER, Gerhard (W. Ger.)
PFLEGER, Helmut (W. Ger.)
PIETZSCH, Wolfgang (E. Ger.)
PLATER, Kazimierz (Poland)
PLECI, Isaias (Arg.)
PORATH, H. Joseph (Israel)
PORRECA, G. (Italy)
PRINS, Lodewijk (Neth.)
PUC, Stojan (Yugo.)
PURDY, C. J. S. (Austral.)
QUINONES, Oscar (Peru)
RABAR, Braslav (Yugo.)
RELLSTAB, Ludwig (W. Ger.)
RICHTER, Emile (Czech.)
RICHTER, Kurt (E. Ger.)
RODL, Dr. Ludwig (W. Ger.)
RUBTSOVA, Olga (USSR)
RUDENKO, Ludmilla (USSR)
SACCONI, Count Antonio (Italy)
SAJTAR, Jaroslav (Czech.)
SANCHEZ, Luis (Colombia)
SANDOR, Bela (Hung.)
SANGUINETI, Raul (Arg.)
SCAFARELLI, F. (Italy)
SCHMIDT, Dr. Paul (U.S.A.)
SCHWEBER, Samuel (Arg.)
SHERWIN, James T. (U.S.A.)
SLIWA, Bogdan (Poland)

SMEDEREVAC, Petar (Yugo.)
STEINER, Lajos (Austral.)
SZABADOS, Eugenio (Italy)
SZILAGYI, Gyorgy (Hung.)
SZILY, Dr. Jozsef (Hung.)
TAN, Hoang L. (Indonesia)
TESCHNER, Rudolf (W. Ger.)
THOMAS, Sir George A. (Eng.)
TORAN ALBERO, Roman (Spain)
TORRE, Carlos (Mexico)
TROIANESCU, Dr. O. (Rum.)
TSVETKOV, Alexandre (Bulg.)
UJTELKY, Max (Czech.)
VAITONIS, P. (Canada)
VAJDA, Dr. A. (Hung.)
VAN DEN BERG, C. B. (Neth.)

VAN GEET, Dirk (Neth.)
VAN SCHELTINGA, Th. D. (Neth.)
VERESOV, Gavril (USSR)
VIDMAR, Milan, Jr. (Yugo.)
VLADIMIROV, Boris (USSR)
VUKOVIC, Vladimir (Yugo.)
WADE, R. G. (Eng.)
WAGNER, Heinrich (W. Ger.)
WEINSTEIN, Raymond (U.S.A.)
WEXLER, Bernardo (Arg.)
WHITAKER, Norman T. (U.S.A.)
YUDOVICH, Mikhail (USSR)
ZAITZEV, Alexander (USSR)
ZITA, Frantisek (Czech.)
ZUIDEMA, Conrad (Neth.)
ZVETKOV—See TSVETKOV.

International Masters (Deceased)

ASZTALOS, Dr. Lajos (Hung.) 1889–1956
ATKINS, Henry E. (Gt. Brit.) 1873–1955
CARLS, Carl (W. Ger.) 1880–1958
FOLTYS, Jan (Czech.) 1908–1952
NAGY, Dr. Geza (Hung.) 1892–1953
NENAROKOV, Vladimir (USSR)
1880–1953

REJFIR, Josef (Czech.) 1909–1962
ROMANOVSKY, Peter (USSR) 1892–1964
STEINER, Herman (U.S.A.) 1905–1955
VERLINSKY, Boris (USSR) 1880–1950
WINTER, William (Eng.) 1898–1955

International Women Masters

ASSENOVA, Venka (Bulg.)
AXT, Helga (W. Ger.)
BAIN, Mary (U.S.A.)
BENINI, Clarice (Italy)
BILEK, Edit (Hung.)
BORISENKO-BELOVA, Valentina (USSR)
BRUCE, Rowena M. (Eng.)
CHAKOVSKAIA, Alla (USSR)
CHAUDÉ, Chantal de Silans (France)
DE BUDINICH, B. Carrasco (Chile)
DE HUGUET, Soledad Gonzales (Arg.)
DE MONTERO, M. Berea (Arg.)
DE MOSCHINI, Celia Baudot (Arg.)
DE SILANS—See CHAUDÉ.
ERETOVA, Kveta (Czech.)
GRESSER, Gisela Kahn (U.S.A.)
GURFINKEL, Josefa (USSR)
HEEMSKIRK, Fannie (Neth.)
HERMANOWA, Roza M. (Poland)
HOLUJ, Krystyna (Poland)
HRUSKOVA-BELSKA, Nina (Czech.)
IGNATIEVA, Olga (USSR)
IVANOVA, Antonia (Bulg.)
JOVANOVIC, Katarina (Yugo.)
KARAKAS, Eva (Hung.)
KARFF, Mona M. (U.S.A.)

KELLER-HERRMANN, Edith (E. Ger.)
KONARKOWSKA-SOKOLOV, H. (Yugo.)
KOSLOVSKAIA, Valentina (USSR)
KUCHNIR, Alla (USSR)
LANE, Lisa (U.S.A.)
LANGOS, Josza (Hung.)
LARSEN, Ingrid (Den.)
LAZAREVIC, Milunka (Yugo.)
MORA, Maria Teresa (Cuba)
NEDELJKOVIC, V. Jovanovic (Yugo.)
NICOLAU, Alexandra (Rum.)
POGOREVICI, Maria (Rum.)
POLIHRONIADE, E. (Rum.)
PRITCHARD, Elaine Saunders (Eng.)
RANNIKU, Maiya (USSR)
REISCHER, Salome (Austria)
RINDER, Friedel (W. Ger.)
ROOTARE, Salme (USSR)
SUCHA, Ruzena (Czech.)
SUNNUCKS, Anne (Eng.)
TCHAJKOVSKAJA—See CHAKOVSKAIA.
TEODORESCU, Margareta (Rum.)
TRANMER, Eileen (Eng.)
VOLPERT, Larisa (USSR)
ZATULOVSKAYA, Tatiana (USSR)
ZVORYKINA, Kira (USSR)

International Women Masters (Deceased)

GRAF-STEVENSON, Sonja (U.S.A.) 1921–1965

International Referees (U.S.A. only)

HOROWITZ, I. A. (Al) (U.S.A.)
KASHDAN, Isaac (U.S.A.)
KMOCH, Hans (U.S.A.)

KOLTANOWSKI, George (U.S.A.)
LASKER, Edward (U.S.A.)
SPANN, Jerry G. (U.S.A.)

International Referees (Deceased)

HELMS, Hermann (U.S.A.) 1870–1963
SIM, Malcolm (Canada) 1880–1956

WERTHEIM, Maurice (U.S.A.) 1886–1950 *

* Title issued posthumously in 1951.

Titleholders by Countries

The distribution of FIDE titleholders living in the various chess-playing countries of the world is indicated in the following list.

Country	Grandmasters	Masters	Women Masters
Argentina	6	14	3
Australia	–	3	–
Austria	1	4	1
Belgium	1	1	–
Brazil	–	1	–
Bulgaria	3	5	2
Canada	1	3	–
Chile	–	1	1
Colombia	–	3	–
Cuba	–	1	1
Czechoslovakia	3	11	3
Denmark	1	2	1
East Germany	1	6	1
Finland	–	3	–
France	–	1	1
Great Britain	–	7	4
Hungary	5	15	3
Iceland	1	1	–
India	–	1	–
Indonesia	–	1	–
Israel	–	3	–
Italy	–	8	1
Mexico	–	1	–
Netherlands	2	13	1
Norway	–	2	–
Peru	–	2	–
Philippines	–	1	–
Poland	–	5	2
Rumania	1	6	4
Spain	1	3	–
Sweden	1	2	–
Switzerland	–	7	–
U.S.A.	10	12	4
USSR	26	33	11
Venezuela	–	1	–
West Germany	4	12	2
Yugoslavia	12	19	4
Totals	80	214	50

CHAPTER VII

World and National Champions

In this chapter we present a complete record of competition for world and United States chess titles from the year each title originated to the present day. So far as we know, this is the first time that all the details have been included in one publication.

Competition for world chess titles has been held under the auspices of the *Fédération Internationale des Échecs* (FIDE) since 1924. This organization, also known as the World Chess Federation, was founded in Paris in 1924 by Pierre Vincent of France (1878-1956). Dr. Alexander Rueb of the Netherlands (1882-1959) was President from 1924 to 1949, and Maurice S. Kuhns of the United States (1859-1949) was Vice President. Congresses were held each year during this period but were discontinued during World War II. In 1946, the FIDE was reorganized and Mr. Folke Rogard of Stockholm became President in 1949. He has held this office with distinction since that time. Annual Congresses have been held since 1946. More than 60 national chess Federations are now affiliated. In addition to its sponsorship and supervision of competition for various world titles, the FIDE formulates and publishes the Laws of Chess, renders decisions on interpretations of the laws, awards international titles to individuals, and authorizes the publication of the *FIDE Revue* as its official publication. FIDE headquarters are at Strandvagen 41, Stockholm, Sweden.

In the United States, competition for the various national titles has been sponsored by the U. S. Chess Federation (USCF) since 1939, when it was organized as the consolidation of the National and American Chess Federations. As the United States Unit of the FIDE, it conducts zonal tournaments (usually combined with national championships) to qualify players into the Interzonal and Women's Candidates' Tournaments of the FIDE. The USCF conducts a rating system and publishes its official organ, *Chess Life,* monthly. Headquarters are at 80 East 11th Street, New York, N. Y.

WORLD CHESS CHAMPIONS

There have been many outstanding players in the long history of chess, but Wilhelm Steinitz, a native of Prague, was the first to bear the official title of World Chess Champion. He won the title in 1886 by defeating Dr. J. H. Zukertort in the first match for the championship of the world.

Before Steinitz, the unofficial world champions were Howard Staunton of England, Adolph Anderssen of Germany, and Paul Morphy of the United States. In 1843, Staunton established himself as the world's leading player by defeating Pierre de Saint-Amant of France in a match which is generally considered as the first to be held under the strict conditions of championship competition, even though a title was not actually at stake. Then Anderssen displaced Staunton by winning the world's first international chess tournament (London, 1851) and scoring notable successes thereafter. In 1858, Paul Morphy went to Europe and defeated in matches all the players he encountered, including Anderssen. During his brief chess career, Morphy was undoubtedly the strongest player in the world.

After Morphy's retirement, Anderssen again became the unofficial world champion. Then, in 1866, Wilhelm Steinitz dethroned Anderssen by defeating him in a set match held in London. Steinitz reigned supreme for twenty-eight years thereafter, defeating all comers until he was finally overthrown by Dr. Emanuel Lasker in 1894.

The Steinitz-Zukertort contest was the first of a long series of world championship matches, listed below. After Steinitz, the title was held successively by Dr. Emanuel Lasker (1894 to 1921), Jose R. Capablanca (1921 to 1927), Alexander Alekhine (1927 to 1935), Dr. Max Euwe (1935 to 1937), and again by Alekhine (1937 to 1946).

1886	Steinitz-Zukertort	10-5	5 drawn
1889	Steinitz-Tchigorin	10-6	1 drawn
1891	Steinitz-Gunsberg	6-4	9 drawn
1892	Steinitz-Tchigorin	10-8	5 drawn
1894	Lasker-Steinitz	10-5	4 drawn
1896	Lasker-Steinitz	10-2	5 drawn
1907	Lasker-Marshall	8-0	8 drawn
1908	Lasker-Tarrasch	8-3	5 drawn
1910	Lasker-Janowski	7-1	2 drawn
1910	Lasker-Schlechter	1-1	8 drawn

1921	Capablanca-Lasker	4-0	10 drawn
1927	Alekhine-Capablanca	6-3	25 drawn
1929	Alekhine-Bogolyubov	11-5	9 drawn
1934	Alekhine-Bogolyubov	8-3	15 drawn
1935	Euwe-Alekhine	9-8	13 drawn
1937	Alekhine-Euwe	11-6	13 drawn

Alekhine died on March 24, 1946, on the eve of a scheduled match with Russia's Mikhail Botvinnik for the world title. This left the status of the world championship in confusion. Did the title revert to ex-champion Euwe, or could Botvinnik claim the title? Should a tournament be held, and if so, who should play in it?

As often happens in such cases, our present system of world championship competition was developed among much strife and tribulation. The World Chess Federation took quick action and announced in July, 1946, that a four-round match-tournament for the world title would be held in the Netherlands in 1947. Botvinnik, Euwe, Fine, Keres, Reshevsky and Smyslov were seeded, and if the winners of the Groningen and Prague tournaments of 1946 were not among the seeded players, they would be allowed to compete with the others for the world title. (Botvinnik won at Groningen, Najdorf at Prague, but the latter did not play in the world title tournament.)

At the same time, the FIDE announced the adoption of a "three-year-cycle" plan for world championship competition in substantially the same form as the system now in existence. The first cycle would start with the year 1947, when preliminary zonal tournaments would be held in the seven zones into which the world was then divided. (At that time, the zones were: 1st European; 2nd European, USSR; 3rd European; U.S.A.; Canada; Central America; South America.) In 1948, the second year of the first cycle, the qualifiers from the zonal tournaments would compete in an Interzonal Tournament. In 1949, the third year of the cycle, there would be a tournament of world championship candidates, comprising the five top players from the Interzonal Tournament and the unsuccessful players from the world title tourney of 1947. In 1950, the winner of the Candidates' Tournament would play a title match with the World Champion (who had earned his title in 1947). In the same year, the second three-year cycle would begin with zonal tournaments.

It is surprising that this plan survived, for there were immediate howls of complaint from all directions. The USCF protested that

Americans had not been given notice of the FIDE meeting at which the decisions were reached, and that our players had no chance to compete at Prague. Vice President Giers of the USCF cabled Dr. Rueb of the FIDE that the USCF had the prerogative of selecting American candidates for the world title tourney and would do so after the forthcoming U. S. Championship. *Chess Review* editorialized that the three-year-cycle scheme "is so complicated that its practicality is very questionable." Botvinnik claimed that a Dutch newspaper had said the Soviet players might work together to put him in first place; he angrily declared that he would not play for the championship in the Netherlands. The Russians wanted the tournament to be held in April; Reuben Fine preferred August. The tournament organizers in the Netherlands saw costs rising steadily.

What with one thing and another, the FIDE backed down completely, withdrew from the organization of the world title tournament, and abandoned its plan for world championship competition. At that time, the FIDE was a relatively weak organization, which makes it even more surprising that the suggested plan was eventually adopted. The 1946 Congress, at which the decisions were first made, was attended by the delegates of only eight countries. The USSR was not affiliated, and the U.S.A. was not represented.

In June of 1947, the world championship situation being still unsettled, Dr. Euwe suggested that Botvinnik assume the title so that candidates would not have to "fight ghosts," but would have someone to challenge. Finally, at the FIDE Congress of 1947, held at The Hague, the tangle was straightened out. The USSR Chess Federation joined the FIDE, and the delegates, including one each from the USSR and the U.S.A., agreed that a title match-tournament of four rounds would be held as originally planned, the six participants being Botvinnik, Euwe, Fine, Keres, Reshevsky, and Smyslov. The idea of qualifying the winner of the Prague tournament was abandoned. Of necessity, the tournament was scheduled for 1948 instead of 1947, and it was decided to play the first half in the Netherlands, the second half in the Soviet Union. The FIDE also revived its three-year-cycle plan for world championship competition, to begin in 1947.

World Championship Tournament, The Hague-Moscow, 1948

The World Championship Tournament began at The Hague on March 1, 1948. All seeded players except Reuben Fine participated.

Fine declined so that he could continue his graduate studies in California. As a result, the five Grandmasters agreed to play five complete rounds instead of the four rounds originally scheduled. This meant that each contestant would play 20 games. The time limit: 40 moves in 2½ hours. Playing sessions: 5.30 to 10.30 P.M., three times a week. Each competitor was allowed a second. Referee was the late Dr. Milan Vidmar of Yugoslavia.

At the end of the first two laps, Botvinnik was leading with 6–2; Reshevsky was in second place with 4½–3½; Keres and Smyslov were tied at 4–4; Dr. Euwe was in last place with 1½–6½. Then the contestants departed for Moscow in a special train. The third lap started on April 11th. By the end of the fourth lap, Botvinnik had taken a commanding lead of 12–4, with Reshevsky and Smyslov tied for second and third with 8½–7½. The last lap was an anticlimax. The contest resulted in a decisive win for Botvinnik, as shown below:

Match-Tourney, 1948	Botvinnik	Smyslov	Keres	Reshevsky	Euwe	Total
1. Botvinnik	....	½ ½ 1 ½ ½	1 1 1 1 0	1 ½ 0 1 1	1 ½ 1 ½ ½	14
2. Smyslov	½ ½ 0 ½ ½	....	0 0 ½ 1 ½	½ ½ 1 ½ ½	1 1 0 1 1	11
3. Keres	0 0 0 0 1	1 1 ½ 0 ½	....	0 ½ 1 0 ½	1 ½ 1 1 1	10½
4. Reshevsky	0 ½ 1 0 0	½ ½ 0 ½ ½	1 ½ 0 1 ½	....	1 ½ ½ 1 1	10½
5. Euwe	0 ½ 0 ½ ½	0 0 1 0 0	0 ½ 0 0 0	0 ½ ½ 0 0	....	4

Soviet Superman Mikhail Botvinnik, born in St. Petersburg (now Leningrad) on August 17, 1911, was the new World Champion. As the outstanding contender, he had earned the title. In 1931, when only 20 years old, he won the seventh USSR Championship. Up to 1948, his greatest successes were at Moscow, 1935, where he tied for first with Salo Flohr ahead of Lasker and Capablanca; Nottingham, 1936, where he tied with Capablanca ahead of Euwe, Fine, Reshevsky, Alekhine, Lasker, and Flohr; Groningen, 1946, first ahead of Euwe, Smyslov, Najdorf, etc. Between 1941 and 1947, he had won first prizes in all of the seven tournaments in which he competed. The Hague-Moscow event made it eight in a row. After winning the title, Botvinnik had a long and distinguished career as World Champion.

The first world championship cycle started in 1947, as originally planned. A zonal tournament was not held in the United States, but the rules permitted players to be nominated into the Interzonal by the affiliated Federations. The USCF named Isaac Kashdan and raised the considerable sum of $1000.00 to pay his expenses, but Kashdan felt that this was not enough and decided not to play. Arnold Denker was chosen by the FIDE as the second U. S. representative, but he declined because he would have had to pay all his own expenses.

With no American players, the first Interzonal Tournament was held in July, 1948, at Saltsjobaden, Sweden, with the following results:

1st Interzonal Tournament, Saltsjobaden, 1948

David Bronstein (USSR)	13½	Eero E. Book (Fin.)	9½
Laszlo Szabo (Hung.)	12½	Svetozar Gligoric (Yugo.)	9½
Isaac Boleslavsky (USSR)	12	Vasja Pirc (Yugo.)	9½
Alexander Kotov (USSR)	11½	Viacheslav Ragozin (USSR)	8½
Andrei Lilienthal (USSR)	11	Dan A. Yanofsky (Canada)	8½
Igor Bondarevsky (USSR)	10½	Dr. X. Tartakover (France)	8
Salo Flohr (USSR)	10½	Ludek Pachman (Czech.)	7½
Miguel Najdorf (Arg.)	10½	Gosta Stoltz (Sweden)	6½
Gideon Stahlberg (Sweden)	10½	Lajos Steiner (Austral.)	5½
Dr. Petar Trifunovic (Yugo.)	10	Erik Lundin (Sweden)	4½

It was a landslide for the Soviet players. The world of chess was astonished to see such famous players as Najdorf and Stahlberg out of the running. The top five in this tournament qualified for the Candidates' Tournament, to compete with Smyslov, Keres, Reshevsky, and Euwe, the unsuccessful participants in the 1947 World Championship Tournament, and Reuben Fine, who was also seeded. However, Reshevsky and Fine could not participate because the State Department banned U. S. citizens from entering Hungary, where the Candidates' Tournament was to be held, and Dr. Euwe could not obtain leave from his teaching duties. The four players who tied with 10½ points in the Interzonal were then allowed to play in the Candidates', but Bondarevsky's ill health prevented him from taking part. Consequently, ten contestants played two complete rounds in the first Candidates' Tournament of the three-year cycle plan, with the following results:

1st Candidates' Tournament, Budapest, 1950

Isaac Boleslavsky (USSR)	12	Alexander Kotov (USSR)	8½
David Bronstein (USSR)	12	Gideon Stahlberg (Sweden)	8
Vassily Smyslov (USSR)	10	Salo Flohr (USSR)	7
Paul Keres (USSR)	9½	Andrei Lilienthal (USSR)	7
Miguel Najdorf (Arg.)	9	Laszlo Szabo (Hung.)	7

The 1950 FIDE Congress at Copenhagen ruled that Boleslavsky and Bronstein must play a twelve-game match for the right to challenge the champion. If the match were indecisive after twelve games, two more games were to be played, and then, if necessary, single sudden-death games until the tie was broken. The match went to fourteen games, and was won by Bronstein who scored 3 wins, 2 losses, and 9 draws.

Botvinnik-Bronstein Championship Match, Moscow, 1951

Starting March 15, 1951, Botvinnik and Bronstein played a twenty-four-game match for the world championship. The match went down to the wire. After 22 games, Bronstein led by one point and could have won the match by drawing the last two, but the champion rallied to win the 23rd, then drew the 24th to tie the match and retain his title. The FIDE rules specify that the challenger must win the match to displace the champion.

Beginning the second three-year cycle, zonal tournaments were held in various parts of the world during the year 1951. The United States did not stage a zonal tournament, but this country was represented in the Interzonal by Herman Steiner of Los Angeles, who held the U. S. Championship title 1948–1950. In 1952, the second Interzonal Tournament was held at Stockholm and Saltsjobaden, Sweden, with the results tabled below:

2nd Interzonal Tournament, Stockholm-Saltsjobaden, 1952

Alexander Kotov (USSR)	16½	Herman Pilnik (Arg.)	10
Tigran Petrosian (USSR)	13½	Herman Steiner (U.S.A.)	10
Mark Taimanov (USSR)	13½	Alexander Matanovic (Yugo.)	9
Ewfim Geller (USSR)	13	Gedeon Barcza (Hung.)	8
Yuri Averbach (USSR)	12½	Gosta Stoltz (Sweden)	7½
Svetozar Gligoric (Yugo.)	12½	Luis Sanchez (Colombia)	7
Gideon Stahlberg (Sweden)	12½	R. G. Wade (N. Z.)	6
Laszlo Szabo (Hung.)	12½	P. Vaitonis (Canada)	5
Wolfgang Unzicker (W. Ger.)	11½	Harry Golombek (Gt. Brit.)	4½
Erich Eliskases (Arg.)	10½	Lodewijk Prins (Neth.)	4½
Ludek Pachman (Czech.)	10		

It was a clean sweep for the Soviet entrants, for the tie among the fifth to eighth places was broken under the Sonnenborn-Berger system in favor of Averbach. The five Soviet players were the only qualifiers from this event and would compete with seeded players Bronstein, Boleslavsky, Euwe, Keres, Najdorf, Reshevsky, and Smyslov in the Candidates' Tournament. This meant that the Candidates' would comprise nine Soviet players and only three from other countries (Euwe, Najdorf, and Reshevsky). Reshevsky protested and refused to play. Then FIDE allowed Gligoric, Stahlberg, and Szabo, who had tied with Averbach in the Interzonal, to enter the Candidates' Tournament. Reshevsky agreed to compete, with some misgivings.

It was felt by many in the Western world that the Soviet players at Saltsjobaden had ganged up on the players from other countries to ensure a practically all-Russian participation in the next Candidates' Tournament. In this country, *Chess Review* claimed that there had been "undeniable collusion by the Russians in a move to freeze out Western competitors." The Australian *Chess World,* speaking of the next Candidates' Tournament, said that "we fear the Russians would put patriotism above the canons of sport, as at Saltsjobaden, and make things a bit easier for the top Russian." These accusations were mainly based on the fact that the five Soviet players at the Interzonal drew all their games with each other. Most of these games were short "Grandmaster" draws, presumably agreed upon in advance.

The largest, most expensive, and possibly the most criticized Candidates' Tournament ever held was staged in Switzerland in 1953. The fifteen contestants played two complete rounds—a total of 28 games for each player. The results are tabled below:

2nd Candidates' Tournament, Neuhausen-Zurich, 1953

Vassily Smyslov (USSR)	18	Mark Taimanov (USSR)	14
David Bronstein (USSR)	16	Yuri Averbach (USSR)	13½
Paul Keres (USSR)	16	Isaac Boleslavsky (USSR)	13½
Samuel Reshevsky (U.S.A.)	16	Laszlo Szabo (Hung.)	13
Tigran Petrosian (USSR)	15	Svetozar Gligoric (Yugo.)	12½
Ewfim Geller (USSR)	14½	Dr. Max Euwe (Neth.)	11½
Miguel Najdorf (Arg.)	14½	Gideon Stahlberg (Sweden)	8
Alexander Kotov (USSR)	14		

Smyslov won the tournament, but Sammy Reshevsky was in there fighting all the way against difficult odds. He tied with Bronstein and Keres for second place—the only non-Russian in the top five. Although he put up a great fight, Reshevsky decided that the conditions were too tough and did not again compete in world championship competitions until 1963. One of his greatest handicaps was the fact that he was the only player in this tournament without a second. When the nine Soviet players arrived in Switzerland they were accompanied by seventeen non-playing officials, including nine Grandmasters who would serve as seconds to the Russian players. Sammy arrived with his wife and two children, but with nobody to help him in the analysis of adjourned games, or the preparation for others.

It was claimed by many that the Soviet players were again guilty of collusion. However, if the USSR players had agreed to boost Smyslov's chances by losing to him, or drawing with him, Alexander Kotov must have been bawled out by the USSR officials, for he had the temerity to beat Smyslov in one game when Smyslov was in the lead, just ahead of Reshevsky, and Kotov himself had no chance for first place. He made up for this lapse in a later round by defeating Reshevsky. (Kotov did the same thing at Groningen in 1946 when he defeated Botvinnik and then won from Euwe. Perhaps he was given the role of the orange pip in the synthetic orangeade, put in to prove the mixture was genuine.) Against the other Russians, Smyslov defeated Keres and Geller twice each, drew all his games with Bronstein, Petrosian, Taimanov, and Averbach.

Botvinnik-Smyslov Championship Match, Moscow, 1954

Smyslov and Botvinnik played a twenty-four game title match in Moscow, starting March 14, 1954. After the 19th game, Botvinnik had a two-point lead and it was considered almost certain that he would win the match, but Smyslov won two of the last five games and the match was drawn. Again Botvinnik retained his title on a tied match.

The 1953 Candidates' Tournament was an expensive affair. It cost the Swiss Chess Federation more than 100,000 Swiss francs. Consequently, the FIDE voted in 1953 to limit the Candidates' Tournament of 1956 to seven contestants, viz., the winner of the previous

Candidates' Tournament (or the runner-up, if the winner had become the World Champion) and the six players who made the best scores in the 1955 Interzonal. New regulations were also adopted covering the procedure to be followed in the arrangements for the world championship match of 1957. Among other rules, it was stipulated that the current champion, if he lost the title in 1954, could take part in a triangular match with the new champion and the challenger qualified from the 1956 Candidates' Tournament.

In correspondence with the FIDE President, Botvinnik criticized some of these new regulations. He felt it was not right to seed only one player from the previous Candidates' Tournament, that a place should be reserved for an ex-champion who had just lost his title. He commented that the number of players in the 1953 Candidates' Tournament had been increased to fifteen in order to make the contest more international in character, and suggested that this result could be achieved by restricting the number of players from any one country.

As a result of these criticisms and other discussions, the FIDE Congress of 1955 decided to seed Smyslov (who in the meantime had drawn his match with Botvinnik) into the Candidates' Tournament of 1956, together with nine players from the Interzonal of 1955. The ten players would compete in a double round tournament. The FIDE also seeded Reshevsky, Bronstein, and Keres into the 1955 Interzonal.

For the future, the Congress decided that, beginning in 1959, the Candidates' Tournament would comprise seven participants, to play four complete rounds, and that the number of players from any one country would be limited to four. The contestants would include five from the previous Interzonal and two from the previous Candidates. However, one of the latter two places would be given instead to a player who had, in the meantime, become ex-champion.

The third championship cycle had started in 1954, when zonal tournaments were held. The United States Championship of that year was also the zonal tournament to qualify two players from this country. U. S. Champion Arthur Bisguier and runner-up Larry Evans, together with Reshevsky, became eligible to play in the 1955 Interzonal Tournament. However, Bisguier was our only representative. Evans and Reshevsky preferred to play in the U. S. Open of that year.

The Interzonal was held at Gothenburg, Sweden, in October of 1955. The results are given below:

3rd Interzonal Tournament, Gothenburg, 1955

David Bronstein (USSR)	15	Carlos E. Guimard (Arg.)	9½
Paul Keres (USSR)	13½	Miguel Najdorf (Arg.)	9½
Oscar Panno (Arg.)	13	Andrija Fuderer (Yugo.)	9
Tigran Petrosian (USSR)	12½	Braslav Rabar (Yugo.)	9
Ewfim Geller (USSR)	12	Wolfgang Unzicker (W. Ger.)	8½
Laszlo Szabo (Hung.)	12	Arthur B. Bisguier (U.S.A.)	8
Miroslav Filip (Czech.)	11	Gideon Stahlberg (Sweden)	8
Herman Pilnik (Arg.)	11	Jan H. Donner (Neth.)	5½
Boris Spassky (USSR)	11	Antonio Medina (Spain)	5½
Georgy Ilivitsky (USSR)	10½	Bogdan Sliwa (Poland)	5½
Ludek Pachman (Czech.)	10½		

The top nine players in this tournament, together with seeded player Vassily Smyslov, took part in the third Candidates' Tournament, held at Amsterdam (16 rounds) and Leeuwarden (2 rounds) from March 27 to May 1, 1956. The contestants played two complete laps with the following results:

3rd Candidates' Tournament, Netherlands, 1956

Vassily Smyslov (USSR)	11½	Boris Spassky (USSR)	9½
Paul Keres (USSR)	10	Laszlo Szabo (Hung.)	9½
David Bronstein (USSR)	9½	Miroslav Filip (Czech.)	8
Ewfim Geller (USSR)	9½	Oscar Panno (Arg.)	8
Tigran Petrosian (USSR)	9½	Herman Pilnik (Arg.)	5

Smyslov-Botvinnik Championship Matches, Moscow, 1957 & 1958

In a scheduled 24-game match, held in Moscow, March 5 to April 28, 1957, challenger Smyslov defeated Botvinnik by a score of 12½ to 9½ and won the title of World Champion.

Under the FIDE Rules, revised again in 1956, a defeated champion was permitted to challenge the winner to a return match. This match was held in Moscow, March 4 to May 9, 1958. Botvinnik regained his title, defeating Smyslov by a score of 12½ to 10½.

The fourth world championship cycle began with the zonal tournaments of 1957. The United States Championship of that year, played from December 17, 1957, to January 8, 1958, was named as the zonal tournament by the USCF. This contest saw the advent of

Bobby Fischer as U. S. Champion at the age of 14. Fischer and Reshevsky qualified to play in the Interzonal of 1958, but Reshevsky declined, and his place was taken by James T. Sherwin, who had finished third. Pal Benko, who became a resident of the United States (and later a citizen), qualified from the West European zonal tournament.

In August of 1958, the 4th Interzonal was held at Portoroz, Yugoslavia, with the following results:

4th Interzonal Tournament, Portoroz, 1958

Mikhail Tal (USSR)	13½	Miroslav Filip (Czech.)	11
Svetozar Gligoric (Yugo.)	13	Oscar Panno (Arg.)	11
Pal Benko (U.S.A.)	12½	Raul Sanguineti (Arg.)	10
Tigran Petrosian (USSR)	12½	Oleg N. Neikirch (Bulg.)	9½
Robert J. Fischer (U.S.A.)	12	Bent Larsen (Den.)	8½
Fridrik Olafsson (Iceland)	12	James T. Sherwin (U.S.A.)	7½
Yuri Averbach (USSR)	11½	Hector Rossetto (Arg.)	7
David Bronstein (USSR)	11½	Rodolfo Cardoso (Phil.)	6
Alexander Matanovic (Yugo.)	11½	Boris de Greiff (Colombia)	4½
Ludek Pachman (Czech.)	11½	Geza Fuster (Canada)	2
Laszlo Szabo (Hung.)	11½		

The top six players in this Interzonal, together with seeded players Vassily Smyslov and Paul Keres, met in the 4th Candidates' Tournament in Yugoslavia, September 6 to October 31, 1959. The United States was represented by Pal Benko and 15-year-old Bobby Fischer, the youngest player in history to earn the title of International Grandmaster.

The number of participants in the Candidates' Tournament was the result of regulations adopted by the FIDE Congress of 1955 and revised by the Congress of 1956. At the latter, it was decided to qualify five players from the Interzonal and two players from the previous Candidates' Tournament. (However, one of the two latter places would be taken instead by an ex-champion who had just lost his title, or by the player who had just drawn his match with the World Champion.) The rules also permitted, in exceptional circumstances, the nomination of an eighth player. This nomination was made because the contestants at the Interzonal had agitated for more qualifiers. Later, at the 1959 Congress, the rules were amended to make mandatory the qualification of six players from the Interzonal.

The final results after four complete rounds:

4th Candidates' Tournament, Bled, Zagreb, & Belgrade, 1959

Mikhail Tal (USSR)	20	Robert J. Fischer (U.S.A.)	12½
Paul Keres (USSR)	18½	Svetozar Gligoric (Yugo.)	12½
Tigran Petrosian (USSR)	15½	Fridrik Olafsson (Iceland)	10
Vassily Smyslov (USSR)	15	Pal Benko (U.S.A.)	8

Mikhail Tal, 22, won the right to play a title match with World Champion Botvinnik. Although Bobby Fischer did not do as well as he had hoped, he finished with plus scores against Benko and Olafsson, even scores of 2–2 against Keres, Smyslov, and Gligoric. The only players who defeated him were Petrosian (3–1) and Tal (4–0).

Tal-Botvinnik Championship Matches, Moscow, 1960 & 1961

The Tal-Botvinnik match was held in Moscow from March 15 to May 10, 1960. At the end of 18 of the 24 scheduled games, Tal led by 10½–7½. The 19th game was postponed for several days. For the second time during the match, Botvinnik requested a five-day adjournment because of illness. After the match was resumed, Tal clinched the title by forcing a draw in 17 moves of the 21st game. The final score was 12½–8½. Mikhail Tal became World Champion at the age of 23. However, Botvinnik challenged Tal to a return match, which ended on May 12, 1961. Botvinnik won the match by the convincing score of 13 to 8, thus regaining his title for the second time, a feat that had never before been achieved in world championship. According to new FIDE rules, this would be the last time that a defeated World Champion would have the right to a return match. If a champion lost his title he would be seeded into the next Candidates' Tournament and would have to earn the right to play a title match with the new champion.

The fifth cycle began with the zonal tournaments of 1960. By this time the number of Federations affiliated with the FIDE had increased to more than fifty, and the number of zones had been increased to nine, as follows: Zone 1—West Europe; Zone 2—Central Europe; Zone 3—Eastern Europe; Zone 4—USSR; Zone 5—U.S.A.; Zone 6—Canada; Zone 7—Central America; Zone 8—South America; Zone 9—Asia.

The 1960-61 U. S. Championship was the zonal tournament for this country. It was again won by Bobby Fischer, with William Lombardy and Raymond Weinstein placing second and third. However, Lombardy and Weinstein were unable to go to the next Interzonal, and their places were taken by Bisguier and Benko.

There was considerable delay in arranging the 5th Interzonal. It was originally supposed to be held in the Netherlands during 1961, but the sponsors were unable to promise the securing of visas for all participants. Attempts to hold the tournament in Moscow, and then Madrid, also collapsed. The tournament was finally held early in 1962 at Stockholm under the direct sponsorship of the FIDE itself. The results are tabled below:

5th Interzonal Tournament, Stockholm, 1962

Robert J. Fischer (U.S.A.)	17½	Julio Bolbochan (Arg.)	11½
Ewfim Geller (USSR)	15	Istvan Bilek (Hung.)	11
Tigran Petrosian (USSR)	15	Gedeon Barcza (Hung.)	11
Miroslav Filip (Czech.)	14	Arthur B. Bisguier (U.S.A.)	9½
Victor Korchnoi (USSR)	14	M. Bertok (Yugo.)	7½
Pal Benko (U.S.A.)	13½	Dan A. Yanofsky (Canada)	7½
Svetozar Gligoric (Yugo.)	13½	Eugenio German (Brazil)	7
Leonid Stein (USSR)	13½	Samuel Schweber (Arg.)	7
Lajos Portisch (Hung.)	12½	Rudolf Teschner (W. Ger.)	6½
Wolfgang Uhlmann (E. Ger.)	12½	Miguel Cuellar (Colombia)	5½
Fridrik Olafsson (Iceland)	12	Manuel Aaron (India)	4
Arturo Pomar (Spain)	12		

It was an outstanding triumph for Bobby Fischer, who finished in first place, 2½ points ahead of a field including some of the strongest players in the world. The top five players qualified, and a three-way match was held among Benko, Gligoric, and Stein for the sixth place. In the double round contest, Stein scored 3 points, Benko 2½, and Gligoric ½. Although Stein won, he was not allowed to play in the Candidates' Tournament. Whereas the FIDE regulations passed in 1956 for the 1957-1959 cycle restricted to four the number of players from any one Federation who could participate in the Candidates' Tournament, the rules adopted in 1959 for the 1960-1962 cycle limited to three the number of players from one Federation who could advance from the Interzonal into the Candidates' Tournament of 1962. Therefore Benko qualified and Stein was in position to play in the Candidates' if Geller, Petrosian or Korchnoi failed to compete.

The six qualifiers from the Interzonal then met with seeded players Tal and Keres in the Candidates' Tournaments at Curaçao.

5th Candidates' Match-Tournament, Curaçao, 1962

Tigran Petrosian (USSR)	17½	Victor Korchnoi (USSR)	13½
Paul Keres (USSR)	17	Pal Benko (U.S.A.)	12
Ewfim Geller (USSR)	17	Mikhail Tal (USSR)	7*
Robert J. Fischer (U.S.A.)	14	Miroslav Filip (Czech.)	7

Bobby Fischer got off to a bad start, losing three of his first five games, including a loss to Benko. He drew up to finish in fourth place.

Petrosian-Botvinnik Championship Match, Moscow, 1963

The match for the World Championship between the titleholder, Dr. Botvinnik, and his challenger, Tigran Petrosian, was held at Moscow from March 23 to May 20, 1963. At first it looked as though Botvinnik would retain his title, since he won the first game in convincing style, and for some time Petrosian could not make up the lost ground. But gradually the advantage veered the other way, and it became apparent that the difference in age between the two players was becoming an increasingly important factor in the contest. Petrosian, 33, had more stamina than Botvinnik, 51. By the time the 19th game was played, Botvinnik was a beaten man. The challenger was three games ahead at 11 to 8 and needed only three draws to win the match. Petrosian then drew the last three games to finish with 12½–9½. So ended a long chapter in the history of the world championship.

Keres and Geller, who tied at Curaçao, played a match for the right to be seeded into the next Candidates' Tournament. The match was won by Keres with a score of 4½–3½.

New Regulations for Candidates' Tournament

Shortly after the conclusion of the 1962 Candidates' Tournament at Curaçao, Bobby Fischer announced that he would boycott FIDE events leading to a world title match. In articles written for *Life* and *Sports Illustrated,* Bobby claimed that the Russians "fixed world chess" by agreeing beforehand to draw with each other and to throw games, if necessary, to ensure a Russian victory.

Probably as a result of Fischer's complaints, the 1962 FIDE Congress voted to change the procedure at future Candidates' Tourna-

* Tal played only 21 games. Illness prevented him from playing the last seven.

ments, beginning in 1965. The changes were proposed by the USSR Federation based on ideas reported to have been suggested by the Yugoslav Federation.

As before, there are to be eight finalists selected under the same rules as those governing the 1962 Candidates' Tournament, but instead of playing a four-lap round robin, the players compete in a knockout match-tournament. First, in the quarter-finals, the eight competitors are paired to play four ten-game matches. The four losers are knocked out and the four winners progress to the two ten-game matches of the semi-finals. In the finals, the two winners of the semi-final matches play a twelve-game match to decide the challenger, and the two losers from the semi-finals play a match to determine the third and fourth places of the tournament.

If any match is tied (except the one to decide third and fourth places), lots are drawn for colors and the match goes into "sudden death" play. However, the winner is decided by a toss-up if a quarter-final match is tied after twelve games, a semi-final match after fourteen games, the final match after twenty games. If the match for third and fourth is tied after the scheduled number of games (usually six, but may be eight or ten under special conditions), the winner is decided by an immediate toss-up.

The regulations provide in detail for the pairings in the quarter-final and semi-final matches. For pairing purposes, the qualified contestants are numbered from 1 to 8. Ordinarily, the winner and runner-up of the previous Candidates' Tournament are Nos. 1 and 2, respectively. However, the No. 1 player may be the previous World Champion, who has just lost his title, or the player who has just drawn his match with the World Champion, in which case the winner of the previous Candidates' Tournament becomes No. 2 and the runner-up is eliminated. Numbers 3 to 8 are given to the six qualifiers from the Interzonal Tournament in the order in which they finished. (If there are tied scores, the order among the tied players is decided either by lot or by Sonnenborn-Berger points.) Lots are drawn for the pairings of the quarter-finals so that each of the players numbered 1 to 4 meets one of the players numbered 5 to 8. Immediately thereafter, lots are drawn to determine the pairings of the quarter-final winners who will meet in the semi-final matches.

If possible, the quarter-final matches are to be arranged simultaneously and in the same place, and are to be followed, after a week of rest, by the semi-finals. However, the FIDE President can make exceptions to this arrangement. The final match of the series must start not more than two months after the end of the semi-finals.

The zonal tournaments of 1963 started the sixth world championship cycle 1963-1965. The world was now divided into ten zones, the ninth being West Asia, the tenth East Asia. The U. S. Championship of 1962-63 was the zonal tournament for the United States. Under FIDE rules, three players could qualify from this tournament into the Interzonal of 1964. Again Bobby Fischer won the U. S. title —for the fifth time. Bisguier placed second and there was a three-way tie for third among Addison, Evans, and Reshevsky. To break the tie, a double-round playoff was held in Los Angeles. It was won by Reshevsky (3-1) who thus qualified as the third representative in the next Interzonal.

Although the new FIDE regulations make collusion impossible in the Candidates' Tournament, and although the rules covering the Interzonal specify that contestants from the same country must play each other as early in the tournament as possible, Bobby Fischer refused to play in the 1964 Interzonal, thereby giving up any chance to play for the world title during this cycle. He has given many reasons for this decision, changing them frequently. It is doubtful that he actually feared collusion in the Interzonal, for he had demonstrated twice that he is quite capable of qualifying for the Candidates' Tournament even if it is true that the Soviet players helped each other by agreeing to short draws.

Fischer's place was taken by Larry Evans. Then Bisguier played a match with Pal Benko and lost decisively. The stakes were $1000.00 to the winner, $500.00 to the loser, with the stipulation that the winner would represent the United States at the Interzonal. This peculiar arrangement was agreed to by Jerry Spann, the FIDE Vice President for the United States. As a result, Benko took Bisguier's place in the Interzonal. Reshevsky, now 52 years old, returned to world championship competition for the first time since 1953.

Ex-champion Mikhail Tal was seeded. The other 23 contestants qualified from ten zonal tournaments held all over the world. The big event was staged in Amsterdam and started on May 20, 1964. The final results are shown in the table on the next page.

6th Interzonal Tournament, Amsterdam, 1964

Vassily Smyslov (USSR)	17	Ludek Pachman (Czech.)	12½
Bent Larsen (Den.)	17	Larry Evans (U.S.A.)	10
Boris Spassky (USSR)	17	Georgi P. Tringov (Bulg.)	9½
Mikhail Tal (USSR)	17	Pal Benko (U.S.A.)	9
Leonid Stein (USSR)	16½	Hector Rossetto (Arg.)	8
David Bronstein (USSR)	16	Alberto Foguelman (Arg.)	8
Borislav Ivkov (Yugo.)	15	Istvan Bilek (Hung.)	8
Lajos Portisch (Hung.)	14½	Oscar Quinones (Peru)	7
Samuel Reshevsky (U.S.A.)	14½	H. Joseph Porath (Israel)	5½
Svetozar Gligoric (Yugo.)	14	Francisco Perez (Cuba)	5
Klaus Darga (W. Ger.)	13½	Bela Berger (Austral.)	4½
Levente Lengyel (Hung.)	13	Zionko Vranesic (Canada)	4

Smyslov, Larsen, Spassky, Tal, Ivkov and Portisch qualified from this tournament to compete with seeded players Botvinnik and Keres in the sixth Candidates' Tournament. Although Stein and Bronstein finished ahead of Ivkov and Portisch, the FIDE regulations do not permit more than three players from any Federation to qualify from the Interzonal. Portisch and Reshevsky tied for the sixth qualification spot and played a four-game match to break the tie. Since Reshevsky was ahead on Sonnenborn-Berger points, he just needed to draw the match to qualify. However, he lost the first game on time, drew the second, lost the third, and Portisch won the match. Reshevsky was eliminated.

Stein and Bronstein, after playing 23 grueling rounds and finishing fifth and sixth, felt it was unfair that players who finished below them were qualified ahead of them. Bronstein proposed to the FIDE President that the number of players in the 1965 Candidates' Tournament be increased from eight to sixteen, including the ex-champion, three from the 1962 Candidates' and twelve from the 1964 Interzonal. This would mean that Botvinnik, Keres, Geller, Fischer, and the top twelve in the 1964 Interzonal would be qualified.

This proposal was submitted in a letter to all affiliated Federations and thoroughly discussed at the 1964 FIDE Congress in Tel Aviv. The delegate of the USSR, among others, felt that no change should be made in regulations which had been adopted for the series of interdependent contests during the three-year cycle 1963-1965. The General Assembly decided by all votes except two to retain the regulations passed in 1962 for the Candidates' Match-Tournament of 1965.

6th Candidates' Knock-Out Match-Tourney, 1965

In 1965 Botvinnik announced that he would not play in the Candidates' Match-Tournament; he objected to the FIDE policy on world championship competition, especially "the annulment of the traditional right of the beaten world champion to a return match." The ex-champion's place was taken by Ewfim Geller, who had tied with Keres in the previous Candidates' at Curaçao.

The pairings of the quarter-final matches were as follows:

Section One: Smyslov vs. Geller and Keres vs. Spassky
Section Two: Tal vs. Portisch and Larsen vs. Ivkov

The Smyslov-Geller match ended in Moscow on April 29th with a surprising victory for Geller by a score of 5½–2½. Former World Champion Smyslov failed to win a single game. Geller won the first, third, and fifth; the other five were drawn. The last two scheduled games were not played, Geller being 3 points ahead.

The Keres-Spassky match began at Riga, capital of Latvia, on April 27th. Although Keres won the first game, and the second was drawn, Spassky forged ahead by winning the third, fourth, and fifth encounters. The sixth and seventh were drawn. Going into the tenth and last game, Spassky led 5–4. In the final game Keres overstepped the time limit in a complicated position and Spassky won the match with a score of 6–4.

In the semi-final match of this section of the tournament, held at Riga from May 27th to June 8th, Spassky turned the tables on Geller by defeating him 5½–2½, the same score with which Geller had upset Smyslov. In this match Geller did not win a single game. Spassky won the second, sixth, and eighth games; five were drawn. At the end of the eighth and last game, Spassky was 3 up and 2 to go.

The quarter-final matches of the second section were held at Bled, Yugoslavia, during June and July. Former World Champion Mikhail Tal and Bent Larsen of Denmark were the victors, each winning by the one-sided score of 5½–2½. Then Tal and Larsen met in the semi-final encounter of this section, starting on July 23rd and ending on August 6th. This was the most exciting of all the matches and was not decided until the tenth and last game. Larsen won the first, Tal the second; the third and fourth were drawn. Then Larsen won the fifth, Tal the sixth. The seventh, eighth, and ninth were drawn, so the two contestants went into the final game with equal scores of 4½–4½ each. The tenth was the most dramatic game of the match. Tal made a brilliant positional sacrifice at his 16th move, followed up with another piece sacrifice at his 34th move. Larsen resigned after White's 37th move and Tal won the match by a score of 5½–4½.

The final twelve-game match of the tournament, between Boris Spassky and Mikhail Tal, started in Tiflis, capital of Georgia in the USSR, on November 1st. The first game was drawn; Tal won the second, Spassky the third. The next five games all ended in draws, two Grandmaster draws and three hard-fought battles. Then Spassky won the last three games of the match to defeat Tal by a final score of 7–4.

The results of the 1965 Candidates' Match-Tourney are summarized below:

Spassky	6	Geller	5½	Tal	5½	Larsen	5½
Keres	4	Smyslov	2½	Portisch	2½	Ivkov	2½

	Spassky	5½		Tal	5½
	Geller	2½		Larsen	4½

		Spassky	7
		Tal	4

Petrosian-Spassky Championship Match, Moscow, 1966

Tigran Petrosian, 36, kept possession of the world title in a 24-game match with Boris Spassky, 29, held in Moscow from May 11 to June 7, 1966. The final score was 12½–11½, but Petrosian clinched the title when he won the 22nd game two up and two to go. The FIDE rules provide that the challenger must defeat the champion to win the title. When he won the 22nd game Petrosian had gained 12 points, making it impossible for Spassky to finish with a plus score. The 23rd and 24th were exhibition games. Spassky defeated the champion in one of these contests; the other was drawn.

The playing sessions of five hours each were held on Mondays, Wednesdays, and Fridays at Moscow's Estrada Theatre, starting at 4.30 P.M. Adjourned games were played on Tuesdays, Thursdays, and Saturdays at the Central Chess Club. A capacity crowd of 1800 spectators attended every game at the theatre.

The rate of play was 40 moves in 2½ hours, with 16 moves every subsequent hour. The World Champion's second was Isaac Boleslavsky, the challenger's Igor Bondarevsky. Alberic O'Kelly de Galway of Belgium was the chief referee, assisted by Dr. Miroslav Filip of Czechoslovakia.

The World Champion had a psychological advantage over his opponent; he could hang on to the title by just drawing every game. He could play safe rather than take unnecessary risks to win games. And it is generally recognized that the champion is a master of defense, an extremely hard man to beat; he demonstrated this quality several times during the match. Spassky, on the other hand, had to take chances and play risky variations. To win the title he had to make a plus score.

The first six games were drawn. The seventh was the only game of the match in which Spassky did not play 1 P-K4 as White. He played 1 P-Q4, then made some weak moves, especially his eleventh. Petrosian seized the opportunity presented to him and proceeded to massacre his opponent with a King-side Pawn advance. The next two games were drawn; then Petrosian went two points up by again defeating the challenger in the tenth. Here the champion, taking advantage of a misplaced Knight and other errors, sacrificed two exchanges and won spectacularly in thirty moves.

When the 11th and 12th games were drawn, the match was half over and Petrosian held the tremendous advantage of being two points ahead. It looked as though he could coast the rest of the way, but Spassky came to life and fought back fiercely. When the 13th game was adjourned, observers considered Petrosian to be "hopelessly lost." Nevertheless, the contest went to 91 moves before the champion conceded defeat. Again, in the 14th game, Spassky was believed to be in a winning position at adjournment; but Petrosian demonstrated his defensive skill and drew the game.

The next four games were drawn. Then Spassky tied up the match by winning the 19th with White. With five games to go, the challenger still had a chance; but Petrosian came right back with a win in the 20th. Again the champion was one up, and the odds were overwhelmingly in his favor when the 21st game was drawn. In the 22nd Spassky could have forced a draw by repetition but at this stage of the match he could not afford another draw; he had to risk failure to play for a win. The attempt failed and Petrosian retained the title.

Future Championship Plans

Although there have been many criticisms of the present system of world championship competition, it was decided at the 1965 FIDE Congress in Wiesbaden to continue the present arrangement with only minor changes. Zonal tournaments were to be held in 1966, the Interzonal in 1967, the same type of Candidates' Match-Tournament in 1968, and the next World Championship Match in 1969.

So far as the complaints of collusion among Soviet players are concerned, it is undoubtedly true that the Soviet contestants in FIDE tournaments, especially in the early competitions, have played as a team and not as individuals. Alexander Kotov admits this in his *Memoirs of a Chessplayer*, published in the USSR in 1960. He apologizes for his victories over Smyslov in 1933 and Botvinnik at Groningen in 1946, and hopes he will be forgiven, since he made up for these lapses by defeating Reshevsky and Euwe respectively in these tournaments.

It is doubtful whether the Soviet players have thrown games, as claimed by Bobby Fischer, but they have certainly played short draws with each other in many tournaments. This may help them in qualifying tournaments such as the Interzonal, in which the top six proceed to the Candidates' Tournament, but it does not help in the Candidates' itself, when it is only the winner who becomes the challenger. In any case, the new type of match-tournament makes collusion impossible.

The FIDE is making a determined effort to prevent unethical players from agreeing in advance to draw their games. The FIDE is also experimenting with methods of eliminating seconds and adjourned game analysis. It is our opinion that the basis for complaints against the Soviet players is gradually disappearing. However, even if we succeed in making it impossible for a player to be unethical or analyze adjourned games, we will still be faced with the problem of how to defeat the Soviet players. The fact remains that they do not have to be unethical to be stronger players than most of their opponents in the rest of the world.

Official World Champions

1886–1894 STEINITZ, Wilhelm (Czechoslovakia)
1894–1921 LASKER, Dr. Emanuel (Germany)
1921–1927 CAPABLANCA, José Raoul (Cuba)
1927–1935 ALEKHINE, Alexander (France)
1935–1937 EUWE, Dr. Max (Netherlands)
1937–1946 ALEKHINE, Alexander (France)
1946–1948 *Vacant*
1948–1957 BOTVINNIK, Mikhail (USSR)
1957–1958 SMYSLOV, Vassily (USSR)
1958–1960 BOTVINNIK, Mikhail (USSR)
1960–1961 TAL, Mikhail (USSR)
1961–1963 BOTVINNIK, Mikhail (USSR)
1963– PETROSIAN, Tigran (USSR)

Winners of World Championship Candidates' Tourneys

Budapest, 1950: BRONSTEIN, David (USSR)
Neuhausen–Zurich, 1953: SMYSLOV, Vassily (USSR)
Amsterdam–Leuwarden, 1956: SMYSLOV, Vassily (USSR)
Bled–Zagreb–Belgrade, 1959: TAL, Mikhail (USSR)
Curaçao, 1962: PETROSIAN, Tigran (USSR)
Moscow–Riga–Bled–Tiflis, 1965: SPASSKY, Boris (USSR)

Winners of FIDE Interzonal Tournaments

Saltsjobaden, 1948: BRONSTEIN, David (USSR)
Stockholm–Saltsjobaden, 1952: KOTOV, Alexander (USSR)
Gothenburg, 1955: BRONSTEIN, David (USSR)
Portoroz, 1958: TAL, Mikhail (USSR)
Stockholm, 1962: FISCHER, Robert J. (U.S.A.)
Amsterdam, 1964: LARSEN, Bent (Denmark); SMYSLOV, Vassily (USSR); SPASSKY, Boris (USSR); TAL, Mikhail (USSR)

WORLD TEAM CHAMPIONSHIPS

The first Chess Olympiad, in which teams representing national chess associations competed, was held in Paris in 1924. There were eighteen teams of three players. The Czechoslovakian team won. Later in the same year, the *Fédération Internationale des Échecs* (FIDE) was inaugurated with headquarters at The Hague.

The first official World Team Championship, for the Hamilton-Russell Trophy, under the auspices of the FIDE, was played in London, 1927. Thereafter, up to the start of World War II, seven World Team Championships were held. In all of these and subsequent FIDE Olympiads, the competing countries were represented by four-man teams; each team was allowed two alternates.

The First Eight Olympiads

No.	Year	Place	Teams	Leading Scorers
1st	1927	London	16	Hungary 40; Denmark 38½; England 36½
2nd	1928	The Hague	17	Hungary 44; U.S.A. 39½; Poland 57
3rd	1930	Hamburg	18	Poland 48½; Hungary 47; Germany 44½ *
4th	1931	Prague	19	U.S.A. 48; Poland 47; Czechoslovakia 46½
5th	1933	Folkestone	15	U.S.A. 39; Czechoslovakia 37½; Poland 34
6th	1935	Warsaw	20	U.S.A. 54; Sweden 52½; Poland 52
7th	1937	Stockholm	19	U.S.A. 54½; Hungary 48½; Poland 47
8th	1939	Buenos Aires	27 **	Germany 36; Poland 35½; Estonia 33½

* U.S.A. sixth with 41½.
** 15 teams in championship finals.

War broke out on the day the championship finals started in Buenos Aires. The British team had qualified, but immediately returned home. At the end of the tournament, South America gained some strong players when Najdorf of Poland, Eliskases of Germany, and some others, did not return to their native lands.

The USSR did not compete in any of the above Olympics. As can be seen by the results, the United States teams were at the top of the heap in those days. The late Frank Marshall, U. S. Champion from 1909 to 1936, led to success such players as Reshevsky, Fine, Kashdan, Dake, Horowitz, Kupchik and Simonson.

9th Olympiad, Dubrovnik, 1950

After the war, world team competition was revived when the 9th Olympiad was held at Dubrovnik, Yugoslavia, August 10 to September 20, 1950. Fifteen teams competed with the following results:

Yugoslavia 45½; Argentina 43½; West Germany 40½; U.S.A. 40; Netherlands 37; Belgium 32; Austria 31½; Chile 30½; France 28½; Finland 28; Sweden 27½; Italy 25; Denmark 22; Peru 21½; Norway 15.

The United States team: Samuel Reshevsky, Herman Steiner, I. A. Horowitz, George Shainswit, George Kramer, Larry Evans. The team was unbeaten, but positions are based on total game points scored.

Since 1950, the World Team Championships have been held regularly at two-year intervals.

10th Olympiad, Helsinki, 1952

Twenty-five teams, including the USSR for the first time, entered the 10th Olympiad at Helsinki. The teams were divided into three preliminary sections. The top three in each group qualified for the Championship Finals, the next three for the Consolation Finals, Group A, the remaining teams for the Consolation Finals, Group B. Results in the finals:

Championship Finals: USSR 21; Argentina 19½; Yugoslavia 19; Czechoslovakia 18; U.S.A. 17; Hungary 16; Sweden 13; West Germany 10½; Finland 10.

Consolation Finals, Group A: Netherlands 21; Israel 19½; East Germany 16½; Poland 16½; Denmark 16; Cuba 15; England 14; Austria 13; Italy 12½.

Consolation Finals, Group B: Brazil 18½; Greece 13½; Norway 13; Switzerland 13; Iceland 12½; The Saar 12½; Luxembourg 1.

There were more strong players in this tournament than ever before. The USSR fielded the most powerful all-Grandmaster team in history up to that time, including Paul Keres, Vassily Smyslov, David Bronstein, Ewfim Geller, and alternates Isaac Boleslavsky, Alexander Kotov. The United States team: Samuel Reshevsky, Larry Evans, Robert Byrne, Arthur Bisguier, and alternates George Koltanowski, Hans Berliner. The USA-USSR teams met in the second round of the finals, finished with tied scores. Reshevsky and Bisguier drew with Keres and Geller; Smyslov defeated Evans; Byrne won from Bronstein. Robert Byrne was hero of the U. S. team at the meet, scoring 5 wins, 3 draws, no losses.

11th Olympiad, Amsterdam, 1954

Twenty-six teams competed in 1954, but the United States did not enter. The teams were organized in four groups for the preliminaries and two groups for the finals. The results are listed below:

Championship Finals: USSR 34; Argentina 27; Yugoslavia 26½; Czechoslovakia 24½; West Germany 23½; Hungary 23; Israel 22; Netherlands 21; England 17; Bulgaria 17; Sweden 15; Iceland 13½.

Consolation Finals: Switzerland 37; Canada 36; Austria 36; Denmark 34½; Italy 28½; Colombia 27½; Belgium 27; Finland 26½; France 26; Saar 24; Norway 22; Greece 21; Ireland 11; Luxembourg 7.

World Champion Mikhail Botvinnik played at board No. 1 for the winning USSR team. The other members of the team were Vassily Smyslov, David Bronstein, Paul Keres, alternates Ewfim Geller and Alexander Kotov. Grandmaster Keres, at board No. 4, scored 13 wins, 1 draw, no losses! Botvinnik led the field of No. 1 board players with 6 wins, 5 draws, no losses. The USSR was demonstrating its chess power. Having won its first two tournaments of this type, the USSR won the next six, for eight in a row (up to 1966).

12th Olympiad, Moscow, 1956

A new record of 34 teams entered in 1956. The teams first competed in four preliminary groups, then finals were played by one group of top three winners, and two consolation groups. The United States did not compete. The results:

Championship Finals: USSR 31; Yugoslavia 26½; Hungary 26½; Argentina 23; West Germany 22; Bulgaria 22; Czechoslovakia 20½; England 20; Switzerland 19; Denmark 19; Rumania 19; Israel 15½.

Consolation Finals, Group A: Austria 28; Iceland 27; Sweden 26½; Belgium 23½; Finland 22½; Colombia 21; Netherlands 21; East Germany 20½; France 19½; Chile 19; Poland 19; Norway 16½.

Consolation Finals, Group B: Philippines 24; The Saar 23; India 20½; Iran 19; Puerto Rico 18½; Mongolia 18½; Scotland 17½; Greece 17; Ireland 13; Luxembourg 9.

The USSR powerhouse team included Botvinnik, Smyslov, Keres, Bronstein, Geller, and Mark Taimanov.

13th Olympiad, Munich, 1958

Again the records were broken as 36 nations, including the United States after a lapse of six years, competed in the 1958 Olympiad. The teams were divided into four preliminary sections. In each section, the top three teams qualified for the Championship Finals, the middle three for the Consolidation Finals, Group A, the bottom three for the Consolation Finals, Group B. The results in the finals:

Championship Finals: USSR 34½; Yugoslavia 29; Argentina 25½; U.S.A. 24; Czechoslovakia 22; East Germany 22; West Germany 22; Switzerland 19; Spain 17½; Bulgaria 17; England 16; Austria 15½.

Consolation Finals, Group A: Hungary 31; Netherlands 28½; Canada 24½; Colombia 24½; Israel 23½; Denmark 23; Poland 22½; Sweden 17; Iceland 16½; Finland 15½; France 14½; Belgium 11.

Consolation Finals, Group B: Norway 30; Philippines 29½; South Africa 28; Italy 26½; Scotland 25½; Greece 25; Portugal 21; Iran 18; Ireland 13½; Tunisia 13; Lebanon 12½; Puerto Rico 11½.

The USSR won by an impressive margin. The winning team included Botvinnik, Smyslov, Keres, and Bronstein, with Mikhail Tal and Tigran Petrosian as alternates! The United States made a good showing. The team included Samuel Reshevsky, William Lombardy, Arthur Bisguier, Larry Evans, and alternate Nicolas Rossolimo. The U. S. and USSR teams met in the first round of the finals. For religious reasons, Reshevsky did not play. Nevertheless, Lombardy, Bisguier, Evans, and Rossolimo all drew their games with the Soviet big four.

14th Olympiad, Leipzig, 1960

Forty teams entered in 1960. Preliminaries divided this big entry list into three final sections, as listed below:

Championship Finals: USSR 34; U.S.A. 29; Yugoslavia 27; Hungary 22½; Czechoslovakia 21½; Bulgaria 21; Argentina 20½; West Germany 19½; East Germany 19; Netherlands 17; Rumania 16½; Great Britain 16½.

Consolation Finals, Group A: Sweden 27½; Israel 26½; Austria 24½; Denmark 23½; Finland 23½; Cuba 23; Norway 23; Spain 22½; Poland 22; Chile 19½; Iceland 16½; India 12.

Consolation Finals, Group B: Philippines 28½; Indonesia 27½; Mongolia 27½; Albania 26½; Ecuador 26; Portugal 25; France 25; Italy 24; Belgium 23½; Tunisia 21½; Greece 20½; Bolivia 19½; Monaco 17½; Ireland 17; Malta 14; Lebanon 8½. (Under FIDE rules, when there are more than 12 teams in a section, this group was played as an 11-round Swiss.)

This was the best postwar showing by a U. S. team. When the two leaders met in the fifth round, Tal drew with Bobby Fischer, Botvinnik with Bill Lombardy, Korchnoi with Robert Byrne, but Smyslov defeated Bisguier. The other two players on the USSR team were Keres and Petrosian. The alternates on the U. S. team were Raymond Weinstein and Rossolimo.

15th Olympiad, Varna, 1962

Thirty-nine countries entered the 15th Olympiad at Golden Sands, near Varna, on the coast of the Black Sea, in Bulgaria. However, the teams representing Ecuador and Indonesia failed to show up. The entrants were divided into four preliminary groups to qualify for the Championship Finals and two Consolation Finals. The results:

Championship Finals: USSR 31½; Yugoslavia 28; Argentina 26; U.S.A. 25; Hungary 23; Bulgaria 21½; West Germany 21; East Germany 20½; Rumania 20½; Czechoslovakia 18½; Netherlands 18; Austria 10½.

Consolation Finals, Group A: Spain 26½; Great Britain 26½; Israel 25; Cuba 22½; Sweden 22½; Poland 22½; Belgium 22; Finland 20½; Mongolia 20; Switzerland 20; Iceland 19; Denmark 17. Although the British team defeated Spain by 3½–½, the tie for first was broken in favor of Spain, the latter having the higher match score.

Consolation Finals, Group B: Norway 32½; Bulgaria B 29½; Albania 28½; Tunisia 28½; India 26½; Iran 25; France 23½; Puerto Rico 22½; Uruguay 22; Greece 18½; Luxembourg 18; Turkey 17; Ireland 14½; Cyprus 1½. Group B was played as an 11-round Swiss. To avoid byes, the host country entered the "Bulgaria B" team, which played *hors de concours*.)

In their individual encounter, the USSR team defeated the U. S. team by 2½–1½. Botvinnik drew with Fischer, although the U. S. Champion had a winning advantage when the game was adjourned. Petrosian drew with Benko, Tal with Donald Byrne, but Boris Spassky defeated Larry Evans. The other members of the teams: Keres and Geller for the USSR, Robert Byrne and Edmar Mednis for the U. S. A.

16th Olympiad, Tel Aviv, 1964

This was the biggest Olympiad to date. Fifty teams entered and taxed the ingenuity of Mr. Folke Rogard, President of the FIDE, in arranging the pairings into seven preliminary sections. The FIDE rules just did not provide for such a large entry list. The top two in each preliminary section qualified to play in the Championship Finals, the next two in the Consolation Finals, Group A, the third two teams in Group B, the remaining eight teams in Group C. The results in the finals:

Championship Finals: USSR 36½; Yugoslavia 32; West Germany 30½; Hungary 30; Czechoslovakia 28½; U.S.A. 27½; Bulgaria 27; Rumania 27; Argentina 26; Poland 24; Netherlands 21; Canada 19; Spain 17½; Israel 17½.

Consolation Finals, Group A: East Germany 38½; Sweden 32; Denmark 31½; England 31; Peru 27½; Austria 27½; Cuba 26; Norway 25½; Mongolia 25½; Chile 24; Philippines 22½; Ecuador 18; Paraguay 17½; Scotland 17.

Consolation Finals, Group B: Iceland 37½; Switzerland 36½; Colombia 35;

Finland 35; Venezuela 30½; France 29; Greece 27½; Iran 23½; India 22; Puerto Rico 21½; Turkey 20½; Mexico 20; Ireland 13; Monaco 12.

Consolation Finals, Group C: Australia 22½; South Africa 18; Bolivia 15½; Uruguay 14½; Portugal 14; Luxembourg 12; Dominica 10½; Cyprus 5.

The USSR won for the seventh time in a row. Their team consisted of Petrosian, Botvinnik, Smyslov, Keres, and alternates Leonid Stein and Boris Spassky. In the preliminaries they massacred six teams, allowing only one draw—to Spain. Then they won the championship finals with ease. However, the USSR team suffered a surprising upset when they were defeated by West Germany in the fifth round. Smyslov lost to Wolfgang Unzicker and Keres to Lothar Schmid; the third and fourth boards were drawn. (This was Keres' first loss in an Olympiad since Helsinki, 1952!) The defeat was the worst the World Champions had ever suffered, and their first for eight years.

The United States team comprised Reshevsky, Benko, Saidy, Bisguier, Donald Byrne, and Addison. In the first eight rounds of the finals the team fared well, having won five matches and drawn the remaining three. In the ninth round, the leading USSR team and the second-place U.S.A. team met in the decisive battle of the Olympics. Although the Soviets did not put in Botvinnik, they were out to win—and they did, in a big way. When it was all over, the American team had lost all four games and were out of the running. Smyslov, Keres, and Stein defeated Benko, Saidy, and Bisguier, respectively, before the session ended. At board No. 1, Reshevsky adjourned against Petrosian, but lost after 74 moves.

Probably as a result of this nerve-shattering debacle, the U. S. team then lost to the Netherlands, but recovered in the last three rounds to finish in sixth place.

17th Olympiad, Havana, 1966

A new record number of fifty-two teams played in the 1966 Olympiad held at the Havana Libre Hotel, Havana, Cuba. The preliminaries, in seven sections, lasted from October 26 to November 2nd, the finals from November 3rd to 20th. The first two teams from each preliminary section qualified for the Championship Finals; the third and fourth teams from each preliminary played in the Consolation Finals, Group A; the fifth and six teams went into Group B, the remaining ten teams into Group C. The results in the finals:

Championship Finals: USSR 39½; U.S.A. 34½; Hungary 33½; Yugoslavia 33½; Argentina 30; Czechoslovakia 29½; Bulgaria 28½; Rumania 27½; East Germany 25½; Denmark 20; Iceland 19; Spain 18; Norway 14; Cuba 12.

Consolation Finals, Group A: Netherlands 37; Poland 31½; Austria 30; Switzerland 28½; Israel 28½; Finland 28; England 27½; Colombia 26½; Canada 25½; Sweden 24½; Belgium 23; France 20; Indonesia 18; Scotland 15½.

Consolation Finals, Group B: Italy 38; Mongolia 33½; Philippines 31; Greece 29; Uruguay 28; Tunisia 26½; Turkey 25½; Venezuela 25; Portugal 25; Chile 23½; Ecuador 23½; Ireland 21; Puerto Rico 18½; Luxembourg 16.

Consolation Finals, Group C: South Africa 28; Mexico 24½; Bolivia 22; Monaco 20; Morocco 19½; Nicaragua 17; Panama 16½; Lebanon 11; Cyprus 11; Hong Kong 10½.

The USSR won the title for the eighth consecutive time since 1952. The winning team included World Champion Tigran Petrosian, 1965 Candidates' Tournament winner Boris Spassky, former World Champion Mikhail Tal, and current USSR Champion Leonid Stein, with Grandmasters Victor Korchnoi and Lev Polugaevsky as alternates. The United States made an excellent showing by placing second and thereby repeating this country's best post-war performance at Leipzig in 1960. The American team included U. S. Champion Bobby Fischer, now 23 years old, and his fellow Grandmasters Robert Byrne, Pal Benko, and Larry Evans, with Grandmaster Nicolas Rossolimo and U. S. Senior Master William G. Addison as alternates. Donald Byrne was the non-playing captain.

Petrosian was awarded the gold medal for the best performance at board No. 1, having scored 11½ out of 13 for a percentage of 88.5. Bobby Fischer was a close second with the outstanding score of 15 out of 17 and a percentage of 88.2.

The Soviet and United States teams were scheduled to meet on Saturday, November 5th, at 4 P.M. The American team asked for a two-hour delay because Bobby Fischer has evened matters with Reshevsky by refusing to play on the "Sabbath" from sunset Friday until dusk on Saturday. Bobby is not an orthodox Jew, but he has become a member of a Christian sect, presumably the Seventh Day Adventists, that requires observance of the same Sabbath. But Alexei Syrov, President of the USSR Chess Federation, refused to accept the delay, and the Czechoslovak director of the tournament awarded the Russians four points when the American team defaulted.

The forfeiting of the American team started an international hullabaloo in a tournament that has traditionally avoided political controversies. Colonel Edmondson of the USCF threatened to withdraw the American team; cables were sent flying to Folke Rogard, president of the FIDE, in Stockholm; a six-nation council was set up to arbitrate the dispute. Mr. Rogard replied, strongly disagreed with the tournament director's ruling, urged the teams to play off the match; the six-nation council also "urgently requested" the Soviet team to reconsider its position and play off the games.

Fortunately, everything ended in sweetness and light, with the USSR and U.S.A. teams toasting each other in brandy, when Mr. Syrov capitulated and agreed to play the match. The teams met on November 14th and the USSR won by 2½–1½. Bobby Fischer had expected to play Petrosian, but the World Champion's place was taken by Boris Spassky, recent challenger for the world title and winner of the second Piatigorsky Cup tournament at Santa Monica, Calif., who has never been defeated by Fischer. The game was drawn after 57 moves. At board 2, Mikhail Tal defeated Robert Byrne in 36 moves; at board 3, Benko and Stein drew in 21 moves; at board 4, Polugaevsky drew with Evans in 52 moves. Although the Soviet players had to give up 1½ of the points they had claimed by forfeit, they proceeded to win the tournament by a margin of five points over the second-place Americans. To complete the story, the three remaining teams the United States had to play on Saturdays—Norway, Spain, and Cuba—agreed to the two-hour delay to 6 P.M.

The 18th Olympiad is scheduled to be held at Lugano, Switzerland, in October and November of 1968. Since Round Robin preliminaries and finals are becoming impractical for the large number of teams now participating in the Olympics, consideration is to be given to the use of the Swiss system when the 38th FIDE Congress meets in Italy in 1967.

Winners of World Team Championships

1927 (London)	Hungary	1952 (Helsinki)	USSR
1928 (The Hague)	Hungary	1954 (Amsterdam)	USSR
1930 (Hamburg)	Poland	1956 (Moscow)	USSR
1931 (Prague)	U.S.A.	1958 (Munich)	USSR
1933 (Folkestone)	U.S.A.	1960 (Leipzig)	USSR
1935 (Warsaw)	U.S.A.	1962 (Varna)	USSR
1937 (Stockholm)	U.S.A.	1964 (Tel Aviv)	USSR
1939 (Buenos Aires)	Germany	1966 (Havana)	USSR
1950 (Dubrovnik)	Yugoslavia		

WORLD STUDENT TEAM CHAMPIONSHIPS

The first international tournament restricted to college students was held in Liverpool, England, in 1952. It was an individual event, won by Bronstein and Taimanov of the USSR. Then an international team tournament for students, won by Norway, was held in Brussels in 1953. These two contests were the forerunners of the official World Student Team Championships, held annually since 1954.

The FIDE Congress of 1954 authorized the International Union of Students (IUS), with headquarters at Prague, Czechoslovakia, to organize the Student Olympiads in collaboration with the FIDE. Regulations governing these contests were adopted by the FIDE Congress of 1957, later revised by the Congress of 1960. In the early tournaments, players up to 30 years of age were qualified, but this was reduced to 27 years of age. Each player must be attending a university or receiving an education of at least the same level with a view to obtaining a professional diploma. Each team must be composed of four players and is allowed two alternates. Final positions in a tournament are determined by the number of game points scored.

1st Student Olympiad, Oslo, 1954

The first official tournament was held at Oslo in 1954. Ten teams competed with the following results:

Czechoslovakia 29½; USSR 28½; Bulgaria 26; England 23; Iceland 19; Sweden 17; Norway 14; Finland 13; Combined team (Italy, Scotland, France) 8½; France 1½.

2nd Student Olympiad, Lyon, 1955

The second official contest of this type was held at Lyon, France, with these results:

USSR 41; Yugoslavia 33; Hungary 32½; Bulgaria 32½; Czechoslovakia 27½; Iceland 26; Poland 25½; Spain 23½; Finland 20½; Netherlands 16½; Sweden 14½; Norway 14½; France 4½.

3rd Student Olympiad, Uppsala, 1956

In 1956, a record number of 16 teams entered, including the United States for the first time. The teams were divided into four preliminary groups. The top two teams from each group qualified for the Championship Finals, the bottom two for the Consolation Finals. The final standings:

Championship Finals: USSR 21½; Hungary 16½; Yugoslavia 15; Bulgaria 15; Spain 12½; Czechoslovakia 11½; Rumania 10½; U.S.A. 9½.
Consolation Finals: Iceland 22; Poland 18½; East Germany 17½; England 15; Finland 12½; France 9; Norway 8½; Sweden 8½.

The United States team: William Lombardy of CCNY, Charles Witte of Columbia, Anthony Saidy of Fordham, Shelby Lyman of Harvard, Edmar Mednis of NYU.

4th Student Olympiad, Reykjavik, 1957

Fourteen teams entered in 1957 and played without preliminaries:

USSR 43½; Bulgaria 37; Czechoslovakia 36; Hungary 34½; U.S.A. 31; Rumania 29; East Germany 28; Iceland 27; England 23½; Denmark 19; Sweden 16; Ecuador 15½; Mongolia 13½; Finland 9½.

The U. S. team: William Lombardy, Edmar Mednis, Arthur Feuerstein (CCNY), Anthony Saidy, Robert Sobel (U. of Pa.).

5th Student Olympiad, Varna, 1958

Sixteen teams entered in 1958 for the contest held at Golden Sands, near Varna, Bulgaria. The teams were divided into four preliminary sections to qualify for two final groups, as follows:

Championship Finals: USSR 19½; Bulgaria 17; Czechoslovakia 14; Yugoslavia 14; Hungary 14; U.S.A. 12½; Argentina 11½; East Germany 9½.
Consolation Finals: Rumania 19; Iceland 17½; Netherlands 17; Poland 16½; Mongolia 13; Sweden 13; Albania 10½; Ireland 5½.

The United States team was the same as in 1957.

6th Student Olympiad, Budapest, 1959

Bulgaria outpointed the USSR in 1959 when 14 teams competed at Budapest. The United States did not participate. The results:

Bulgaria 40½; USSR 39; Hungary 37½; Rumania 36; East Germany 32½; Czechoslovakia 31; England 26½; Mongolia 21½; Poland 21½; Israel 20; France 19; Sweden 18½; Finland 15; Ireland 5½.

7th Student Olympiad, Leningrad, 1960

At Leningrad, in 1960, the United States finally won the championship. Fourteen teams competed, with the following results:

U.S.A. 41; USSR 39½; Yugoslavia 37; Czechoslovakia 31½; Bulgaria 31; Rumania 30; East Germany 28½; Netherlands 25½; Hungary 24½; Great Britain 24; Sweden 16; Mongolia 16; Finland 10; Belgium 9½.

The winning team: William Lombardy, Charles Kalme, Raymond Weinstein, Anthony Saidy, Edmar Mednis, Eliot Hearst.

8th Student Olympiad, Helsinki, 1961

The USSR regained the title in 1961 when thirteen teams competed at Helsinki. The United States placed second. Complete results:

USSR 39½; U.S.A. 34½; East Germany 31; Czechoslovakia 31; Bulgaria 29; Hungary 28½; Netherlands 25; England 20; Mongolia 20; Denmark 19; Finland 18½; Sweden 10; Tunisia 6.

The U. S. team: William Lombardy, Raymond Weinstein, James T. Sherwin, Charles Kalme, Edmar Mednis, Lawrence C. Gilden.

9th Student Olympiad, Marienbad, 1962

The ninth tournament was scheduled to take place in London, but the British Chess Federation could not guarantee visas for all participants. The gap was filled by the Czechoslovakian Federation, and the contest was staged at Marienbad. A record number of 18 teams competed. Divided into three preliminary groups, the top three from each group qualified for the Championship Finals, the bottom three for the Consolation Finals. The United States did not send a team. The results:

Championship Finals: USSR 24½; Yugoslavia 20; Czechoslovakia 19; East Germany 17; Rumania 16½; Bulgaria 14½; Hungary 13½; Poland 12½; Mongolia 6½.
Consolation Finals: Netherlands 23; England 21½; Israel 21½; Denmark 21; Finland 17; Cuba 11½; Belgium 10; Sweden 9½; Scotland 9.

10th Student Olympiad, Budva, 1963

The 1963 tournament was held at Budva in Yuvoslavia. Nineteen teams entered and played in preliminaries to qualify for two final sections. The USSR slipped to a tie for third-fourth with Bulgaria. In fifth place was the U. S. team of William Lombardy of St. Joseph's Seminary, Raymond Weinstein and Bernard Zuckerman of Brooklyn College, Mitchell Sweig of the University of Chicago and Walter Cunningham of Los Angeles State.

Championship Finals: Czechoslovakia 24; Yugoslavia 23½; Bulgaria 22; USSR 22; U.S.A. 19½; Netherlands 17½; Mongolia 16; Poland 16; Hungary 13; Italy 6½.
Consolation Finals: England 25½; East Germany 24½; Finland 20½; Sweden 17½; Tunisia 16; Cuba 15; Belgium 11; Turkey 9; Scotland 5.

11th Student Olympiad, Cracow, 1964

In 1964, at Cracow, Poland, the USSR regained the title. The United States team of William Lombardy, Raymond Weinstein, Charles Kalme, Bernard Zuckerman, Michael Valvo, and Mitchell Sweig finished in fourth place. Twenty-one teams entered the contest. The resuults in the finals were as follows:

Championship Finals: USSR 31½; Czechoslovakia 29½; Hungary 29; U.S.A. 28; Yugoslavia 27; Poland 21½; Israel 19; East Germany 18; Bulgaria 18; Mongolia 16½; Denmark 15½; Austria 10½.

Consolation Finals: Rumania 23; Great Britain 22½; Finland 19½; Netherlands 19; Sweden 18; Cuba 15½; Iceland 15; Italy 11; Belgium ½.

12th Student Olympiad, Sinaia, 1965

The 12th tournament was held at Sinaia, a beautiful mountain resort in Rumania, from July 23 to August 9, 1965. Seventeen teams competed, but the United States was not represented. Other notable absentees were Yugoslavia, Poland, and Mongolia. Three teams from each of three preliminary sections qualified for the championship finals. The USSR team retained the title.

Championship Finals: USSR 21; Israel 20; Denmark 18; Rumania 17½; Czechoslovakia 17½; England 14½; East Germany 14; Hungary 12; Netherlands 9½.

Consolation Finals: Bulgaria 22½; Austria 19½; Finland 19; Sweden 16; Tunisia 12; Scotland 10; Cuba 7; Belgium 6.

13th Student Olympiad, Orebro, 1966

The 1966 event, held July 30 to August 14 at Orebro, Sweden, was won by the USSR. The United States did not participate. Results were as follows:

Championship Finals: USSR 34; Czechoslovakia 28½; Denmark and Yugoslavia 27½; Rumania 23; Israel 21½; England 20; East Germany 19; Bulgaria 18½; Hungary 17½; Netherlands 15; Finland 12.

Consolation Finals: Sweden 21; Cuba 20; Puerto Rico 19½; Scotland 19; Switzerland 17; Iceland 16; Tunisia 13; Belgium 9½; Ireland 9.

Winners of World Student Team Championships

1954 (Oslo)	Czechoslovakia	1961 (Helsinki)	USSR
1955 (Lyon)	USSR	1962 (Marienbad)	USSR
1956 (Uppsala)	USSR	1963 (Budva)	Czechoslovakia
1957 (Reykjavik)	USSR	1964 (Cracow)	USSR
1958 (Varna)	USSR	1965 (Sinaia)	USSR
1959 (Budapest)	Bulgaria	1966 (Orebro)	USSR
1960 (Leningrad)	U.S.A.		

WORLD JUNIOR CHAMPIONSHIPS

The first World Junior Chess Championship (for players under 20 years of age) was held at Coventry and Birmingham, England, in 1951. The eighteen contestants played eleven rounds under the Swiss System. The title was won by Borislav Ivkov of Yugoslavia.

1st Junior Championship, Coventry & Birmingham, 1951

Borislav Ivkov (Yugo.)	9½	E. Selzer (Austria)	6
Malcolm N. Barker (Eng.)	8	G. Berriman (Austral.)	5½
R. C. Cruz (Arg.)	7	Fridrik Olafsson (Iceland)	5½
P. Harris (Eng.)	6½	L. Joyner (Canada)	5
Bent Larsen (Den.)	6½	A. Eikrem (Norway)	3½
E. Nyreen (Fin.)	6½	J. J. Walsh (Ire.)	3½
Edwin Bhend (Switz.)	6	J. A. Jackson (Scot.)	3
S. Burstein (France)	6	S. Asker (Sweden)	2½
W. Rosen (W. Ger.)	6	B. Coosemans (Belg.)	2½

Under the sponsorship of the FIDE, a Round Robin tournament has since been held biennially.

2nd Junior Championship, Copenhagen, 1953

The second tournament was held at Copenhagen in 1953. The twenty entrants were divided into two preliminary groups of ten. The top four from each group met in the championship finals with the following results:

Oscar Panna (Arg.)	5½	Jonathan Penrose (Eng.)	2½
Klaus Darga (W. Ger.)	5½	Dieter Keller (Switz.)	2½
Borislav Ivkov (Yugo.)	3½	James T. Sherwin (U.S.A.)	2½
Fridrik Olafsson (Iceland)	3½	Bent Larsen (Den.)	2½

Consolation Finals: F. Scafarelli (Italy) 5; Miguel Farre (Spain) 4½; H. Heikkila (Fin.), R. Persitz (Israel) & F. Roessel (Neth.) 4; M. B. Mellberg (Sweden), E. Reichel (Austria), & Ross E. Siemms (Canada) 3½; J. Boey (Belg.) 3; Y. Barda (Norway) & J. Herbin (France) 2½; Petri (Saar) 2.

The rules provided that all ties (in preliminaries and finals) must be broken under the so-called Sonnenborn-Berger system. On this basis, the title was awarded to Oscar Panno of Argentina.

It is interesting to note that the top four in this tournament, together with Bent Larsen, are now International Grandmasters. The remaining three are International Masters.

3rd Junior Championship, Antwerp, 1955

In 1955 there were 24 entrants, including two from Belgium, the host country. The players were divided into three preliminary groups of eight. The top three from each group, and the player in fourth place who made the best score (Portisch) qualified for the Championship Finals. The remaining 14 contestants played in the Consolation Finals. The title was won by Boris Spassky of the USSR; the runner-up was Edmar Mednis of the United States. The complete results:

Boris Spassky (USSR)	8	Dieter K. Keller (Switz.)	4
Edmar Mednis (U.S.A.)	7	J. Van Oosterom (Neth.)	3½
Miguel Farre (Spain)	6½	J. Hallstrom (Fin.)	2½
Lajos Portisch (Hung.)	5½	Svein Johannessen (Norway)	1½
Gueorguy P. Tringov (Bulg.)	5	Samuel Schweber (Arg.)	1½

Consolation Finals: D. Ciric (Yugoslavia) 7½; Ingi R. Johannsson (Iceland) 6½; Broden (Sweden) 6½; K. W. Lloyd (England) 6½; Jorgenssen (Denmark) 5½; Klages (West Germany) 4½; Van Hoorne (Belgium) 4; Kreppenhofer (Austria) 4; Somers (Belgium) 4; Purdy (Australia) 3½; Muller (France) 3; Philippe (Luxembourg) 3; Donia (Saar) 2½; Deiseach (Ireland) 2.

4th Junior Championship, Toronto, 1957

William Lombardy of the United States won the title in 1957, making a perfect score of 11–0. There were twelve contestants, including two from Canada, the host country. The final results:

William Lombardy (U.S.A.)	11	F. Jobin (Canada)	4½
M. Gerusel (W. Ger.)	9	J. Aldrete (Mexico)	4
A. K. P. Jongsma (Neth.)	8½	T. Makelainen (Fin.)	3½
V. Selimanov (USSR)	8	B. Rabinovitch (S. Africa)	2½
R. Cardoso (Phil.)	6½	J. M. Bahgat (Egypt)	2
R. Hallerod (Sweden)	5	P. Bates (Canada)	1½

5th Junior Championship, Munchenstein, 1959

The 5th was sponsored by the Swiss Chess Federation. Twenty-six players entered and were divided into three preliminary groups. The top four in each group qualified for the Championship Finals, the next three for the Consolation Finals, Group A, the others for Consolation Group B. The final results:

Carlos Bielicki (Arg.)	8½	D. Hamann (Den.)	5½
Bruno Parma (Yugo.)	6½	N. Naranja (Phil.)	5
D. Rumens (Eng.)	6½	A. Tomson (USSR)	5
J. Stevanov (Bulg.)	6½	F. Kuijpers (Neth.)	4½
C. Clemens (W. Ger.)	5½	R. Philipps (N. Z.)	4
U. Kuttner (E. Ger.)	5½	W. Erny (Switz.)	3

Consolation Finals, Group A: Hoen (Norway) 6; Hohler (Switzerland) 5½; Grimshaw (Canada) 5; Anguera (Spain) 4½; Saren (Finland) 4; Wostyn (Belgium) 4; Halen (Sweden) 3; Primavera (Italy) 2½; Weinwurm (Austria) 1½.

Consolation Finals, Group B: Velasco (Cuba) 6; Maalouf (Lebanon) 5½; Cassidy (Ireland) 5½; Biever (Luxembourg) 2; Tcherniak (France) 1.

6th Junior Championship, The Hague, 1961

A new record of thirty juniors played at The Hague in 1961. Raymond Weinstein of the United States tried to enter but was ruled too old to compete. The contestants played in four preliminary groups. The top three from each group qualified for the Championship Finals, the next three for the Consolation Finals, Group A, the others for Consolation Group B. Two dropped out after the preliminaries. The final results:

Bruno Parma (Yugo.)	9	R. Calvo (Spain)	5
Florin Gheorghiu (Rum.)	8½	A. Gulbrandsen (Norway)	4½
A. Kuindzhi (USSR)	8	B. Nagy (Hung.)	4
H. Pfleger (W. Ger.)	7	G. Larusson (Iceland)	3
C. Zuidema (Neth.)	7	O. Kinnmark (Sweden)	2½
H. Westerinen (Fin.)	5½	D. Thomson (Scot.)	2

Consolation Finals, Group A: Rodney Philipps (New Zealand) 8½; O. Jakobsen (Denmark) 7; U. Kuttner (East Germany) 6½; Larry Gilden (U.S.A.) 6; J. Minaya (Colombia) 5½; H. Holaszek (Austria) 5; D. Smith (England) 4½; J. Rubinetti (Argentina) 3½; J. Diekstra (Netherlands) 3; A. Rosino (Italy) 3; E. Keogh (Ireland) 2½.

Consolation Finals, Group B: W. Schmidt (Poland) 7½; M. Markus (Switzerland) 6; C. Maalouf (Lebanon) 3; R. Wostyn (Belgium) 2; R. Rischette (Luxembourg) 1½.

7th Junior Championship, Vrnjacka Banja, 1963

Again thirty juniors competed in the 1963 tournament, held in Yugoslavia. Under the new regulations for the Junior Championship, adopted by the FIDE Congress of 1962, the entrants were divided into five preliminary groups of six. The top two in each group qualified for the Championship Finals, the next two for the Consolation Finals, Group A, the last two for the Consolation Finals, Group B. The final results:

Florin Gheorghiu (Rum.)	7½	A. Zaharov (USSR)	4
Mihail Janata (Czech.)	7½	A. Zwaig (Norway)	4
B. Kurajica (Yugo.)	4	P. N. Lee (Eng.)	4
J. Adamski (Poland)	4	H. Westerinen (Fin.)	3
Ann Lian Tan (Singapore)	4	S. Bojkovic (Yugo.)	2½

Consolation Finals, Group A: H. Holaszek (Austria) 7; P. Ostermeyer (West Germany) 6; I. Gat (Israel) 5½; M. Moe (Denmark) 5½; V. Musil (Yugoslavia) 5; D. Friedgood (South Africa) 5; M. Fuller (Australia) 4½; H. Bohlig (East Germany) 3; R. Alvarez (Cuba) 2; R. Litsberger (Sweden) 1½. *Consolation Finals, Group B:* C. Amado (Argentina) 7; N. Kirilov (Bulgaria) 7; Walter Cunningham (U.S.A.) 6½; B. Kristiansson (Iceland) 5½; E. C. Scholl (Netherlands) 5; H. Glauser (Switzerland) 4½; Z. Kovacs (Hungary) 4½; N. Dietrich (Luxembourg) 2½; J. Cordovil (Portugal) 2; J. Burstow (Canada) ½.

The new FIDE rules required a four-game playoff match between the two tied leaders. Gheorghiu won the match and the title.

8th Junior Championship, Barcelona, 1965

There were 28 entries for the tournament held at Barcelona from August 14 to September 1, 1965. The title was won by B. Kurajica of Yugoslavia. The final results:

B. Kurajica (Yugo.)	6½	R. Hubner (W. Ger.)	4½
Hartoch (Neth.)	6	Schoneberg (E. Ger.)	4½
V. Tukmakov (USSR)	6	Farago (Hung.)	4
A. Zwaig (Norway)	5	L. Bronstein (Arg.)	3½
J. Bleiman (Israel)	4½	Simon (Spain)	½ *

* Withdrew after fifth round.

Consolation Finals, Group A: D. Suttles (Canada) 6½; R. D. Keene (England) 6; J. Cordovil (Portugal) 4½; S. Pedersen (Denmark) 4; Weissbacher (Austria) 4; R. Eggman (Switzerland) 3½; Makles (France) 3½; Jamieson (Scotland) 3; Platzack (Sweden) 1.
Consolation Finals, Group B: Gonzales (Spain) 6; Bou Aziz (Tunis) 4½; Belistri (Uruguay) 4; Capece (Italy) 3½; H. Broman (Finland) 3; R. P. Brent (Australia) 3; Haldanarson (Iceland) 2½; Rooze (Belgium) 1½.

9th Junior Championship, 1967

The 1967 tournament will be organized by the Israeli Chess Federation, probably in Jerusalem from the end of August to the middle of September.

World Junior Champions

1951–1953	IVKOV, Borislav (Yugo.)	1959–1961	BIELICKI, Carlos (Arg.)
1953–1955	PANNO, Oscar (Arg.)	1961–1963	PARMA, Bruno (Yugo.)
1955–1957	SPASSKY, Boris (USSR)	1963–1965	GHEORGHIU, Florin
1957–1959	LOMBARDY, William		(Rum.)
	(U.S.A.)	1965–	KURAJICA, Bojan (Yugo.)

WOMEN'S WORLD CHAMPIONSHIPS

Before World War II, individual tournaments for the Women's World Chess Championship and custody of the Lady Hamilton-Russell Cup were held at two-year intervals at the same time and place as the Chess Olympiads. The outstanding woman master of that time was Vera Menchik, probably the most famous woman player in the history of chess, who won the Women's World Championship in 1927 when she was 21 years of age. Male masters who lost to her belonged to what was known as the "Vera Menchik Club." The members included Dr. Euwe, Sultan Khan, Reshevsky, Colle, Lajos Steiner, Saemisch, Becker, Thomas, and Yates. Miss Menchik, the daughter of an English mother and a Czechoslovak father, lived in Russia as a girl and learned chess there. She left Russia in 1923 and lived in Czechoslovakia until 1934, when she took up residence in England. In 1937 she married R. H. S. Stevenson, secretary of the British Chess Federation.

Vera Menchik was the undefeated woman Champion from 1927 to 1944. She won the biennial Women's World Championship Tournaments seven successive times from 1927 to 1939. On June 27, 1944, Vera Menchik-Stevenson was killed in a German air attack on southern England. After her death, the women's title remained vacant until 1950.

Post-War Championship Tourney, Moscow, 1950

Regular competition for the title of Woman Chess Champion of the World, suspended after the 1939 tournament at Buenos Aires, was reorganized by the FIDE after the war. With the cooperation of the USSR Chess Federation, a tournament was held in 1950 at Moscow to determine which of the leading women players of the world would be recognized as champion. Ludmilla Rudenko of the USSR won the tournament and became the new World Champion. The final standings:

Ludmilla Rudenko (USSR)	11½	Clarice Benini (Italy)	7
Olga Rubtsova (USSR)	10½	Josza Langos (Hung.)	6
V. Borisenko-Belova (USSR)	10	Maria Teresa Mora (Cuba)	6
Elizaveta Bykova (USSR)	10	Gisela K. Gresser (U.S.A.)	5
Edith Keller-Herrmann (E. Ger.)	9½	Mona M. Karff (U.S.A.)	5
C. de Silans Chaudé (France)	9½	Nina Hruskova-Belska (Czech.)	5
Eileen Tranmer (Eng.)	9½	Ingrid Larsen (Den.)	4½
Fannie Heemskirk (Neth.)	8	Rosa Germanowa (Poland)	3

According to regulations set up by the FIDE, competition for the women's title follows in three-year cycles. Qualifying zonal tournaments are held in the first year of each cycle; a Candidates' Tournament is played in the second year. The contestants in the latter include three players seeded from the preceding Candidates' Tournament and qualifiers from the zonal tournaments. (In the rules of 1956 and 1959, fifteen players qualified from the zonals; in 1962 this number was increased to sixteen.) In the third year, the winner of the Candidates' plays a match with the champion for the title (originally a 14-game match but changed in 1956 to 16 games). Provision is made for the procedure to be followed if the champion or the qualified challenger refuses or is unable to play a title match.

The first cycle began with the zonal tournaments of 1951. The United States failed to hold such a tournament, but the USCF designated Mary Bain, U. S. Woman Champion, and Mona M. Karff as the representatives of the United States at the Candidates' Tournament. The FIDE rules provided for such a procedure if a zonal tournament is not held.

1st Women Candidates' Tournament, Moscow, 1952

The first Candidates' Tournament for women was held at Moscow late in 1952. The results are tabled below:

Elizaveta Bykova (USSR)	11½	Josza Langos (Hung.)	8
Fannie Heemskirk (Neth.)	10½	Olga Rubtsova (USSR)	8
Olga Ignatieva (USSR)	10½	Mona M. Karff (U.S.A.)	7
V. Borisenko-Belova (USSR)	10	Rowena M. Bruce (Eng.)	5
Edith Keller-Herrmann (E. Ger.)	10	Nina Hruskova-Belska (Czech.)	4½
Kira Zvorykina (USSR)	10	Mary Bain (U.S.A.)	3½
Eileen Tranmer (Eng.)	9	M. Berea de Montero (Arg.)	3
C. de Silans Chaudé (France)	8	Salome Reischer (Austria)	1½

Bykova-Rudenko Championship Match, Leningrad, 1953

Elizaveta Bykova earned the right to challenge Ludmilla Rudenko for the title. The match was played at Leningrad in 1953 and won by Mrs. Bykova with a score of 8–6. The new champion held the title until 1956.

The U. S. Women's Championship of 1954 was named the zonal tournament of the second world championship cycle. Gisela K. Gresser, Mona M. Karff, and Sonja Graf qualified for the Candidates' Tournament of 1955.

2nd Women Candidates' Tournament, Moscow, 1955

The qualifiers from the various zonal tournaments and the players seeded from the first Candidates' Tournament met at Moscow in 1955. The results are given below:

Olga Rubtsova (USSR)	15	Gisela K. Gresser (U.S.A.)	9½
Larisa Volpert (USSR)	14½	Sonja Graf (U.S.A.)	9½
Edith Keller-Herrmann (E. Ger.)	14	Olga Ignatieva (USSR)	9½
Kira Zvorykina (USSR)	13½	Eva Karakas (Hung.)	7
V. Borisenko-Belova (USSR)	13	Josefa Gurfinkel (USSR)	6½
Verica Nedeljkovic (Yugo.)	12½	Krystyna Holuj (Poland)	6½
Milunka Lazarevic (Yugo.)	12	Mona M. Karff (U.S.A.)	5½
Antonia Ivanova (Bulg.)	11½	Celia B. de Moschini (Arg.)	4½
Fannie Heemskirk (Neth.)	10	Ruzena Sucha (Czech.)	4
C. de Silans Chaudé (France)	9½	B. Carrasco de Budinich (Chile)	2

World Championship Matches, Moscow, 1956 and 1958

Olga Rubtsova had earned the right to challenge the titleholder, Elizaveta Bykova; but Ludmilla Rudenko, the ex-champion, claimed the right to participate in the competition for the world title, and a triangular match was arranged with the champion, ex-champion, and the challenger as participants, each to play 16 games. The contest was held in Moscow and ended on September 23, 1956, with a victory for Olga Rubtsova, who scored 10 points, while Mrs. Bykova scored 9½ and Mrs. Rudenko 4½. Thus the title was won by Olga Rubtsova.

In accordance with provisions made in 1955, Mrs. Bykova challenged Mrs. Rubtsova to a return match. In this match, held in Moscow February 4 to March 12, 1958, Elizaveta Bykova regained her title, defeating Olga Rubtsova by a score of 8½ to 5½.

The third cycle began with the zonal tournaments of 1957. In Zone 5 (U.S.A.), Gisela K. Gresser and Sonja Graf qualified from the tournament held in Los Angeles during November 1957, but Sonja Graf did not play in the next Candidates' Tournament.

3rd Women Candidates' Tournament, Plovdiv, 1959

This tournament was supposed to have been held in 1958, but financial difficulties forced a postponement. It was staged in Bulgaria May 1 to 26, 1959, with the following results:

Kira Zvorykina (USSR)	11½	Olga Rubtsova (USSR)	6½
Verica Nedeljkovic (Yugo.)	10½	Kveta Eretova (Czech.)	6
Larisa Volpert (USSR)	9½	Gisela K. Gresser (U.S.A.)	5½
Salme Rootare (USSR)	9	Friedel Rinder (W. Ger.)	4½
Edith Keller-Herrmann (E. Ger.)	9	Maria Pogorevici (Rum.)	4½
Milunka Lazarevic (Yugo.)	8	Paunka Todorova (Bulg.)	4½
Eva Karakas (Hung.)	7½	S. G. de Huguet (Arg.)	2½
V. Borisenko-Belova (USSR)	7		

Bykova-Zvorykina Championship Match, Moscow, 1959

Kira Zvorykina, as the qualified challenger, played a match with World Champion Elizaveta Bykova. The match was held in Moscow, started on December 2, 1959. Mrs. Bykova won by a score of 8½–4½, thus keeping her title for another three years.

The fourth cycle started in 1960. The U. S. Women's Championship of the previous year was named the zonal tournament for this country. Lisa Lane, the new U. S. Champion, and Gisela K. Gresser qualified to compete in the Candidates' Tournament.

4th Women Candidates' Tournament, Vrnjacka Banja, 1961

This tournament, held in Yugoslavia, saw the emergence of a newcomer in women's chess, the twenty-year-old Nona Gaprindashvili of the USSR. The final results were as follows:

Nona Gaprindashvili (USSR)	13	Elizabeta Polihroniade (Rum.)	7
V. Borisenko-Belova (USSR)	11	Henryka Konarkowska (Poland)	7
Kira Zvorykina (USSR)	10	Lisa Lane (U.S.A.)	6
Milunka Lazarevic (Yugo.)	9½	Gisela K. Gresser (U.S.A.)	6
Verica Nedeljkovic (Yugo.)	9½	C. de Silans Chaudé (France)	6
Tatiana Zatulovskaya (USSR)	9½	Fannie Heemskirk (Neth.)	5½
Larisa Volpert (USSR)	9	Friedel Rinder (W. Ger.)	5½
Eva Karakas (Hung.)	9	S. Hundsuren (Mongolia)	2½
Alexandra Nicolau (Rum.)	9		

Gaprindashvili-Bykova Championship Match, Moscow, 1962

The young winner of the Candidates' Tournament played a scheduled 16-game match with Elizaveta Bykova, starting September 17th in Moscow, and won by the overwhelming score of 9–2. Thus Nona Gaprindashvili became the new World Champion. Mrs. Bykova had held the title from 1953 to 1956 and again from 1958 to 1962.

As the U. S. Championship Tournaments, for men and women respectively, had also become the zonal tournaments, the USCF attempted to arrange a Women's Championship on an annual basis. However, no championship was scheduled for 1963, beginning the fifth cycle of world title competition, so the 1962 Women's Championship was named as the zonal tournament to qualify for the Candidates' event of 1964. The two qualifiers were Gisela K. Gresser, the current champion, and Lisa Lane, the runner-up.

5th Women Candidates' Tournament, Sukhumi, 1964

The 1964 tournament, with eighteen contestants, was held in September at the Black Sea resort of Sukhumi in the USSR. The results:

Alla Kuchnir (USSR)	12½	Kveta Eretova (Czech.)	8½
Milunka Lazarevic (Yugo.)	12½	Elizaveta Bykova (USSR)	8
Tatiana Zatulovskaya (USSR)	12½	Lisa Lane (U.S.A.)	7
Katarina Jovanovic (Yugo.)	11	Gisela K. Gresser (U.S.A.)	6½
Kira Zvorykina (USSR)	11	Eva Karakas (Hung.)	6½
Maiya Ranniku (USSR)	10½	Margareta Teodorescu (Rum.)	6½
V. Borisenko-Belova (USSR)	10	Antonia Ivanova (Bulg.)	6
Henryka Konarkowska (Poland)	10	M. Tsend (Mongolia)	4
Verica Nedeljkovic (Yugo.)	9	C. B. de Moschini (Arg.)	1

The Yugoslav representative, Milunka Lazarevic, was the pacesetter and seemed an almost certain winner. After fourteen rounds she led the field by 2½ points; then she collapsed and scored only half a point in the last three rounds. The tournament ended in a three-way tie for first place when Mrs. Gresser defeated the Yugoslav player in the final round.

Under FIDE rules, the triple tie had to be broken to determine the next challenger. The tie was played off at Moscow in December, 1964. Milunka Lazarevic of Yugoslavia forged ahead, defeating both of her opponents in the first lap of the double round contest; but again she collapsed and lost to both in the second lap. Alla Kuchnir won the event with a score of 2½–1½. Tatiana Zatulovskaya was third with 1½–2½.

Gaprindashvili-Kuchnir Championship Match, Riga, 1965

Although Alla Kuchnir is a talented player, she was outclassed in the title match with Nona Gaprindashvili. The Champion retained her title by a score of 8½–4½. The young Champion continues to improve her technique. In December 1964, at Tiflis, she won the Soviet Women's Championship with a score of 15–4.

Women World Champions

1927–1944	MENCHIK, Vera (Czech.–Eng.)
1944–1950	*Vacant*
1950–1953	RUDENKO, Ludmilla (USSR)
1953–1956	BYKOVA, Elizaveta (USSR)
1956–1958	RUBTSOVA, Olga (USSR)
1958–1962	BYKOVA, Elizaveta (USSR)
1962–	GAPRINDASHVILI, Nona (USSR)

Winners of Women Candidates' Tournaments

1952 (Moscow) BYKOVA, Elizaveta (USSR)
1955 (Moscow) RUBTSOVA, Olga (USSR)
1959 (Plovdiv) ZVORYKINA, Kira (USSR)
1961 (Vrnjacka Banja) GAPRINDASHVILI, Nona (USSR)
1964 (Sukhumi) KUCHNIR, Alla (USSR)

WOMEN'S WORLD TEAM CHAMPIONSHIPS

The first official tournament of this type was held at Emmen in 1957 under the sponsorship of the Netherlands Chess Federation. Twenty-one teams of two players took part. They were divided into three preliminary sections. The top three teams in each section qualified for the Championship Finals, the next two for the Consolation Finals, Group A, the last two for the Consolation Finals, Group B.

1st Women's Olympiad, Emmen, 1957

Championship Finals: USSR 10½; Rumania 10½; East Germany 10; Hungary 8½; Bulgaria 8; Yugoslavia 7½; England 7; West Germany 6; Netherlands 4.
Consolation Finals, Group A: U.S.A. 8; Czechoslovakia 8; Poland 7½; Denmark 4½; Ireland 1; Scotland 1.
Consolation Finals, Group B: France 8½; Austria 7½; Finland 6; Norway 4½; Belgium 2½; Luxembourg 1.

The USSR team was awarded the title, having won four of its matches while Rumania had won only three. The U. S. representatives, Gisela K. Gresser and Jacqueline Piatigorsky, did not qualify for the Championship Finals, but won the Group A Consolation Finals on a Sonnenborn-Berger tie-break with Czechoslovakia.

2nd Women's Olympiad, Split (Yugoslavia), 1963

The Women's Olympiad was supposed to be held once every four years. The second was scheduled for Emmen in 1961, but had to be abandoned owing to visa difficulties. It was then switched to Poland, but in November 1961 the Poland Chess Federation announced it could not sponsor the event. A sponsor was found eventually, and the second Olympiad for women was held at Split, Yugoslavia, in 1963. Gisela K. Gresser and Mary Bain were the U. S. representatives. Fifteen teams competed with the results shown below.

USSR 25; Yugoslavia 24½; East Germany 21; Rumania 18½; Bulgaria 17½; Hungary 17; Netherlands 15½; Poland 15; U.S.A. 12½; Mongolia 10½; West Germany 10½; Austria 8; Belgium 5; Monaco 5; Scotland 4½.

The Woman World Champion, Nona Gaprindashvili, made the impressive score of 11½–½ at top board for the USSR. Verica Nedeljkovic, at second board for Yugoslavia, made a perfect score of 12–0.

3rd Women's Olympiad, Oberhausen, 1966

Sponsored by the West German Chess Federation, the third Olympiad was held at Oberhausen from October 3rd to 15th, 1966. Fourteen teams of two players (and one alternate) competed with the results shown below:

USSR 22; Rumania 20½; East Germany 17; Yugoslavia 16½; Netherlands 16; Czechoslovakia 15; Hungary 15; Bulgaria 14; England 12; U.S.A. 9½; Poland 9; West Germany 6½; Denmark 5; Austria 4.

The USSR team won for the third time. At first board, World Champion Nona Gaprindashvili scored 9 out of 11; at second board, USSR Woman Champion Valentina Koslovskaia scored 4 out of 5; the team's alternate, Tatiana Zatulovskaya, scored 9 out of 10. The United States was represented by co-champions Gisela K. Gresser and Lisa Lane, with Eva Aronson as alternate.

Although the American team finished in tenth place, Mrs. Gresser and Miss Lane defeated both members of the Rumanian team in the ninth round. The Rumanians were leading the field at that time, having beaten the USSR team 2–0 in the first round. Grandmaster Alexander Kotov is reported to have commented that "only the United States would have helped Russia."

Winners of Women's World Team Championships

1957 (Emmen)	USSR
1963 (Split)	USSR
1966 (Oberhausen)	USSR

UNITED STATES CHESS CHAMPIONS

Paul Morphy of New Orleans was the winner of the first national chess tournament held in the United States (New York, 1857). Although the title of U. S. Chess Champion was not then in existence, Morphy was recognized as the strongest player in the country and later became the unofficial champion of the world. Morphy's successor, Capt. George H. Mackenzie, was referred to as "the national champion" but the title did not become official until 1890, when it was won by Jackson W. Showalter. Thereafter the championship was held by Simon Lipschuetz, Albert B. Hodges, Harry Nelson Pillsbury, and Frank J. Marshall.

Marshall held the title for 27 years and retired undefeated in 1936 when the first U. S. Championship Tournament was arranged. The Marshall Chess Club donated the Frank J. Marshall Trophy as the emblem of the national title. Since 1936 the championship has been decided by tournament play, with occasional matches between tournaments.

1st U. S. Championship Tournament, New York, 1936

The first tournament was held in 1936 under the auspices of the National Chess Federation. The committee seeded Arthur W. Dake, Reuben Fine, I. A. Horowitz, Isaac I. Kashdan, Alexander Kevitz, Abraham Kupchik, Samuel Reshevsky, Herman Steiner. In addition, preliminaries were held in which forty-eight players competed in four sections. The top two players from each section qualified for the finals. The results:

Samuel Reshevsky (N. Y.)	11½	I. A. Horowitz (N. Y.)	7
Albert C. Simonson (N. Y.)	11	Samuel D. Factor (Ill.)	6½
Reuben Fine (N. Y.)	10½	Herman Steiner (Calif.)	6
G. N. Treysman (N. Y.)	10½	Arnold S. Denker (N. Y.)	6
Isaac Kashdan (N. Y.)	10	Sidney Bernstein (N. Y.)	5
Arthur W. Dake (Ore.)	9	Milton Hanauer (N. Y.)	4½
Abraham Kupchik (N. Y.)	9	Weaver W. Adams (Mass.)	3
Alexander Kevitz (N. Y.)	7½	Harold Morton (Mass.)	3

The following six championships were held at two-year intervals.

2nd U. S. Championship Tournament, New York, 1938

Ten players were seeded and seven others qualified from preliminaries in which thirty players competed. Reshevsky won again.

Samuel Reshevsky (N. Y.)	13	A. E. Santasiere (N. Y.)	7
Reuben Fine (N. Y.)	12½	G. N. Treysman (N. Y.)	7
Albert C. Simonson (N. Y.)	11	S. S. Cohen (N. Y.)	6½
I. A. Horowitz (N. Y.)	10	Milton Hanauer (N. Y.)	6½
Isaac Kashdan (N. Y.)	9½	Fred Reinfeld (N. Y.)	6½
Arthur W. Dake (Ore.)	9	George Shainswit (N. Y.)	5½
David Polland (N. Y.)	9	Harold Morton (Mass.)	5
Abraham Kupchik (N. Y.)	8½	Walter B. Suesman (R. I.)	2
Sidney Bernstein (N. Y.)	7½		

In 1939, the National Chess Federation and the American Chess Federation (successor to the Western Chess Association) amalgamated to become the United States Chess Federation. Thereafter, all championships were held under the auspices of the USCF.

3rd U. S. Championship Tournament, New York, 1940

Twenty-five players competed in three preliminary sections to qualify six for the finals with eleven seeded players. Reshevsky won for the third time.

Samuel Reshevsky (N. Y.)	13	Fred Reinfeld (N. Y.)	7½
Reuben Fine (N. Y.)	12½	George Shainswit (N. Y.)	7½
Isaac Kashdan (N. Y.)	10½	Weaver W. Adams (Mass.)	7
Albert S. Pinkus (N. Y.)	10	Herbert Seidman (N. Y.)	7
Albert C. Simonson (N. Y.)	10	Matthew Green (N. Y.)	6
Abraham Kupchik (N. Y.)	9½	Milton Hanauer (N. Y.)	6
Arnold S. Denker (N. Y.)	9½	Philip Woliston (Calif.)	3
Sidney Bernstein (N. Y.)	7½	G. Littman (Ill.)	2
David Polland (N. Y.)	7½		

In 1941, Reshevsky played a 16-game match for the title with I. A. Horowitz. Reshevsky defeated the challenger without losing a game. He won three and drew thirteen.

4th U. S. Championship Tournament, New York, 1942

Isaac Kashdan (N. Y.)	12½	Louis Levy (N. Y.)	6½
Samuel Reshevsky (N. Y.)	12½	Irving Chernev (N. Y.)	6
Arnold S. Denker (N. Y.)	10½	Carl Pilnick (N. Y.)	6
Albert S. Pinkus (N. Y.)	10½	Norman Lessing (N. Y.)	5½
Herman Steiner (Calif.)	10	Harry Baker (N. Y.)	5½
I. A. Horowitz (N. Y.)	9	Benjamin Altman (N. Y.)	4
Herbert Seidman (N. Y.)	7	Matthew Green (N. Y.)	4 *
Jacob Levin (Pa.)	6½	Herman Hahlbohm (Ill.)	4

* Illness forced Green to withdraw and forfeit seven games.

Twenty-three players competed in three preliminary sections to qualify seven for the finals with nine seeded players. Kashdan and Reshevsky tied for first, then played a scheduled 14-game match to break the tie. The match ended with the eleventh game when Reshevsky had scored 7½ points to regain the undisputed title. Reshevsky won six games, Kashdan two; three games were drawn.

5th U. S. Championship Tournament, New York, 1944

Nine players qualified from only 18 preliminary entries in three sections to compete with nine seeded players in the finals. Neither Reshevsky nor Kashdan competed, and the title was won by Arnold Denker, who defeated Reuben Fine in their individual encounter.

Arnold S. Denker (N. Y.)	15½	Atillio DiCamillo (Pa.)	7
Reuben Fine (N. Y.)	14½	Sol Weinstock (N. Y.)	7
I. A. Horowitz (N. Y.)	14	Lewis J. Isaacs (Ill.)	6½
Herman Steiner (Calif.)	14	Leon Neidich (N. J.)	6½
Albert S. Pinkus (N. Y.)	13½	Aaron A. Rothman (N. Y.)	6½
George Shainswit (N. Y.)	10½	Bernard Stromberg (N. Y.)	5
Benjamin Altman (N. Y.)	9	Irving Chernev (N. Y.)	4½
Weaver W. Adams (Mass.)	8	David Gladstone (N. Y.)	2½
Sven Almgren (N. Y.)	8	Louis J. Persinger (N. Y.)	½

Early in 1946, Denker retained his title in a match with Herman Steiner of California. Denker won by a score of 6–4.

6th U. S. Championship Tournament, New York, 1946

In an attempt to broaden participation in the U. S. Championship, the USCF adopted a regional system of qualification for the 1946 contest. The country was divided into seven geographical areas in which efforts were to be made to hold qualifying tournaments. At first, the USCF seeded only the reigning champion, Arnold Denker, into the finals, but later yielded to a storm of protest and agreed to seed Fine, Horowitz, Kashdan, Pinkus, Reshevsky, and Steiner in addition to Denker. Although only three of the seven areas held special qualifying tournaments, representatives from all but one of the areas came to New York and played in the championship. Six of the seven seeded masters also entered the event. Denker lost his title and Reshevsky regained it. The final results are given in the table on the next page.

Samuel Reshevsky (Mass.)	16	Olaf Ulvestad (Wash.)	7½
Isaac Kashdan (N. Y.)	13½	Sol Rubinow (Va.)	7
A. E. Santasiere (N. Y.)	13	Weaver W. Adams (Mass.)	6½
Jacob Levin (Pa.)	12½	Atillio DiCamillo (Pa.)	6½
Arnold S. Denker (N. Y.)	12	Aaron A. Rothman (N. Y.)	6½
I. A. Horowitz (N. Y.)	12	Walter B. Suesman (R. I.)	6½
Herman Steiner (Calif.)	11	George Drexel (Fla.)	5
Albert S. Pinkus (N. Y.)	10½	A. Fink (Calif.)	4
George Kramer (N. Y.)	9½	S. Kowalski (N. J.)	3½
Albert Sandrin, Jr. (Ill.)	8		

7th U. S. Championship Tournament, South Fallsburg, N. Y., 1948

For the 1948 championship, the USCF seeded only Fine, Kashdan, Reshevsky, and either Herman Steiner or the winner of the U. S. Open Championship of that year. The other sixteen contestants qualified from preliminaries held in all seven USCF areas of the United States. As it turned out, Steiner qualified from one of the area preliminaries and Weaver Adams, who won the U. S. Open, qualified from another preliminary. Isaac Kashdan was the only seeded master to take part in the championship. Fine and Reshevsky made financial demands which the committee was unable to meet. Most of the leading U. S. masters boycotted the tournament, refusing to play in the preliminaries. It was freely predicted that the U. S. Championship would soon become an amateur event. At the last moment, Reshevsky found a patron willing to put up the fee demanded, and Sammy announced that he was now able to play in the championship. However, all arrangements had been made and the time for acceptance of invitations had elapsed, so the tournament director ruled that Reshevsky was too late.

In the finals, Herman Steiner won the title, finishing one-half point ahead of Kashdan. The standings:

Herman Steiner (Calif.)	15	Albert Sandrin, Jr. (Ill.)	10½
Isaac Kashdan (N. Y.)	14½	A. E. Santasiere (N. Y.)	10½
George Kramer (N. Y.)	13	Paul Poschel (Ill.)	8
Olaf Ulvestad (Wash.)	13	Dr. Joseph Platz (N. Y.)	7½
Herman V. Hesse (Pa.)	12	Irving Heitner (N. Y.)	7
Sol Rubinow (Pa.)	12	N. T. Whitaker (Md.)	6
George Shainswit (N. Y.)	12	Franklin J. Howard (N. J.)	5½
Weaver W. Adams (Mass.)	11½	Sven Almgren (Calif.)	4
Larry Evans (N. Y.)	11½	Anthony Suraci (Conn.)	3
Walter Shipman (N. Y.)	11½	Wm. H. Janes (Texas)	2

8th U. S. Championship Tournament, New York, 1951

The USCF found it impossible to arrange a regular biennial championship tournament in 1950. Instead, an invitational tournament was held in 1951. The number of invited players dwindled from as many as fifty to an eventual twenty-four who were then divided into four preliminary groups. The top three in each group qualified for the finals. The current champion, Herman Steiner, did not compete. The title was won by Larry Evans, with Reshevsky in second place. Larry was eighteen years old—the youngest U. S. Champion up to that time. The standings in the finals:

Larry Evans (N. Y.)	9½	A. E. Santasiere (N. Y.)	5
Samuel Reshevsky (N. Y.)	8½	Dr. A. Mengarini (N. Y.)	4½
Max Pavey (N. Y.)	7	George Shainswit (N. Y.)	4
Herbert Seidman (N. Y.)	6½	Milton Hanauer (N. Y.)	3½
I. A. Horowitz (N. Y.)	5½	Albert S. Pinkus (N. Y.)	3½
Sidney Bernstein (N. Y.)	5	Albert C. Simonson (N. Y.)	3½

In 1952, Larry Evans retained his title in a match with ex-champion Herman Steiner of Los Angeles. The score was 10–4.

9th U. S. Championship Tournament, New York, 1954

In 1950 the USCF had adopted a complicated three-year cycle plan for the U. S. Championship, but it was never carried out. After the Harkness Rating System had been adopted by the USCF and the first rating list was published in 1950, it was decided to hold a Challengers' Tournament, based on national ratings, to qualify six players into the next championship. Twenty-three rated masters and experts took part in this ten-round Swiss System tournament, held in 1953 at Philadelphia. The players who qualified were Arthur Bisguier, Hans Berliner, Karl Burger, Atillio DiCamillo, Paul Brandts, and Saul Wachs. With the exception of DiCamillo, who was unable to play, these qualifiers met in the 1954 championship with four qualifiers from the U. S. Open, two seeded from the 1951 championship, and Larry Evans, the reigning champion. The final results:

Arthur Bisguier (N. Y.)	10	Hans Berliner (Wash., D. C.)	6½
Larry Evans (N. Y.)	9	Saul Wachs (Phila., Pa.)	6½
Herbert Seidman (N. Y.)	8	Eliot Hearst (N. Y.)	6
Max Pavey (N. Y.)	7½	Karl Burger (N. Y.)	5½
James T. Sherwin (N. Y.)	7½	Carl Pilnick (N. Y.)	5
Sidney Bernstein (N. Y.)	7	Paul Brandts (N. Y.)	3
Nicolas Rossolimo (N. Y.)	7	Dr. A. Mengarini (N. Y.)	2½

10th U. S. Championship Tournament, New York, 1957-58

A new era began in 1957 when the U. S. Chess Federation joined with the American Chess Foundation in sponsoring the 4th annual Lessing J. Rosenwald Trophy Tournament. The USCF announced its recognition of this tournament as the United States Championship. It also designated the 1957-58 event as the FIDE zonal tournament in World Championship competition. The players who finished first and second would represent the United States in the FIDE Interzonal Tournament of 1958. The U. S. Championship thus became an annual event. A tournament was held each year up to and including 1963.

The USCF abandoned its previous methods of qualification by means of preliminaries. Players were invited to compete on the basis of their USCF ratings. The United States Junior Champion was seeded. The final results of this first annual championship, starting in December of 1957 and finishing in January of 1958, were as follows:

Robert J. Fischer (N. Y.)	10½	Edmar Mednis (N. Y.)	6½
Samuel Reshevsky (N. Y.)	9½	Herbert Seidman (N. Y.)	6
James T. Sherwin (N. Y.)	9	Sidney Bernstein (N. Y.)	5
William Lombardy (N. Y.)	7½	Arthur B. Bisguier (N. Y.)	5
Hans Berliner (Wash., D. C.)	7	A. DiCamillo (Pa.)	4½
Arnold S. Denker (N. Y.)	6½	Abe Turner (N. Y.)	4½
Arthur W. Feuerstein (N. Y.)	6½	George Kramer (N. J.)	3

This tournament saw the emergence of Bobby Fischer as U. S. Champion at the age of 14. He also won the U. S. Junior Championships of 1956 and 1957, and the U. S. Open Championship of 1957.

11th U. S. Championship, New York, 1958-59

Competing against most of the top players of the United States, including four International Grandmasters, Bobby Fischer again won the championship of 1958-59. He did not lose a single game, winning six and drawing five.

Robert J. Fischer (N. Y.)	8½	William Lombardy (N. Y.)	6
Samuel Reshevsky (N. Y.)	7½	Pal Benko (N. Y.)	5½
James T. Sherwin (N. Y.)	6½	Robert Byrne (Ind.)	4
Arthur B. Bisguier (N. Y.)	6	Charles Kalme (Pa.)	4
Donald Byrne (Pa.)	6	Edmar Mednis (N. Y.)	3
Larry Evans (N. Y.)	6	Raymond Weinstein (N. Y.)	3

12th U. S. Championship, New York, 1959-60

For the third successive time, Fischer won the championship in 1959-60, again with no losses.

Robert J. Fischer (N. Y.)	9	Herbert Seidman (N. Y.)	5½
Robert Byrne (Ind.)	8	James T. Sherwin (N. Y.)	5
Samuel Reshevsky (N. Y.)	7½	Edmar Mednis (N. Y.)	4½
Pal Benko (N. Y.)	7	Sidney Bernstein (N. Y.)	4
Arthur B. Bisguier (N. Y.)	6½	Arnold S. Denker (N. Y.)	3
Raymond Weinstein (N. Y.)	6	Robin Ault (N. J.)	0

13th U. S. Championship, New York, 1960-61

Fischer did it again in the tournament of 1960-61. For the fourth time in a row, he won the U. S. Championship, again without losing a game.

Robert J. Fischer (N. Y.)	9	Charles Kalme (Pa.)	6
William Lombardy (N. Y.)	7	Pal Benko (N. Y.)	4½
Raymond Weinstein (N. Y.)	6½	Hans Berliner (Wash., D. C.)	4½
Arthur B. Bisguier (N. Y.)	6	Robert Byrne (Ind.)	4½
Samuel Reshevsky (N. Y.)	6	Anthony F. Saidy (N. Y.)	4½
James T. Sherwin (N. Y.)	6	Herbert Seidman (N. Y.)	2½

Fischer-Reshevsky Match, 1961

In 1961, a non-title match was held between Fischer and Reshevsky. Although the championship was not at stake, the importance of this match justifies its inclusion in this record of U. S. Championship competition. Fischer was the reigning champion and Reshevsky had won the title many times in the past.

After eleven of the scheduled sixteen games had been completed, the score was tied. Each player had won two games; the other seven were drawn. Unfortunately, the match then broke up in a squabble. Fischer was forfeited when he refused to appear for the 12th game, which had been re-scheduled to start at 11 A.M. on a Sunday, to meet the convenience of one of the financial patrons of the match. Fischer refused to continue the match unless the 12th game was cancelled. The officials of the American Chess Foundation, organizers of the match, awarded victory to Reshevsky when Fischer did not show up for the 13th game in New York.

14th U. S. Championship, New York, 1961-62

Several of the leading United States masters, including Fischer, Reshevsky, Bisguier and Lombardy, declined to play in the 14th Championship. It was won by Larry Evans, who had previously taken the title in 1951.

Larry Evans (N. Y.)	7½	Eliot Hearst (Va.)	5½
Robert Byrne (Ind.)	7	Donald Byrne (Pa.)	5
Pal Benko (N. Y.)	6½	Raymond Weinstein (N. Y.)	4½
Edmar Mednis (N. Y.)	6½	Abe Turner (N. Y.)	4
Herbert Seidman (N. Y.)	6½	George Kramer (N. J.)	3½
James T. Sherwin (N. Y.)	6½	Sidney Bernstein (N. Y.)	3

15th U. S. Championship, New York, 1962-63

Returning to the championship wars, Fischer won the title for the fifth time in the tournament of 1962-63.

Robert J. Fischer (N. Y.)	8	Hans Berliner (Wash., D. C.)	5
Arthur B. Bisguier (N. Y.)	7	Edmar Mednis (N. Y.)	5
William Addison (Calif.)	6½	Pal Benko (N. Y.)	4½
Larry Evans (N. Y.)	6½	Nicolas Rossolimo (N. Y.)	4½
Samuel Reshevsky (N. Y.)	6½	R. H. Steinmeyer (Mo.)	4
Robert Byrne (Ind.)	6	James T. Sherwin (N. Y.)	2½

16th U. S. Championship Tournament, New York, 1963-64

Bobby Fischer made chess history when he won the 16th Championship Tournament with a perfect score of 11–0. It was the sixth time he had won the title. The final results:

Robert J. Fischer (N. Y.)	11	Raymond Weinstein (N. Y.)	5
Larry Evans (N. Y.)	7½	Arthur B. Bisguier (N. Y.)	4½
Pal Benko (N. Y.)	7	Edmar Mednis (N. Y.)	3½
Samuel Reshevsky (N. Y.)	6½	William Addison (Calif.)	3½
Anthony F. Saidy (N. Y.)	6½	R. H. Steinmeyer (Mo.)	3
Robert Byrne (Ind.)	5½	Donald Byrne (Pa.)	2½

In 1964 the sponsors announced that a championship tournament would not be held that year. International commitments, including the sending of a team to Tel Aviv, made it impractical to stage a championship event.

17th U. S. Championship Tournament, New York, 1965

Bobby Fischer, now 22, won the championship for the seventh time in 1965. Although Bobby won the event, he lost to Reshevsky and Robert Byrne and drew with William Addison for a final score of 8½–2½. With the exception of the International Tournament at Havana in which he competed by teletype from New York, Fischer had not played against any strong competition for a couple of years. Observers felt that lack of practice had an unfavorable effect on his playing strength. However, the fact remains that he did win the tournament and became the first to win the title outright seven times.

Robert J. Fischer (N. Y.)	8½	Pal Benko (Calif.)	5
Robert Byrne (Ind.)	7½	Larry Evans (Nev.)	5
Samuel Reshevsky (N. Y.)	7½	Anthony Saidy (Calif.)	5
William Addison (Calif.)	6½	Arthur Bisguier (N. Y.)	3
Bernard Zuckerman (N. Y.)	6½	Karl Burger (N. Y.)	3
Nicolas Rossolimo (N. Y.)	6	Duncan Suttles (B. C.)	2½

18th U. S. Championship Tournament, New York, 1966

Bobby made it the eighth time in 1966, drawing three games (with Evans, Addison and Robert Byrne) but losing none.

Robert J. Fischer (N. Y.)	9½	Anthony Saidy (N. Y.)	5
Larry Evans (Nev.)	7½	Robert Byrne (Ind.)	4½
Pal Benko (Calif.)	6	Samuel Reshevsky (N. Y.)	4½
James T. Sherwin (N. Y.)	6	Nicolas Rossolimo (N. Y.)	4½
Arthur B. Bisguier (N. Y.)	5½	Donald Byrne (Pa.)	4
William Addison (Calif.)	5	Bernard Zuckerman	4

Official United States Chess Champions

1890–1892	Jackson W. Showalter	1946–1948	Samuel Reshevsky
1892–1894	Simon Lipschuetz	1948–1951	Herman Steiner
1894–1896	Albert B. Hodges	1951–1954	Larry Evans
1897–1906	Harry Nelson Pillsbury	1954–1958	Arthur Bisguier
1906–1909	Jackson W. Showalter *	1958–1962	Robert J. Fischer
1909–1936	Frank J. Marshall	1962–1963	Larry Evans
1936–1944	Samuel Reshevsky **	1963–	Robert J. Fischer
1944–1946	Arnold S. Denker		

* Pillsbury died in 1906. Marshall was then generally accepted as U. S. Champion, but technically the title reverted to Showalter, according to Marshall. He did not feel that he had a clear right to the title until he defeated Showalter in 1909.

** Reshevsky and Isaac Kashdan were recognized as co-champions when they tied for first in the tournament of 1942, but Reshevsky then defeated Kashdan in a match to break the tie.

U. S. OPEN CHAMPIONSHIPS

Since 1900, an open national chess tournament has been held annually in the United States. Up to the year 1938, these tournaments were conducted by the Western Chess Association and its successor, the American Chess Federation (1934-1938). Since 1939, they have been held under the auspices of the United States Chess Federation.

Prior to 1947, the number of contestants was relatively small. The tournaments were conducted as Round Robins with preliminaries, Championship Finals, and Consolation Finals. To accommodate the increasing number of entrants, the Swiss System was adopted in 1947 and has been used ever since. As a result, the tournaments have become increasingly popular, despite the fact that each tournament is scheduled for 12 or 13 rounds and lasts almost two weeks.

At Milwaukee in 1953, all previous records were broken when 181 players took part in the Open. At Cleveland in 1957 there were 184 entries. A new record was set at San Francisco in 1961 when 198 players participated. The 1963 Open at Chicago, with 266 players, was the largest chess tournament ever held in the United States. At Boston in 1964 there were 229 players—a slight decrease, but still well over the 200 mark.

The awarding of large and numerous cash prizes is one of the big attractions. The first prize is usually $1000.00, the second prize $500.00, and other prizes for the top fifteen to twenty players range down to $15.00. There are also cash prizes for the top women entrants and for the highest ranking players in the Expert, A, B, and C classes. The junior entrant with the best score gets a cash prize. In recent years, special handicap prizes have also been awarded.

U. S. Open Champions

The complete list of tournaments and national open champions is given below:

No.	Year	Place	Champions
1	1900	Excelsior, Minn.	L. Uedemann
2	1901	Excelsior, Minn.	N. M. MacLeod
3	1902	Excelsior, Minn.	L. Uedemann
4	1903	Chicago, Ill.	Max Judd
5	1904	St. Louis, Mo.	S. Mlotkowski

AMERICAN OPEN CHAMPIONSHIPS

This new four-day Swiss System tournament was inaugurated in 1965. According to *Chess Life,* "the tournament, with a prize fund of $2,400, was conceived by USCF President Ed Edmondson and joins the United States Open and the National Open as one of the top nation-wide chess events."

The first contest, with 124 entrants, was held at the Del Mar Club in Santa Monica, Calif., November 25-28, 1965, and was won by Grandmaster Pal Benko. Mrs. Lena Grumette won the women's prize.

The second tournament of the series, with a prize fund of $3,000, was held at the same place as the first, November 24-27, 1966.

American Open Champions

No.	Year	Place	Champions
1	1965	Santa Monica, Calif.	Pal Benko
2	1966	Santa Monica, Calif. (tie)	Larry Kaufman
			Robion Kirby

U. S. JUNIOR CHAMPIONSHIPS

In April of 1966 the USCF announced that an annual invitational U. S. Junior Championship would be held in cooperation with the Piatigorsky Foundation. The first tournament of the series was played June 20-26, 1966, at the Henry Hudson Hotel, New York, N. Y. The eight contestants, all younger than 21, had been invited to compete on the basis of their latest USCF ratings. One game of the Round Robin was played each day, and adjourned games were played off each evening. The final results are shown in the table below:

Walter Browne (Brooklyn, N. Y.) .... 5 –2
Robert Wachtel (Parlin, N. J.) 4½–2½
David Blohm (San Francisco, Calif.) 4½–2½
Alan Baisley (Hatboro, Pa.) 3½–3½
Marc Yoffie (New York, N. Y.) .... 3 –4
Brendan Godfrey (Minneapolis, Minn.) 2½–4½
Ralph Tobler (Chicago, Ill.) 2½–4½
Jeffrey Harris (Philadelphia, Pa.) 2½–4½

Walter Browne, a 17-year-old senior at Brooklyn's Erasmus High School, came from behind to win the title. For unexplained personal reasons, Browne failed to show up for his second round game against tailender Harris and lost by forfeit. He also lost the fourth round game (over the board) to runner-up Wachtel, but won his last three games to take the title.

The 1966 U. S. Junior Champion was awarded an all-expenses-paid trip to play in the U. S. Open at Seattle, Wash., August 14-26, 1966. His name was engraved on a permanent cup donated by the Piatigorsky Foundation, and trophies were presented to the top three finishers. All players in the invitational U. S. Junior Championship have their expenses paid to participate.

In 1967 and 1969, first prize in the U. S. Junior Championship will be qualification into and an all-expenses-paid trip to the World Junior Chess Championship held in those years. Second prize will be an all-expenses-paid trip to the U. S. Open. All other arrangements will be as in 1966.

U. S. Junior Champions

No.	Year	Place	Champions
1	1966	New York, N. Y.	Walter Browne

U. S. JUNIOR OPEN CHAMPIONSHIPS *

The first United States Junior Open Chess Championship, restricted to players under 20 (later raised to 21), was held at Chicago in 1946. The 32 entrants were divided into six preliminary sections. Twelve players qualified for the Championship Finals, nine for each of two Consolation Finals. The championship was won by Larry Friedman of Cleveland with 8½-2½.

The second Junior Open Championship was held in Cleveland in 1947. As the number of entrants had risen to 45, the plan followed in the U. S. Open Championship of 1946 was followed, viz., an eight-round Swiss System preliminary and Round Robin finals, with preliminary scores carried over to the finals. The top twelve competed for the championship; the others played in three groups of Con-

---

* In 1966, when the invitational Junior Championship was inaugurated, the older annual contest was renamed the U. S. Junior Open Championship.

solation Finals. Larry Friedman again won the title with a preliminary score of 6½–1½ and a final score of 9–2, for a total of 15½–3½. The third Junior Open Championship at Oak Ridge, Tenn., in 1948, with 50 entrants, was conducted as a straight ten-round Swiss System tournament. Arthur B. Bisguier, 18-year-old champion of New York's Manhattan Chess Club, and Frank Anderson, 20-year-old Toronto City and Provincial Champion, tied for first at 8–2. Bisguier was awarded the title under the tie-breaking rules.

All succeeding annual championships have been conducted as nine- or ten-round Swiss System tournaments. In recent years, the Champion is given custody of the John W. Collins Trophy. (Jack Collins has encouraged and developed many youthful players, including Bobby Fischer and Robert and Donald Byrne.) Up to 1964, the number of entrants in the Junior Open Championships steadily increased. In 1963 and 1964, 72 young players competed for the title. The complete list of tournaments and U. S. Junior Open Champions is given below:

U. S. Junior Open Champions

No.	Year	Place	Champions
1	1946	Chicago, Ill.	Larry Friedman
2	1947	Cleveland, Ohio	Larry Friedman
3	1948	Oak Ridge, Tenn.	Arthur B. Bisguier
4	1949	Fort Worth, Tex.	Arthur B. Bisguier
5	1950	Milwaukee, Wis.	James Cross
6	1951	Philadelphia, Pa.	Saul Wachs
7	1952	Omaha, Neb.	Curt Brasket
8	1953	Kansas City, Mo.	Saul Yarmak
9	1954	Long Beach, Calif.	Ross E. Siemms
10	1955	Lincoln, Neb.	Charles Kalme
11	1956	Philadelphia, Pa.	Robert J. Fischer
12	1957	San Francisco, Calif.	Robert J. Fischer
13	1958	Homestead, Fla.	Raymond Weinstein
14	1959	Omaha, Neb.	Robin Ault
15	1960	West Orange, N. J.	Robin Ault
16	1961	Toledo, Ohio	Robin Ault
17	1962	Tucson, Ariz.	Larry Gilden
18	1963	University Park, Pa.	Peter Irwin
19	1964	Towson State College, Md.	John Meyer
20	1965	Boston, Mass.	William Martz
21	1966	Minneapolis, Minn.	Charles Alden

U. S. AMATEUR CHAMPIONSHIPS

Four Round Robin tournaments for the title of United States Amateur Chess Champion were held in New York during the war years 1942 through 1945. The finalists qualified from preliminaries. The title was originated, and these tournaments were directed, by the late L. Walter Stephens, Vice President of the USCF. A player was considered an "amateur" and eligible to compete if he had not played in the finals of any U. S. Championship Tournament.

After a lapse of ten years, the writer of this book, as Business Manager of the USCF, revived competition for the amateur title. A Swiss System tournament, with a modest entry fee, open to all players except rated masters, was held at Lake Mohegan, N. Y., over the weekend of May 21-23, 1955. There were 57 entrants. The idea of a holiday weekend tournament, without masters and with no cash prizes, was an immediate success.

From 1955 to 1964, tournaments of six or seven rounds were held annually over the Memorial Day weekend at Asbury Park, N. J., with trophies and book prizes awarded to the top three winners, and the first- and second-place winners in Classes A, B, and C. The woman entrant with the highest score is recognized as Woman Amateur Chess Champion of the United States and gets a special trophy. Being an amateur event, the time limit is 50 moves in two hours, and unfinished games are adjudicated after each player has made his 50 moves. Each tournament is rated by the USCF so that contestants can obtain a national rating or strive to improve their existing rankings.

These amateur tournaments have become increasingly popular events among chessplayers and their families. The number of entrants grew steadily until 1959, when 163 players from sixteen states competed for the title. In 1965, when the tournament returned to New York City after ten years at Asbury Park, an all-time record of 242 players took part in the event.

The complete list of tournaments and champions is given below:

No.	Year	Men Champions	Women Champions
1	1942	E. Schuyler Jackson, Jr.	
2	1943	Dr. Ariel Mengarini	
3	1944	E. Schuyler Jackson, Jr.	
4	1945	Paul Ellis	
	1946 to 1954: No tournaments held.		

No.	Year	Men Champions	Women Champions
5	1955	Clinton L. Parmelee	Kathryn Slater
6	1956	John Hudson	Kathryn Slater
7	1957	Harry Lyman	Rosalie de Serrano
8	1958	Eric W. Marchand	Greta Fuchs
9	1959	L. Russell Chauvenet	Lisa Lane
10	1960	Raoul L. Benedicto	Greta Fuchs
11	1961	Edgar T. McCormick	Greta Fuchs
12	1962 (tie)	{ Ben Greenwald and { Dr. Max Cohen	Adele Goddard
13	1963	Kenneth Clayton	Cecilia Rock
14	1964	Michael Hailparn	Zenaida Huber
15	1965	Frank Street	Eclesia Cestone
16	1966	Thomas Lux	Zenaida Huber Wagner

U. S. TEAM CHAMPIONSHIPS

The USCF inaugurated a national team championship tournament in 1961. The Swiss System is used and the contest is held over a weekend. Each team has four members and not more than two alternates. Cash prizes are awarded to the high-scoring teams and players. Positions are determined by match points, ties being broken by game points. Up to this writing, three tournaments have been held as listed below:

No.	Year	Place	Winning Team
1	1961	Raleigh, N. C.	District of Columbia
2	1962	Tacoma Park, Md.	District of Columbia
3	1964	Chevy Chase, Md.	U. S. Students

In 1961, eleven teams competed, and there was a tie between the District of Columbia and Scarlet Knights of N. J. teams. Each team scored 5½–½ match points, but the title went to the District of Columbia on the basis of its higher game points. The same two teams again tied on match points of 5–1 in 1962, and the D. C. team again won the title on game points. The winning team in 1964 comprised the members of the U. S. Students team in a warm-up prior to participation in the World Students Team Championship. The team breezed through the five-round Swiss with ease, winning all its matches. The winning team: William Lombardy, Charles Kalme, Bernard Zuckerman, and Michael Valvo.

U. S. WOMEN'S CHAMPIONSHIPS

In 1937, the National Chess Federation recognized the winner of the women's tournament held annually by the Marshall Chess Club of New York as the woman champion of the NCF. In 1934, 1937, and 1938, the American Chess Federation held open tournaments for women at the same time and places as the ACF Open Championships, now called the U. S. Open Championship.

For the purposes of identification, in the following list of tournaments we refer to the NCF-endorsed events of 1937 and 1938 as the first and second U. S. Women's Championships. The tournaments conducted by the ACF are included in the list of U. S. Women's Open Championships in the next section of this chapter. In 1939, the NCF and ACF combined to form the U. S. Chess Federation. All tournaments after this date in the following list, starting with the 3rd Championship of 1940, were held under the auspices of the USCF.

1st Women's Championship, New York, 1937: Adele Rivero won the title and the Hazel Allen Trophy with a score of 8½–½. The other players scored as follows: Mary Bain 7; Mrs. R. McCready 5; Kathryn Slater 5; Adele Raettig 5; Helen White 4; Mrs. Wm. Davey 3; Elsie Rogosin 3; Edith L. Weart 2; Elizabeth Wray 2.

2nd Women's Championship, New York, 1938: Miss Karff won the tournament held at the same time and place as the men's championship under the auspices of the NCF. The final standings: Mona M. Karff 9½; Mary Bain 8½; Adele Rivero 7½; Edith L. Weart 7; Mrs. R. McCready 5; Mathilda Harmath 4; Adele Raettig 4; Edna Harrison 3½; Helen Kashdan 3; Mrs. W. E. Jackson 2; Elizabeth Wray 1.

3rd Women's Championship, New York, 1940: The 1940 contest and all subsequent championships were held under the sponsorship of the U. S. Chess Federation. Adele Rivero regained the title. The final standings: Adele Rivero 7; Mona M. Karff 5½; Gisela K. Gresser 5; Helen Weissenstein 5; Mary Bain 4½; Mrs. R. McCready 4½; Mathilda Harmath 2½; Adele Raettig 1; Elizabeth Wray 1.

In 1941, Mrs. Rivero lost her title in a match with Miss Karff. The latter won the match by a score of 5–1. Adele married Donald Belcher of New York the day before the match began.

Miss Karff retained her title convincingly in the championship of 1942.

4th Women's Championship, New York, 1942: Mona M. Karff 8; Adele Belcher 6; Nancy Roos 6; Gisela K. Gresser 5½; Mary Bain 4; Mathilda Harmath 2½; Elizabeth Wray 2½; Adele Raettig 1; Cecilia Fawns ½.

5th Women's Championship, New York, 1944: The title was won by Gisela K. Gresser, who scored eight straight victories. The other scores: Mona M. Karff 7; Kate Henschel 5; Wally Henschel 4; Adele Raettig 4; Nancy Roos 4; Elizabeth Wray 3; Mildred Peters ½; Maude M. Stephens ½.

6th Women's Championship, New York, 1946: Mona M. Karff scored an easy victory and regained the title, winning all but her last game for a final score of 8½–½. Mary Bain was a good second with 7½–1½, while ex-champion Gisela K. Gresser placed third with 6½–2½.

7th Women's Championship, South Fallsburg, N. Y., 1948: Miss Karff and Mrs. Gresser became co-champions when they tied with scores of 6½–½. The six other contestants, who had qualified from various sections of the country, scored as follows: Mary Bain (Fla.) 4–3; Lena Grumette (N. Y.) 3½–3½; Lucille Kellner (Mich.) 2½–4½; Adele Raettig (N. J.) 2–5; Mary Selensky (Pa.) 2–5; Elizabeth Wray (N. Y.) 1–6.

8th Women's Championship, New York, 1951: The title was won by Mary Bain of New York and Miami, Fla., with a score of 8½–½. Mrs. Gresser and Miss Karff, the previous co-champions, were second and third respectively. The Edith L. Weart Trophy was awarded as the emblem of the women's title.

9th Women's Championship, New York, 1953: Miss Karff again won the championship with a score of 7½–½. Mrs. Gresser was second, having scored 7–0 up to the last round, when she lost to Miss Karff. The other players: Rosalie de Serrano 5½; Kate and Wally Henschel 4½ each; Adele Raettig and Henrietta Rogers 2½ each; Mrs. M. Babakin 2; Margaret Story 0.

10th Women's Championship, New York, 1955: The tournament ended in a tie between Gisela K. Gresser of New York and Nancy Roos of Los Angeles. The co-champions scored 9–2 each. Other scores: Mona M. Karff 8½; Mrs. Kenneth S. Vines 7½; Lucille Kellner 6½; Lena Grumette, Willa Owens and Mary Selensky 4 each; Rosalie de Serrano 2½; Wally Henschel 2; Kate Henschel 1.

11th Women's Championship, Los Angeles, 1957: Gisela K. Gresser of New York and Sonja Graf of Palm Springs, Calif., became co-champions in 1957, each scoring 9½–1½ in the twelve-player tournament at Los Angeles. Other scores: Eva Aronson (Chicago) 7½; Mona M. Karff (New York) 7; Kathryn Slater (New York) 6½; Lena Grumette (Los Angeles) and Nancy McLeod (San Francisco) 6 each; Lucille Kellner (Detroit) 5; Mary Selensky (Philadelphia) 4; Olga Higgins (Santa Barbara) 2½; Mildred Morrell (Haddonfield, N. J.) 2; Lenore Simon (Los Angeles) ½. As this was the women's zonal tournament, the co-champions qualified to play in the next Women's Candidates' Tournament.

12th Women's Championship, New York and W. Orange, N. J., 1959: Lisa Lane of Philadelphia outpointed former champions Gisela Gresser and Mona Karff to take the title in 1959. Sonja Graf did not compete. The final scores: Lisa Lane (Philadelphia) 7; Gisela K. Gresser (New York) 6½; Mona M. Karff (New York) 5½; Eva Aronson (Chicago) 5; Mary Selensky (Philadelphia) 4; Nancy McLeod (Millbrae, Calif.) 2½; Mildred Morrell (Gary, Ind.) 2½; Lena Grumette (Hollywood, Calif.) 2; Mabel Burlingame (Phoenix, Ariz.) 1.

13th Women's Championship, New York, 1962: When U. S. Woman Champion Lisa Lane had lost four games in the Christmas Tournament at Hastings, England, she quit the tournament and announced that she could not concentrate because she was in love. She was giving up chess, she said. However, she came back to compete in the U. S. Women's Championship of 1962. Whether or not she was still in love is not known, but she failed to retain her title. Gisela Gresser won it with a score of 8½–1½. Lisa Lane was second with

7½. Miss Karff and Eva Aronson tied with 7 points each, followed by Mary Bain with 6–4; Lucille Kellner 5–5; Jacqueline Piatigorsky 4–6; Mary Selensky and 14-year-old Kate Sillars, 3½–6½ each; Mildred Morrell 2–8; Greta Fuchs 1–9.

14th Women's Championship, New York, 1964: After a lapse of four years, Sonja Graf came back into competition and won the championship with 8½–1½ points. Remainder of the field scored as follows: Gisela K. Gresser 7½; Mona M. Karff 6½; Eva Aronson 5½; Jacqueline Piatigorsky 5½; Cecilia Rock 5; Mary Selensky 4½; Zenaida Z. Huber 4; Mary Bain 3½; Sara Kaufman 2½; Adele Goddard 2.

Sonja Graf died in New York on March 6th, 1965, at the early age of 44. Although married to Vernon Stevenson, and the mother of a son, Alexander, she preferred to be known by her maiden name. Gisela K. Gresser regained the championship in the tournament of 1965.

15th Women's Championship, New York, 1965: Gisela K. Gresser 8–2; Jacqueline Piatigorsky 7½–2½; Ruth Herstein 6–4; Mona M. Karff 6–4; Kate Sillars 6–4; Dr. Helen Weissenstein 5½–4½; Rachel Guinan 4–6; Zenaida Huber 4–6; Anna-Lisa Korhonen 3–7; Mary Selensky 3–7; Mildred Morrell 2–8.

In 1966, Mrs. Gresser and Lisa Lane became co-champions. As a result, they qualified to play in the World Women Candidates' Tournament of 1967.

16th Women's Championship, New York, 1966: Gisela K. Gresser 8½–1½; Lisa Lane 8½–1½; Eva Aronson 6–4; Dr. Helen Weissenstein 5–5; Kate Sillars 5–5; Mona M. Karff 4½–5½; Mabel Burlingame 4½–5½; Jacqueline Piatigorsky 4–6; Zenaida Huber Wagner 3½–6½; Mildred Morrell 3½–6½; Mary Bain 2–8.

Official U. S. Women Chess Champions

1937–1938	Adele Rivero	1955–1957 (tie)	{ Gisela K. Gresser / Nancy Roos
1938–1940	Mona M. Karff		
1940–1941	Adele Rivero	1957–1959 (tie)	{ Gisela K. Gresser / Sonja Graf
1941–1944	Mona M. Karff		
1944–1946	Gisela K. Gresser	1959–1962	Lisa Lane
1946–1948	Mona M. Karff	1962–1964	Gisela K. Gresser
1948–1951 (tie)	{ Gisela K. Gresser / Mona M. Karff	1964–1965	Sonja Graf
		1965–1966	Gisela K. Gresser
1951–1953	Mary Bain	1966– (tie)	{ Gisela K. Gresser / Lisa Lane
1953–1955	Mona M. Karff		

U. S. WOMEN'S OPEN CHAMPIONSHIPS

Open Championship Tournaments for women have been held irregularly in connection with the annual U. S. Open Championships. Prior to 1951, the women's tournaments were conducted as separate Round Robin contests. Thereafter, with the exception of the 1954 tournament, the ladies usually played in the same Swiss System tournament as the men, the title of U. S. Woman Open Champion being awarded to the woman player who finished with the highest score. If necessary, ties were usually broken under the rules of the tournament.

Complete records of the Women's Open Championship are difficult to locate and are not always available. Subject to possible omissions, the list of titleholders is given below.

No.	Year	Place	Open Champions
1	1934	Chicago, Ill.	Virginia Sheffield
2	1937	Chicago, Ill.	Jean M. Grau
3	1938	Boston, Mass.	Mona M. Karff
4	1939	New York, N. Y.	Mona M. Karff *
5	1948	Baltimore, Md.	Mona M. Karff
6	1950	Detroit, Mich. (tie)	Mona M. Karff / Lucille Kellner
7	1951	Fort Worth, Tex.	Maxine Cutlip
8	1953	Milwaukee, Wis.	Eva Aronson
9	1954	New Orleans, La.	Gisela K. Gresser **
10	1955	Long Beach, Calif.	Sonja Graf
11	1956	Oklahoma City, Okla.	Sonja Graf
12	1957	Cleveland, Ohio	Sonja Graf
13	1958	Rochester, Minn.	Kathryn Slater
14	1959	Omaha, Neb.	Sonja Graf
15	1960	St. Louis, Mo.	Lisa Lane
16	1961	San Francisco, Calif.	Eva Aronson
17	1962	San Antonio, Tex.	Kathryn Slater
18	1963	Chicago, Ill.	Kate Sillars
19	1964	Boston, Mass.	Kathryn Slater / Cecilia Rock
20	1965	Rio Piedras, P. R. (tie)	Mary Bain / Kathryn Slater
21	1966	Seattle, Wash.	Mary Bain

* The 1939 tournament ended in a three-way tie, but Miss Karff won the playoff with Mary Bain and Dr. Helen Weissenstein.

** The 1954 tournament was a separate round robin of eleven players. It was the women's zonal tournament for that year. Mrs. Gresser scored 8–2. Miss Karff and Sonja Graf tied at 7–3, but the latter had more Sonnenborn-Berger points and qualified, with Mrs. Gresser, to play in the Women's World Championship Candidates' Tournament.

U. S. INTERCOLLEGIATE CHAMPIONSHIPS

Team tournaments for the championship of the Intercollegiate Chess League and custody of the Harold M. Phillips Trophy have been conducted during Christmas vacations since the beginning of the 20th century. Individual championships were also held during the Easter vacations. However, the reduction of chess activities durnig World War II resulted in the decision to alternate the team and individual championships annually. This practice was continued until 1964, the tournaments being held at Christmastime.

In 1945 the intercollegiate tournaments were endorsed by the USCF as national championships. The first official event was an individual tournament held in 1945. This was the first national tournament to be conducted under the Swiss System and was directed by Milton Finkelstein, who was appointed to supervise college chess activities.

Since 1945, individual championships have been held biennially. With the exception of the first and eighth tournaments, when only six rounds were played, the entrants competed in seven-round Swiss System contests, ties for the title being broken under existing rules. From 23 entrants in 1945, the number of players rose to 40 in 1949, then fell off for a few years. In 1961 there were 50 entrants; in 1963, a new high of 103 players from 31 colleges competed. In 1965, the individual and team championships were combined in one eight-round event and the number of entrants jumped to a record-breaking 183 from 49 North American colleges and universities. Marc Yoffie of the CCNY team made the highest score and became the individual champion.

The first USCF-endorsed Intercollegiate Team Championship was held in 1946. It was conducted as a modified Swiss System tournament of eight rounds under the direction of Milton Finkelstein. Thirteen colleges entered, including teams representing Harvard, Yale, and Princeton. Previously, the Ivy League colleges had competed only in the team tournaments of the HYPD League (Harvard, Yale, Princeton, and Dartmouth). The first team championship was won by CCNY with a total game score of 25–7.

The team championships were held biennially from 1946 to 1964. After the first tournament, the number of Swiss System rounds was changed to seven, in 1958 to six, then back to seven in 1964. Up to and including the sixth championship of 1956, the final positions of the team were determined by the total game score (as in the FIDE World Team Championships). In 1956 the University of Chicago won the title with 22½–5½ game points, and CCNY placed second with 21½–6½. However, the CCNY team won all its seven matches, including the one with Chicago, whereas the latter team scored only 6–1 in match points. The rules were then changed to make the match-point score decisive, with ties broken by game points. Oddly enough, in the next team event of 1958, the University of Chicago retained the title in a six-round Swiss with a match score of 5–1, ahead of Harvard's 4½–1½, although Harvard topped the field in game points, scoring 17–7.

In 1965, when the individual and team championships were combined in one event, the positions of the teams were determined by their total game scores. The University of Toronto took first place with 23–9 points; M.I.T. was second with 22–10.

The eight-round 1966 tournament, held December 26–30 at Penn State University, was also a combined individual and team championship. This type of contest, which will probably be continued in the future, is conducted as an individual Swiss System tournament, and the player who makes the highest score becomes the U. S. Intercollegiate Individual Champion. The Team Championship is won by the players from a single college or university whose four top scorers, regarded as a team, make a higher total number of game points than any other similar team in the tournament.

The details of the individual and team championships since 1945 are listed below:

U. S. Intercollegiate Individual Championships

No.	Year	Place	Champions
1	1945	New York, N. Y.	Kiven Plessit (CCNY)
2	1947	New York, N. Y.	Robert Byrne (Yale)
3	1949	New Brunswick, N. J.	Paul L. Dietz (Pittsburgh)
4	1951	Philadelphia, Pa.	James T. Sherwin (Columbia)
5	1953	New York, N. Y.	Albert Weissman (NYU)
6	1955	New York, N. Y.	Edmar Mednis (NYU)
7	1957	Erie, Pa.	Charles Kalme (U. of Pa.)
8	1959	Sanford Greene, Pa.	Leslie H. Ault (Columbia)
9	1961	Washington, D. C.	Larry Gilden (U. of Md.)
10	1963	South Bend, Ind.	Henry Davis (U. of Tex.)
11	1965	New York, N. Y.	Marc Yoffie (CCNY)

(Continued)

U. S. Intercollegiate Team Championships

No.	Year	Place	Winning Team
1	1946	New York, N. Y.	CCNY
2	1948	New York, N. Y.	CCNY
3	1950	New York, N. Y.	Columbia
4	1952	New York, N. Y.	Columbia
5	1954	New York, N. Y.	Fordham
6	1956	New York, N. Y.	U. of Chicago
7	1958	New York, N. Y.	U. of Chicago
8	1960	New York, N. Y.	Columbia
9	1962	Philadelphia, Pa.	Brooklyn "A"
10	1964	Los Angeles, Calif.	San Jose State
11	1965	New York, N. Y.	U. of Toronto

Index

304 INDEX